Teach Yourself VISUALLY™

Dreamweaver® 4

by Mike Wooldridge

Visual™

From

maranGraphics®

&

Hungry Minds™   HUNGRY MINDS, INC.
New York, NY • Cleveland, OH • Indianapolis, IN

Teach Yourself VISUALLY™ Dreamweaver® 4

Published by
Hungry Minds, Inc.
909 Third Avenue
New York, NY 10022
www.hungryminds.com

maranGraphics, Inc.
5755 Coopers Avenue
Mississauga, Ontario, Canada L4Z 1R9

Library of Congress Control Number: 2001089358

ISBN: 0-7645-0851-2

Printed in the United States of America

10 9 8 7 6 5 4 3 2 1

1K/RT/QW/QR/IN

Distributed in the United States by Hungry Minds, Inc.

Distributed by CDG Books Canada Inc. for Canada; by Transworld Publishers Limited in the United Kingdom; by IDG Norge Books for Norway; by IDG Sweden Books for Sweden; by IDG Books Australia Publishing Corporation Pty. Ltd. for Australia and New Zealand; by TransQuest Publishers Pte Ltd. for Singapore, Malaysia, Thailand, Indonesia, and Hong Kong; by Gotop Information Inc. for Taiwan; by ICG Muse, Inc. for Japan; by Intersoft for South Africa; by Eyrolles for France; by International Thomson Publishing for Germany, Austria and Switzerland; by Distribuidora Cuspide for Argentina; by LR International for Brazil; by Galileo Libros for Chile; by Ediciones ZETA S.C.R. Ltda. for Peru; by WS Computer Publishing Corporation, Inc., for the Philippines; by Contemporanea de Ediciones for Venezuela; by Express Computer Distributors for the Caribbean and West Indies; by Micronesia Media Distributor, Inc. for Micronesia; by Chips Computadoras S.A. de C.V. for Mexico; by Editorial Norma de Panama S.A. for Panama; by American Bookshops for Finland.

For corporate orders, please call maranGraphics at 800-469-6616 or fax 905-890-9434.

For general information on Hungry Minds' products and services please contact our Customer Care Department within the U.S. at 800-762-2974, outside the U.S. at 317-572-3993 or fax 317-572-4002.

For sales inquiries and reseller information, including discounts, premium and bulk quantity sales, and foreign-language translations, please contact our Customer Care Department at 800-434-3422, fax 317-572-4002, or write to Hungry Minds, Inc., Attn: Customer Care Department, 10475 Crosspoint Boulevard, Indianapolis, IN 46256.

For information on licensing foreign or domestic rights, please contact our Sub-Rights Customer Care Department at 212-884-5000.

For information on using Hungry Minds' products and services in the classroom or for ordering examination copies, please contact our Educational Sales Department at 800-434-2086 or fax 317-572-4005.

For press review copies, author interviews, or other publicity information, please contact our Public Relations department at 317-572-3168 or fax 317-572-4168.

For authorization to photocopy items for corporate, personal, or educational use, please contact Copyright Clearance Center, 222 Rosewood Drive, Danvers, MA 01923, or fax 978-750-4470.

Screen shots displayed in this book are based on pre-released software and are subject to change.

Trademark Acknowledgments

Permissions

Hungry Minds™ is a trademark of Hungry Minds, Inc.

U.S. Corporate Sales	U.S. Trade Sales
Contact maranGraphics at (800) 469-6616 or Fax (905) 890-9434.	Contact Hungry Minds at (800) 434-3422 or fax (317) 572-4002.

Some comments from our readers...

"I have to praise you and your company on the fine products you turn out. I have twelve of the *Teach Yourself VISUALLY* and *Simplified* books in my house. They were instrumental in helping me pass a difficult computer course. Thank you for creating books that are easy to follow."

—*Gordon Justin (Brielle, NJ)*

"I commend your efforts and your success. I teach in an outreach program for the Dr. Eugene Clark Library in Lockhart, TX. Your *Teach Yourself VISUALLY* books are incredible and I use them in my computer classes. All my students love them!"

—*Michele Schalin (Lockhart, TX)*

"Thank you so much for helping people like me learn about computers. The Maran family is just what the doctor ordered. Thank you, thank you, thank you."

—*Carol Moten (New Kensington, PA)*

"I would like to take this time to compliment maranGraphics on creating such great books. Thank you for making it clear. Keep up the good work."

—*Kirk Santoro (Burbank, CA)*

"I write to extend my thanks and appreciation for your books. They are clear, easy to follow, and straight to the point. Keep up the good work!"

—*Seward Kollie (Dakar, Senegal)*

"What fantastic teaching books you have produced! Congratulations to you and your staff. You deserve the Nobel prize in Education in the Software category. Thanks for helping me to understand computers."

—*Bruno Tonon (Melbourne, Australia)*

"Over time, I have bought a number of your 'Read Less, Learn More' books. For me, they are THE way to learn anything easily."

—*José A. Mazón (Cuba, NY)*

"I was introduced to maranGraphics about four years ago and YOU ARE THE GREATEST THING THAT EVER HAPPENED TO INTRODUCTORY COMPUTER BOOKS!"

—*Glenn Nettleton (Huntsville, AL)*

"Compliments To The Chef!! Your books are extraordinary! Or, simply put, Extra-Ordinary, meaning way above the rest! THANK YOU THANK YOU THANK YOU! for creating these.

—*Christine J. Manfrin (Castle Rock, CO)*

"I'm a grandma who was pushed by an 11-year-old grandson to join the computer age. I found myself hopelessly confused and frustrated until I discovered the Visual series. I'm no expert by any means now, but I'm a lot further along than I would have been otherwise. Thank you!"

—*Carol Louthain (Logansport, IN)*

"Thank you, thank you, thank you....for making it so easy for me to break into this high-tech world. I now own four of your books. I recommend them to anyone who is a beginner like myself. Now....if you could just do one for programming VCR's, it would make my day!"

—*Gay O'Donnell (Calgary, Alberta, Canada)*

"You're marvelous! I am greatly in your debt."

—*Patrick Baird (Lacey, WA)*

maranGraphics is a family-run business
located near Toronto, Canada.

At **maranGraphics**, we believe in producing great computer books — one book at a time.

maranGraphics has been producing high-technology products for over 25 years, which enables us to offer the computer book community a unique communication process.

Our computer books use an integrated communication process, which is very different from the approach used in other computer books. Each spread is, in essence, a flow chart — the text and screen shots are totally incorporated into the layout of the spread.

Introductory text and helpful tips complete the learning experience.

maranGraphics' approach encourages the left and right sides of the brain to work together — resulting in faster orientation and greater memory retention.

Above all, we are very proud of the handcrafted nature of our books. Our carefully-chosen writers are experts in their fields, and spend countless hours researching and organizing the content for each topic. Our artists rebuild every screen shot to provide the best clarity possible, making our

screen shots the most precise and easiest to read in the industry. We strive for perfection, and believe that the time spent handcrafting each element results in the best computer books money can buy.

Thank you for purchasing this book. We hope you enjoy it!

Sincerely,

Robert Maran
President
maranGraphics
Rob@maran.com
www.maran.com
www.hungryminds.com/visual

CREDITS

Acquisitions, Editorial, and Media Development

Project Editor
Jade L. Williams

Acquisitions Editor
Jen Dorsey

Product Development Supervisor
Lindsay Sandman

Copy Editor
Timothy Borek

Technical Editor
Yolanda Burrell

Editorial Manager
Rev Mengle

Media Development Manager
Laura Carpenter

Permissions Editor
Carmen Krikorian

Media Development Coordinator
Marisa Pearman

Production

Book Design
maranGraphics®

Production Coordinator
Maridee Ennis

Layout
LeAndra Johnson, Kristin Pickett

Screen Artists
Mark Harris, Jill A. Proll

Illustrators
Ronda David-Burroughs, David E. Gregory,
Suzana G. Miokovic, Steven Schaerer

Proofreaders
Dave Faust, Susan Moritz, Angel Perez,
Marianne Santy, Sossity R. Smith, Charles Spencer

Indexer
TECHBOOKS Production Services

Special Help
Macromedia, Inc.

ACKNOWLEDGMENTS

General and Administrative

Hungry Minds, Inc.: John Kilcullen, CEO; Bill Barry, President and COO; John Ball, Executive VP, Operations & Administration; John Harris, CFO

Hungry Minds Technology Publishing Group: Richard Swadley, Senior Vice President and Publisher; Mary Bednarek, Vice President and Publisher; Walter R. Bruce III, Vice President and Publisher; Joseph Wikert, Vice President and Publisher; Mary C. Corder, Editorial Director; Andy Cummings, Publishing Director, General User Group; Barry Pruett, Publishing Director, Visual Group

Hungry Minds Manufacturing: Ivor Parker, Vice President, Manufacturing

Hungry Minds Marketing: John Helmus, Assistant Vice President, Director of Marketing

Hungry Minds Production for Branded Press: Debbie Stailey, Production Director

Hungry Minds Sales: Roland Elgey, Senior Vice President, Sales and Marketing; Michael Violano, Vice President, International Sales and Sub Rights

The publisher would like to give special thanks to Patrick J. McGovern,
without whom this book would not have been possible.

ABOUT THE AUTHOR

Mike Wooldridge is a technology writer and Web designer in the San Francisco Bay Area. He has a day job at Namesecure, which registers domain names. He is the author of several other books in the Visual series, including *Teach Yourself Visually Photoshop 6*. For more information about using Dreamweaver, visit his site at www.mediacosm.com/dreamweaver.

AUTHOR'S ACKNOWLEDGMENTS

Thanks to the many people at Hungry Minds and maranGraphics who helped make this book happen, including project editor Jade Williams, acquisitions editors Martine Edwards and Jennifer Dorsey, copy editors Jill Mazurczyk and Tim Borek, technical editor Yolanda Burrell, editorial manager Rev Mengle, and artists Ronda David-Burroughs, David E. Gregory, Mark Harris, Suzana G. Miokovic, Jill Ann Proll, and Steven Schaerer. Thanks to Jesse Reklaw (www.slowwave.com) for his wonderful illustrations. Also, thanks to the friends and relatives who let me use their pictures in the examples.

To Linda. Thanks for all the great advice, and for putting up with the messy home office.

TABLE OF CONTENTS

Chapter 4

SETTING UP YOUR WEB SITE

Chapter 5

FORMATTING AND STYLING TEXT

Chapter 6

WORKING WITH IMAGES AND GRAPHICS

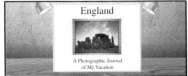

TABLE OF CONTENTS

Chapter 7

CREATING HYPERLINKS

Chapter 8

CREATING TABLES

Chapter 9

CREATING FORMS

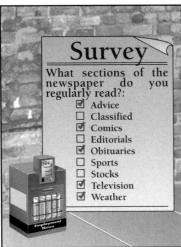

Chapter 10

CREATING FRAMES

TABLE OF CONTENTS

Chapter 14

IMPLEMENTING TIMELINES

Chapter 15

PUBLISHING A WEB SITE

Chapter 16

SITE MAINTENANCE

Bird Watchers' Home Page

NATURE
- Wildlife
- Rainforests
- Memberships

Steve's
TOTALLY AMAZING WORLD OF
GAMES

Mid-Western Farms

XOTIC Automobiles

Travel the World

Country Kitchen Template

Your Internet source for recipes, cooking tips and more!

Home

Recipes

Cooking Tips

Vegetarian Specials

Healthy Snacks

E-Mail the Chef

Site maintained by: Jane Wilson

New Releases

Top Ten

Concerts

BCG music store

About BCG

CHAPTER 1

Getting Started with Dreamweaver

This chapter describes the World Wide Web, introduces the different types of information you can put on a Web site, and tells you how to start Dreamweaver.

INTRODUCTION TO THE WORLD WIDE WEB

You can use Dreamweaver to create and publish Web pages on the World Wide Web.

World Wide Web

The *World Wide Web (Web)* is a global collection of documents located on Internet-connected computers that you can access by using a Web browser. Web pages are connected to one another through clickable hyperlinks.

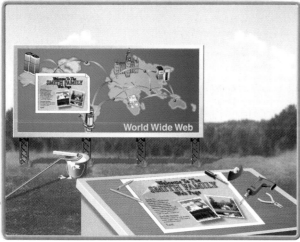

Dreamweaver

Dreamweaver is a program that enables you to create Web pages that feature text, images, and multimedia. It also helps you link your pages together, and includes tools that let you transfer the finished files to a Web server where others can then view them.

HTML

Hypertext Markup Language (HTML) is the formatting language used to create Web pages. Every Web page you see has an associated page of HTML that gives it its structure. You can use Dreamweaver to create Web pages without knowing HTML, because Dreamweaver writes the HTML for you behind the scenes.

Web Browser

A *Web browser* is a program that can download Web documents from the Internet, interpret their HTML, and then display the Web page text and any associated images and multimedia as a Web page. Two popular Web browsers are Microsoft Internet Explorer and Netscape Navigator.

Web Server

A *Web server* is an Internet-connected computer that makes Web documents available to Web browsers. Each Web page that you view on the World Wide Web comes from a Web server somewhere on the Internet. When you are ready to publish your pages on the Web, Dreamweaver can connect to a Web server and transfer your files to it.

Web Site

A *Web site* is a collection of linked Web pages stored on a Web server. Most Web sites have a *home page* that describes the information located on the Web site and provides a place where people can start their exploration of the site. The pages of a good Web site are intuitively organized and have a common theme.

PARTS OF A WEB PAGE

You can communicate your message on the Web in a variety of ways. The following are some of the common elements found on Web pages.

Text

Text is the simplest type of content you can publish on the Web. Dreamweaver lets you change the size, color, and font of Web-page text and organize it into paragraphs, headings, and lists. Perhaps the best thing about text is that practically everyone can view it, no matter what type of browser or Internet connection a person may have, and it downloads very quickly.

Images

You can shoot photos for your Web site with a digital camera. Or you can prepare drawings, logos, and other art for the Web using a scanner. You can then place these images on your Web pages with Dreamweaver. Images are a must if you want your pages to stand out visually.

Hyperlinks

Often simply called a link, a *hyperlink* is text or an image that has been associated with another file. You can access the other file by clicking the hyperlink. Hyperlinks usually link to other Web pages, but they can also link to other locations on the same page or to other types of files.

Tables

Tables organize information in columns and rows on your Web page. By turning off a table's borders and setting it to span an entire page, you can use a table to organize the layout of a page. The commands in Dreamweaver give you an easy way to create complex tables.

Softball Standings

Team	Games	Wins	Losses	Ties	Points
The Chargers	10	9	1	0	18
Sluggers	10	8	1	1	17
The Champs	10	7	2	1	15
The Eagles	10	5	5	0	10
Barry's Battalion	10	3	7	0	6
The Professionals	10	2	8	0	4
Baseball Borders	10	1	9	0	2

Forms

Forms reverse the information flow on Web sites enabling visitors to your site to send information back to you. Dreamweaver lets you create forms that include text fields, drop-down menus, radio buttons, and other elements.

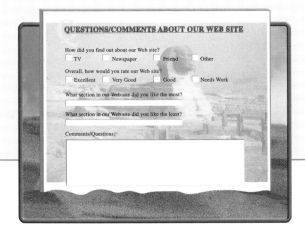

Frames

In a framed Web site, the browser window is divided into several rectangular frames, and a different Web page is loaded into each frame. Users can scroll through content in each frame, independently of the content in the other frames. Dreamweaver offers visual tools for building frame-based Web sites.

PLAN YOUR WEB SITE

Carefully planning your pages before you build them can help ensure that your finished Web site looks great and is well organized.

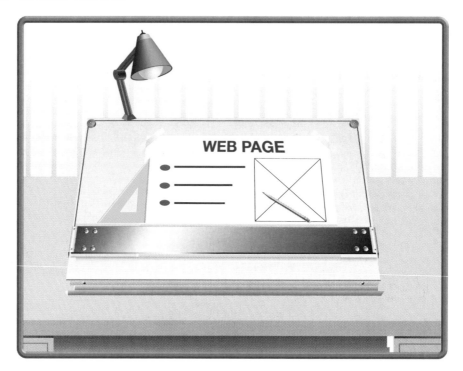

Organize Your Ideas

Build your site on paper before you start building it in Dreamweaver. Sketching out a site map, with rectangles representing Web pages and arrows representing hyperlinks, can help you visualize the size and scope of your project.

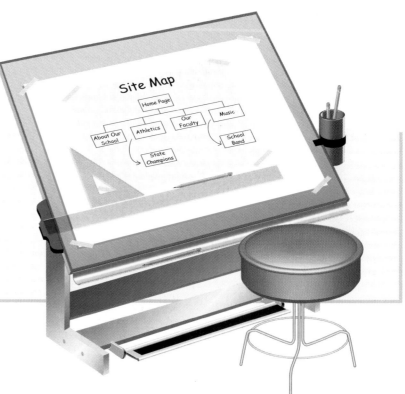

Gather Your Content

After you decide what types of Web pages you want to create, you have to generate content that will appear on them. This process can involve writing text, shooting photos, and designing graphics. It can also involve producing multimedia content such as audio and video files. Having lots of content to choose from will make it easier to create pages that are interesting to read and look at.

Define Your Audience

Carefully defining your audience can help you decide what kind of content to offer on your Web site. Some advanced Dreamweaver features — such as cascading style sheets and layers — can only be viewed using the most recent versions of Web browsers. Knowing how technologically advanced your audience is can help you decide whether to include more advanced features on your pages.

Host Your Finished Web Site

For your finished site to be accessible on the Web, you will need to have it stored (or hosted) on a Web server. Most people have their Web sites hosted on a Web server at a commercial *Internet service provider* (ISP) or at their company.

TOUR THE DREAMWEAVER INTERFACE ON A PC

You build Web pages in Dreamweaver on a PC by using various windows, panels, and inspectors.

DOCUMENT WINDOW

Provides you with a work area to insert and arrange text, images, and other elements of your Web page.

TOOLBAR

Contains shortcuts to many of the document window commands, and a text field where you can specify a title for your page.

MENUS

Contains the available command choices for the Document window.

OBJECTS PANEL

Allows you to add images, tables, and multimedia to your Web pages.

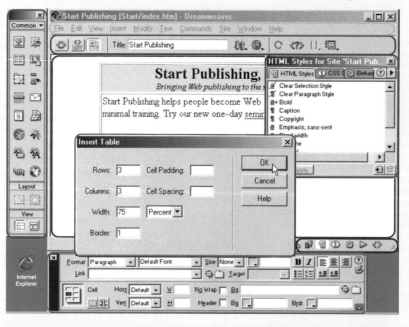

PANEL

An accessory window that enables you to manage the features of your Web page, or apply commands.

DIALOG BOX

Allows you to enter specific information when executing a Dreamweaver command.

PROPERTY INSPECTOR

A window where you can view and modify properties of an object that is selected in the Document window.

LAUNCHER BAR

Contains icons that you can click to open and close panels and inspectors.

You build Web pages in Dreamweaver on a Macintosh by using various windows, panels, and inspectors.

DOCUMENT WINDOW

Provides you with a work area to insert and arrange text, images, and other elements of your Web page.

TOOLBAR

Contains shortcuts to many of the Document window commands, and a text field where you can specify a title for your page.

MENUS

Contains the available command choices for the Document window.

OBJECTS PANEL

Allows you to add images, tables, and multimedia to your Web pages.

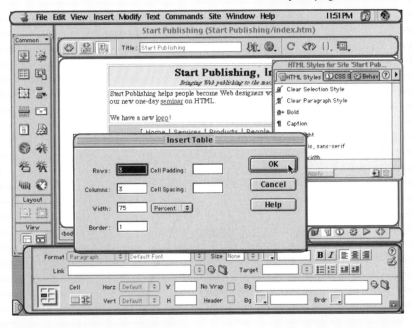

PANEL

An accessory window that enables you to manage the features of your Web page, or apply commands.

DIALOG BOX

Allows you to enter specific information when executing a Dreamweaver command.

PROPERTY INSPECTOR

A window where you can view and modify properties of an object that is selected in the Document window.

LAUNCHER BAR

Contains icons that you can click to open and close panels and inspectors.

Note: The screen shots you see in this book were taken on a PC. Except for minor differences, the icons, menus and commands are the same on a Macintosh. When PC and Macintosh commands are different, the Macintosh commands are in parentheses, for example: Press Enter *(* Return *).*

START DREAMWEAVER ON A PC

You can start
Dreamweaver on a PC
and begin building
pages that you can
publish on the Web.

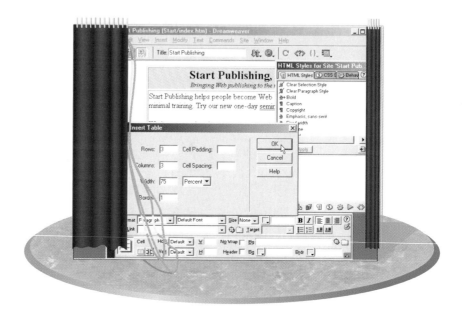

START DREAMWEAVER ON A PC

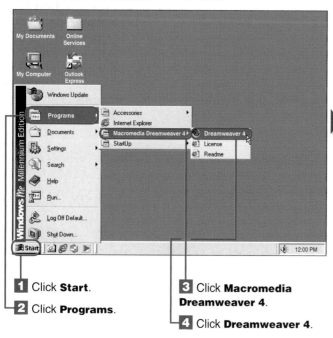

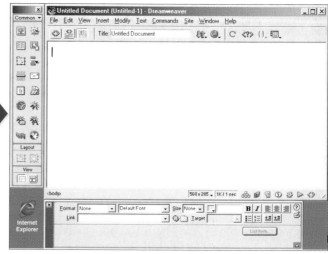

1 Click **Start**.

2 Click **Programs**.

3 Click **Macromedia Dreamweaver 4**.

4 Click **Dreamweaver 4**.

Note: Your path to the Dreamweaver application may be different, depending on how you installed your software.

■ An untitled Web page appears in a Document window.

You can start
Dreamweaver on a
Macintosh and begin
building pages that
you can publish on
the Web.

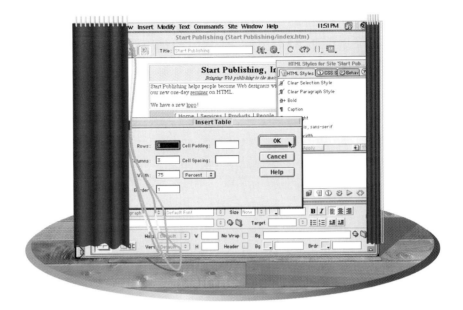

START DREAMWEAVER ON A MACINTOSH

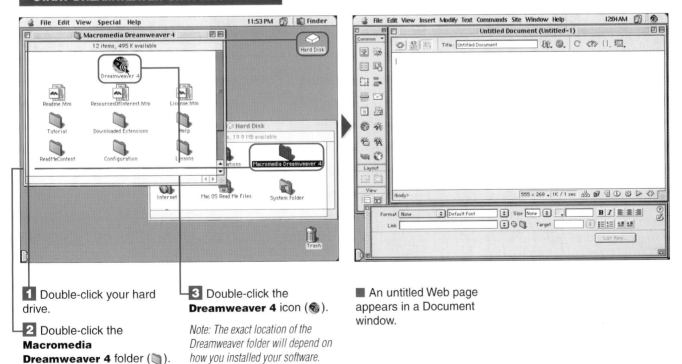

1 Double-click your hard drive.

2 Double-click the **Macromedia Dreamweaver 4** folder (📁).

3 Double-click the **Dreamweaver 4** icon (🖐).

Note: The exact location of the Dreamweaver folder will depend on how you installed your software.

■ An untitled Web page appears in a Document window.

SHOW OR HIDE A WINDOW

You can show or hide accessory windows, also called panels and inspectors, by using commands in the Window menu.

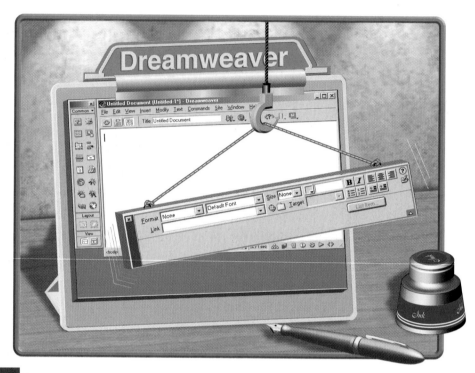

SHOW OR HIDE A WINDOW

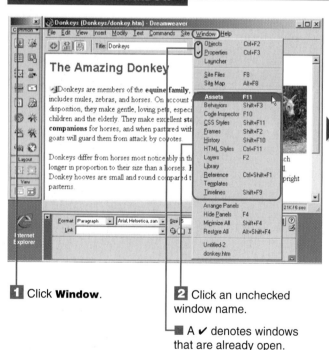

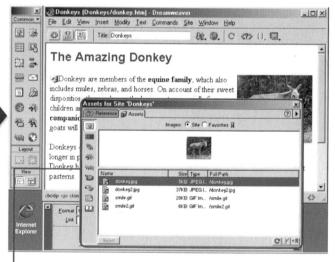

1 Click **Window**.

2 Click an unchecked window name.

■ A ✔ denotes windows that are already open.

■ Dreamweaver shows the window.

■ To hide a window, click **Window** and the checked window name.

■ You can click **Window** and **Hide Panels** to hide everything except the Document window.

EXIT DREAMWEAVER

You can exit
Dreamweaver after
you finish using the
program.

You should always
exit Dreamweaver
and all other
programs before
turning off your
computer.

EXIT DREAMWEAVER

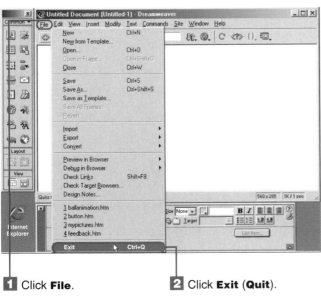

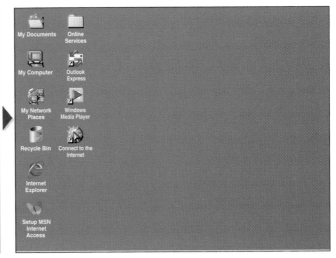

1 Click **File**.

2 Click **Exit** (**Quit**).

■ Dreamweaver exits.

■ Before exiting,
Dreamweaver will alert you
to any documents open that
have unsaved changes,
allowing you to save them.

You can use the help tools built into Dreamweaver to get answers to your questions.

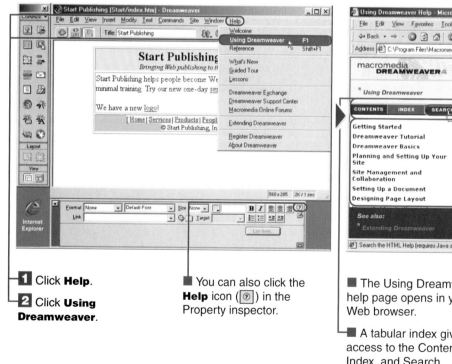

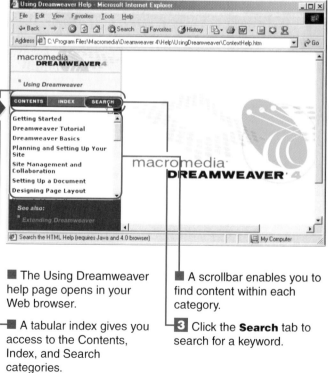

1 Click **Help**.

2 Click **Using Dreamweaver**.

■ You can also click the **Help** icon (⊚) in the Property inspector.

■ The Using Dreamweaver help page opens in your Web browser.

■ A tabular index gives you access to the Contents, Index, and Search categories.

■ A scrollbar enables you to find content within each category.

3 Click the **Search** tab to search for a keyword.

Are there different ways of getting the same thing done in Dreamweaver?

Very often, yes. For example, you may be able to access a command one way through a Dreamweaver menu, another way through the Object panel or Property inspector, and yet another way by right-clicking (control-clicking) an object with the mouse.

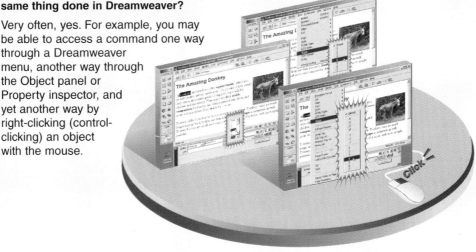

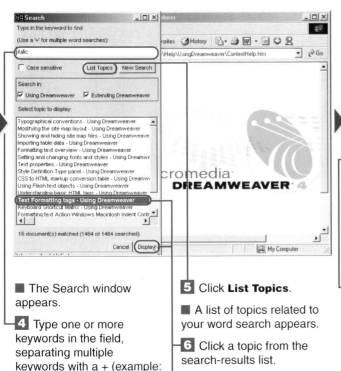

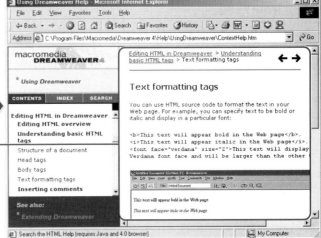

■ The Search window appears.

4 Type one or more keywords in the field, separating multiple keywords with a + (example: **frame + borders**).

5 Click **List Topics**.

■ A list of topics related to your word search appears.

6 Click a topic from the search-results list.

7 Click **Display**.

■ Information on your topic appears in the Web browser.

CHAPTER 2

Exploring the Dreamweaver Interface

This chapter familiarizes you with the Web-building tools that you will use often in Dreamweaver. You also learn different ways to view your Web page information.

CUSTOMIZE THE DOCUMENT WINDOW

The Document window is the main workspace in Dreamweaver, where you insert and arrange the text, images, and other elements of your Web page. For every page you open in Dreamweaver, a separate Document window will appear.

CUSTOMIZE THE DOCUMENT WINDOW

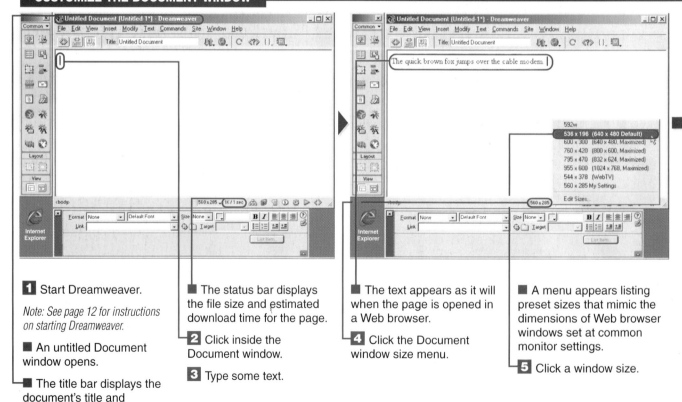

1 Start Dreamweaver.

Note: See page 12 for instructions on starting Dreamweaver.

■ An untitled Document window opens.

■ The title bar displays the document's title and filename.

■ The status bar displays the file size and estimated download time for the page.

2 Click inside the Document window.

3 Type some text.

■ The text appears as it will when the page is opened in a Web browser.

4 Click the Document window size menu.

■ A menu appears listing preset sizes that mimic the dimensions of Web browser windows set at common monitor settings.

5 Click a window size.

What Is WYSIWYG?

WYSIWYG (pronounced wizzy-wig) stands for **W**hat **Y**ou **S**ee **I**s **W**hat **Y**ou **G**et. Because you build Web pages visually in the Document window and see the content approximately as it will appear in a Web browser, Dreamweaver is a WYSIWYG Web editor. This is in contrast to text-based Web editors, which only let you create Web pages by writing HTML code.

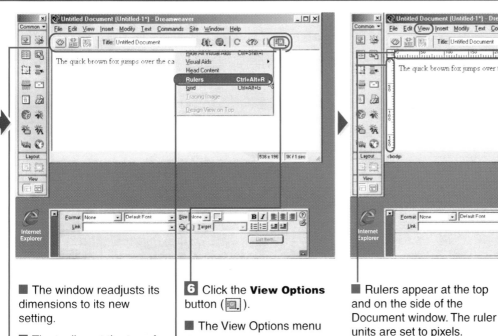

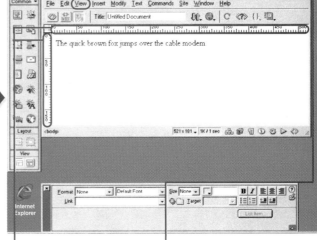

■ The window readjusts its dimensions to its new setting.

■ The toolbar at the top of the Document window gives you easy access to various commands.

6 Click the **View Options** button ([image]).

■ The View Options menu appears.

7 Click **Rulers**.

■ Rulers appear at the top and on the side of the Document window. The ruler units are set to pixels.

■ You can change the ruler units by clicking **View**, **Rulers**, and then a units setting from the menu bar.

The Property inspector lets you view the properties associated with the object or text that is currently selected in the Document window. Text fields, drop-down menus, buttons, and other form elements in the Property inspector allow you to modify these properties.

FORMAT CONTENT WITH THE PROPERTY INSPECTOR

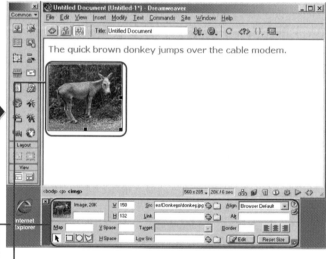

1 Click **Window**.

2 Click **Properties**.

■ The Property inspector appears.

3 Click and drag the mouse ⬚ to select some text.

■ The Text Property inspector appears.

■ You can format the text size, font, link, and more in the inspector.

■ You can click ⬚ to switch between standard and expanded modes of the inspector.

4 Click an image.

■ Image properties, such as dimensions, filename, and alignment, appear in the Property inspector.

■ You can change options in the Property inspector to modify the image.

ADD OBJECTS WITH THE OBJECTS PANEL

The Objects panel lets you insert objects such as images, tables, and layers into the Document window. The panel has a drop-down menu at the top, allowing you to view different sets of object-insertion buttons.

ADD OBJECTS WITH THE OBJECTS PANEL

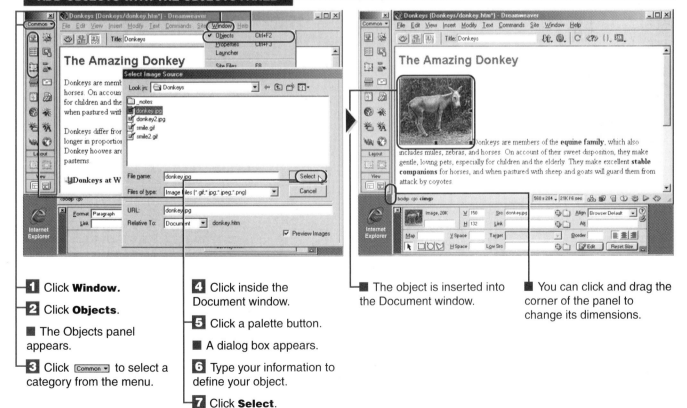

1 Click **Window**.

2 Click **Objects**.

■ The Objects panel appears.

3 Click Common to select a category from the menu.

4 Click inside the Document window.

5 Click a palette button.

■ A dialog box appears.

6 Type your information to define your object.

7 Click **Select**.

■ The object is inserted into the Document window.

■ You can click and drag the corner of the panel to change its dimensions.

CORRECT ERRORS WITH THE HISTORY PANEL

The History panel keeps track of the commands you perform in Dreamweaver and allows you to return your page to a previous state by backtracking through those commands. This is a convenient way to correct errors.

CORRECT ERRORS WITH THE HISTORY PANEL

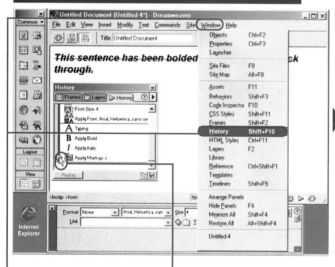

-1 Click **Window**.

-2 Click **History**.

■ The History panel appears.

■ The History panel records the commands you perform in Dreamweaver.

3 To undo one or more commands, click and drag the slider ▷ upward.

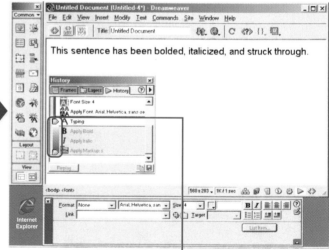

■ The page reverts to its previous state.

■ To redo the commands, click and drag the slider ▷ downward.

REARRANGE PANELS

To keep your onscreen workspace from being cluttered, you can combine or dock windows to create multi-tab windows. This enables you to click the tabs to switch between different windows.

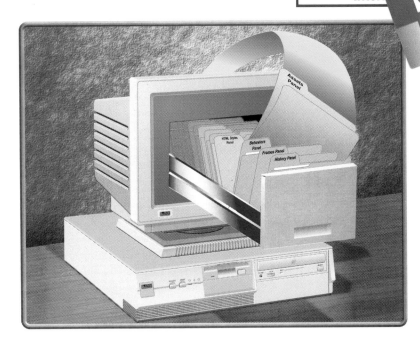

REARRANGE PANELS

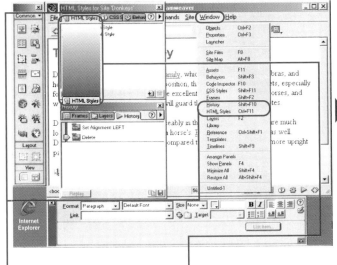

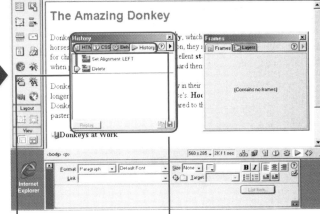

1 Click **Window**.

2 Click two panels or inspectors from the Window menu.

Note: You cannot combine the Property inspector, Site window, or Launcher with other windows.

3 Click and drag a tab from one window to another.

■ The first window is docked (combined) with the second.

■ You can select between the different tools in the window by clicking the tabs.

CREATE AND APPLY A CUSTOM COMMAND

You can select a
sequence of commands
that has been recorded
in the History panel and
save as a custom
command. The new
command will appear
under the Commands
menu.

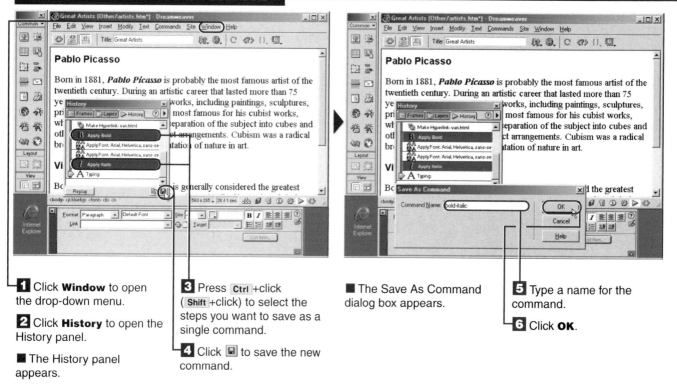

1 Click **Window** to open
the drop-down menu.

2 Click **History** to open the
History panel.

■ The History panel
appears.

3 Press `Ctrl` +click
(`Shift` +click) to select the
steps you want to save as a
single command.

4 Click 🖫 to save the new
command.

■ The Save As Command
dialog box appears.

5 Type a name for the
command.

6 Click **OK**.

How do I change the name of a custom command?

Select **Commands**, then **Edit Command List**. Dreamweaver displays a dialog box that lists the custom commands and lets you edit their names.

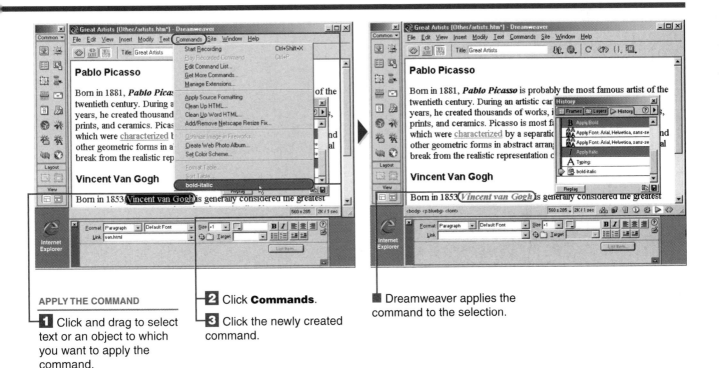

APPLY THE COMMAND

1 Click and drag to select text or an object to which you want to apply the command.

2 Click **Commands**.

3 Click the newly created command.

■ Dreamweaver applies the command to the selection.

CREATE A KEYBOARD SHORTCUT

You can use the Keyboard Shortcut Editor to define your own shortcut commands or edit existing shortcuts. This allows you to assign easy-to-remember keyboard combinations to commands that you use often in Dreamweaver.

To start defining your own shortcuts in Dreamweaver, you first have to create your own custom set, which you can do by duplicating an existing set.

CREATE A KEYBOARD SHORTCUT

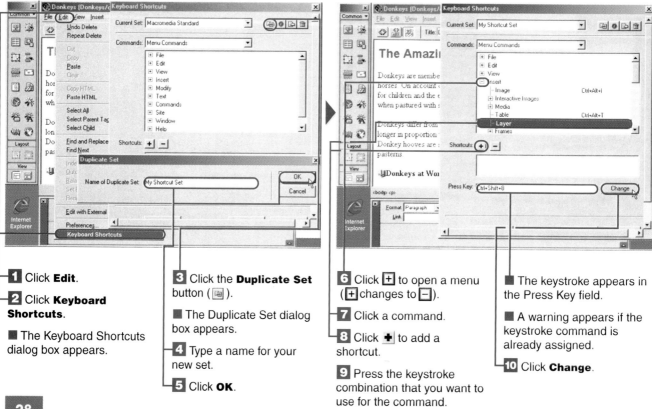

■1 Click **Edit**.

■2 Click **Keyboard Shortcuts**.

■ The Keyboard Shortcuts dialog box appears.

■3 Click the **Duplicate Set** button ( ).

■ The Duplicate Set dialog box appears.

■4 Type a name for your new set.

■5 Click **OK**.

■6 Click ⊞ to open a menu (⊞ changes to ⊟).

■7 Click a command.

■8 Click ✚ to add a shortcut.

■9 Press the keystroke combination that you want to use for the command.

■ The keystroke appears in the Press Key field.

■ A warning appears if the keystroke command is already assigned.

■10 Click **Change**.

Can I reassign a keyboard shortcut that is already being used?

Yes. Dreamweaver will warn you about it already being used, but you can still dismiss the warning and have the shortcut reassigned.

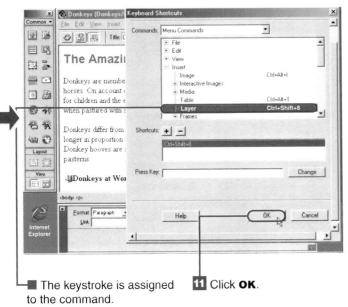

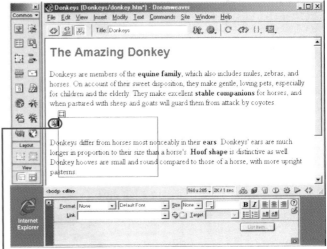

■ The keystroke is assigned to the command.

11 Click **OK**.

EXECUTE A KEYBOARD SHORTCUT

1 Click inside the Document window, or click and drag to select an object if necessary.

2 Press the keystroke combination.

■ The command executes.

SET PREFERENCES

You can easily change
the default appearance
and behavior of
Dreamweaver by
specifying settings in the
Preferences dialog box.
Preferences let you
modify the user interface
of Dreamweaver to
better suit how you like
to work.

SET PREFERENCES

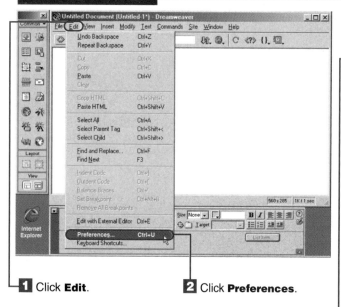

1 Click **Edit**.

2 Click **Preferences**.

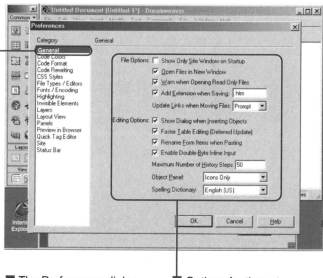

■ The Preferences dialog
box appears.

3 Click a Preferences
category.

■ Options for the category
appear.

How do I ensure that Dreamweaver does not change my HTML or other code?

You can select options under the Code Rewriting category in Preferences to ensure that Dreamweaver does not automatically correct or modify your code. You can turn off its error-correcting functions, specify files that it should not rewrite based on file extension, or disable its character encoding features.

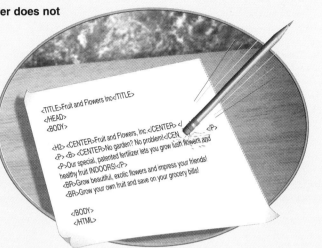

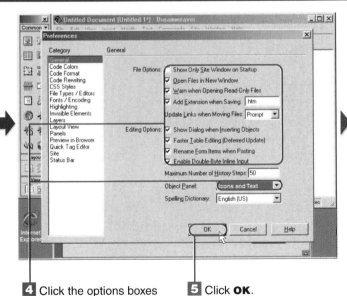

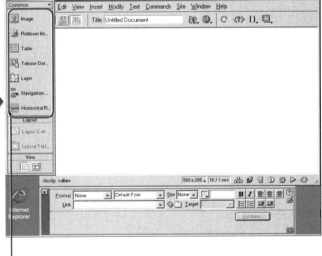

4 Click the options boxes (☑ select or ☐ deselect) or click ⏷ to make changes to the options (example: Set the Objects panel to display both icons and text descriptions).

5 Click **OK**.

■ The preference changes take effect.

```
<HTML>
<HEAD>
<TITLE>Fruit and Flowers Inc</TITLE>
</HEAD>
<BODY>

<H2> <CENTER>Fruit and Flowers, Inc.</CENTER> </H2>
<P> <B> <CENTER>No garden? No problem!</CENTER> </B> </P>
<P>Our special, patented fertilizer lets you grow lush flowers and
healthy fruit INDOORS!</P>
<BR>Grow beautiful, exotic flowers and impress your friends!
<BR>Grow your own fruit and save on your grocery bills!

</BODY>
</HTML>
```

CHAPTER 3

Working with HTML

Dreamweaver helps you build your Web pages by writing HTML. This chapter introduces the important features of this language and the tools in Dreamweaver that let you edit HTML.

INTRODUCTION TO HTML

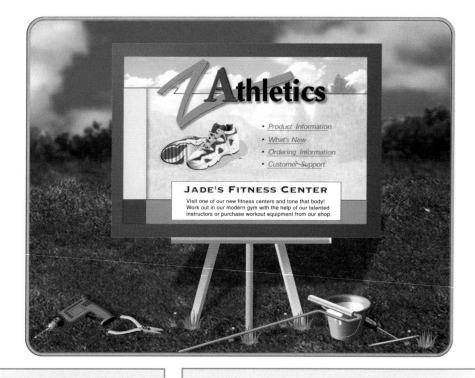

Dreamweaver creates your Web pages by writing HTML. This saves you time by not having to write the code yourself.

HTML

Hypertext Markup Language (HTML) is the formatting language that you use to create Web pages. When you open a Web page in a browser, it is HTML code telling the browser how to display the text, images, and other content on the page. At its most basic level, Dreamweaver is an HTML-writing application (although it can do many other things as well).

HTML Tags

The basic unit of HTML is a *tag*. You can recognize HTML tags by their angle brackets:

```
<p>Today the weather was
<b>nice</b>.<br>Tomorrow it may
<i>rain</i>.</p>
```

You can format text and other elements on your page by placing it inside HTML tags.

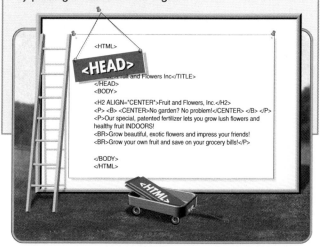

How Tags Work

Some HTML tags work in twos: Opening and closing tags surround content in a document and control the formatting of the content. For example, `<b>` tags cause text to be bold. Closing tags are distinguished by a forward slash (/). Other tags can stand alone. For example, `<br>` tags add a line break. HTML tags are not case sensitive; they can be uppercase, lowercase, or mixed case.

HTML Documents

Because HTML documents are plain text files, you can open and edit them with any text editor. In fact, in the early days of the Web, most people created their pages with simple editors such as Notepad (Windows) and SimpleText (Macintosh). But writing HTML by hand can be a slow, tedious process, especially when creating advanced HTML elements such as tables, forms, and frames.

Create Web Pages Without Knowing Code

Dreamweaver streamlines the process of creating Web pages by giving you an easy-to-use, visual interface with which to generate HTML. You specify formatting with menu commands and button clicks, and Dreamweaver takes care of writing the HTML code behind the scenes. When you build a Web page in the Document window, you see your page as it will eventually appear in a Web browser, instead of as HTML.

Direct Access to the Code

Dreamweaver gives you direct access to the raw HTML code if you want it. This can be an advantage for people who know HTML and want to do some formatting of their page by typing tags. The Code View mode, Code Inspector, and Quick Tag Editor in Dreamweaver enable you to edit your page by adding HTML information manually. Access to the code also means you can add HTML features that Dreamweaver does not yet support.

VIEW AND EDIT THE SOURCE CODE

You can switch to Code View in the Document window to inspect and edit the HTML and other code of a Web page.

You will probably do most of you work in Design View, which displays your page approximately as it will be viewed in a Web browser.

VIEW AND EDIT THE SOURCE CODE

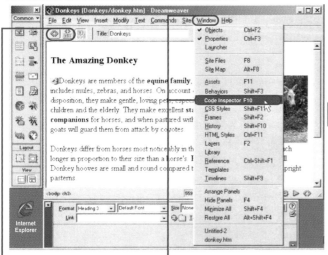

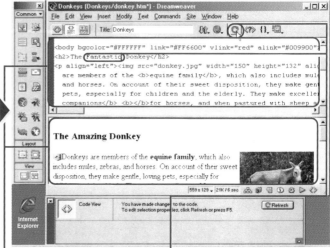

■ **1** Click a code-viewing option (example: **Code and Design Views** button).

■ Clicking the **Code View** button (⬚) displays the source code of your page in the Document window.

■ Clicking the **Code and Design Views** button (⬚) splits the window and displays both your source code and the design in the Document window.

■ Selecting **Code Inspector** under the Window menu displays the code in a separate window.

■ The Code and Design Views appear in the Document window.

■ The HTML and other code appear in one pane.

■ The design view appears in the other pane.

■ **2** Click in the code to edit the text, or add or modify the HTML.

■ **3** Click the **Refresh** button (⬚).

How do I turn on line numbers in Code View, or make code wrap at the right edge of the window?

Both of these options (and others) are available by clicking the **Options** button at the top of the Document window when you are in Code View.

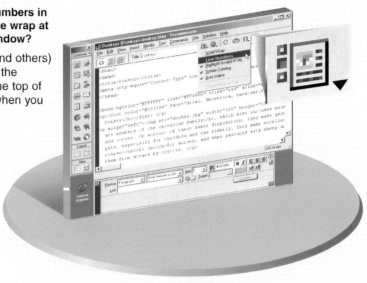

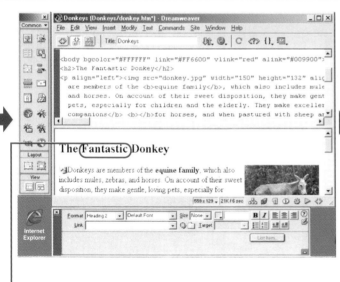

The content in Design View updates to reflect the code changes.

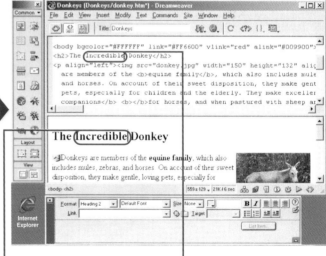

4 Click in the Design View window and type to make changes.

■ The content in Code View updates dynamically as you make your changes.

EXPLORE STRUCTURAL TAGS

You define the basic structure of every HTML document with several basic tags. To view the HTML of a Web page, click Code View, or the Code View and Design View button in the Document window, or Code Inspector in the Window menu.

<html> TAGS

Opening and closing <html> tags begin and end every HTML document.

<head> TAGS

Opening and closing <head> tags surround descriptive and accessory information for a page. This includes <title> and <meta> tag content.

<body> TAGS

Opening and closing <body> tags surround content that appears inside the Web browser window. The bgcolor attribute of the <body> tag defines the background color, and the text attribute of the <body> tag defines the text color.

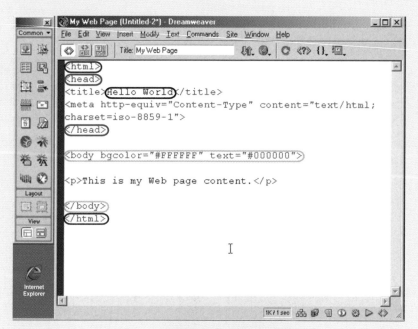

PAGE TITLE

The content inside the opening and closing <title> tags is displayed in the Document window title bar.

Block-formatting tags let you organize information in your Web page. To view the HTML of a Web page, click a Code View button in the Document window or Code Inspector in the Window menu.

CODE VIEW

DESIGN VIEW

This page features a heading, a paragraph, and an unordered list.

<p> TAG

The <p> tag organizes information into a paragraph.

<ul> AND <li> TAGS

The <ul> tag defines an unordered list. Each list item is defined with an <li> tag.

HEADING

PARAGRAPH

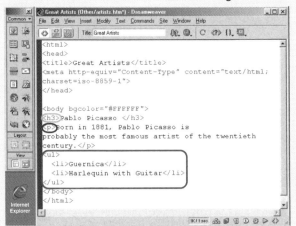

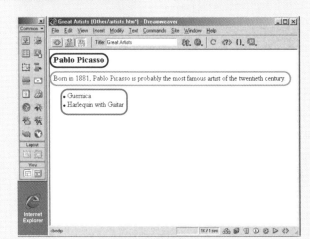

<h> TAG

An <h> tag organizes information into a heading. There are six levels of headings, <h1> (the largest) through <h6> (the smallest).

, <ol>, AND <pre> TAGS

Other block-formatting tags include
 (line break) <ol> (ordered list) and <pre> (preformatted text).

UNORDERED LIST

EXPLORE TEXT-FORMATTING TAGS

You can format the style of sentences, words, and characters with text-formatting tags. To view the HTML of a Web page, click a Code View button in the Document window or Code Inspector in the Windows menu.

CODE VIEW

`<font>` TAG

The `<font>` tag controls various characteristics of text on a Web page.

`<size>` ATTRIBUTE

The `<size>` attribute goes inside the `<font>` tag and specifies the size of text.

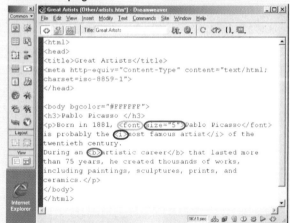

`<b>` TAG

The `<b>` tag defines text as bold.

`<i>` TAG

The `<i>` tag defines text as italic.

DESIGN VIEW

This page features text with a different font size, as well as bold and italic text.

FONT SIZE

ITALIC TEXT

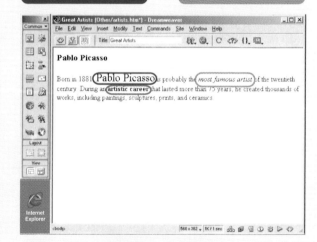

BOLD TEXT

The `<img>` tag lets you add an image to your page and the `<a>` tag lets you create a hyperlink. To view the HTML of a Web page, click a Code View button in the Document window or Code Inspector in the Window menu.

CODE VIEW

DESIGN VIEW

This page features a right-aligned image and a text hyperlink.

`<img>` TAG

The `<img>` tag inserts an image into a page.

`<src>` ATTRIBUTE

The `<src>` attribute specifies an image file to insert.

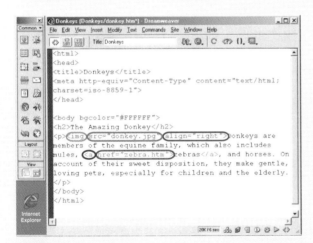

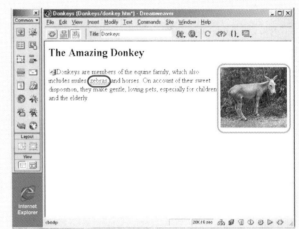

`<align>` ATTRIBUTE

The `<align>` attribute specifies the alignment of an image.

`<a>` TAG

The `<a>` tag specifies the content that will serve as a hyperlink.

`<href>` ATTRIBUTE

The `<href>` attribute specifies the hyperlink destination.

TEXT HYPERLINK

RIGHT-ALIGNED IMAGE

CLEAN UP YOUR HTML

Dreamweaver can optimize the HTML in your Web page by deleting extraneous or nonfunctional tags. This can decrease a page's file size and make the source code easier to read in Code View.

It is a good idea to run the Clean Up HTML command when editing documents originally created in other HTML editors.

CLEAN UP YOUR HTML

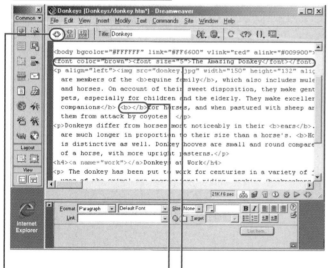

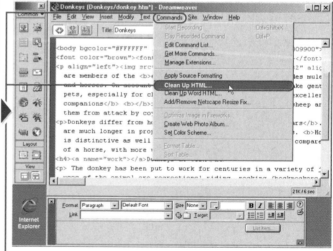

1 Click ◇ to display the HTML of the page.

■ In this example, combined `<font>` tags appear in the code, saving you space.

■ This example also includes an empty `<b>` tag in the code. This tag serves no purpose and can be deleted.

2 Click **Commands**.

3 Click **Clean Up HTML**.

How do empty tags end up appearing in Dreamweaver's HTML?

Sometimes if you heavily edit Web-page text in the Document window (cutting and pasting sentences, reformatting words, and so on), Dreamweaver will inadvertently remove text from inside tags without removing the tags themselves.

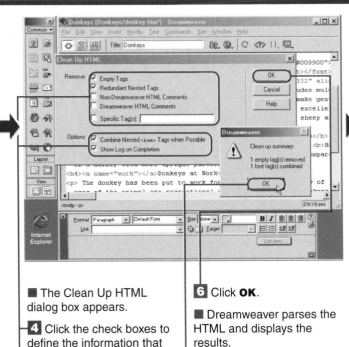

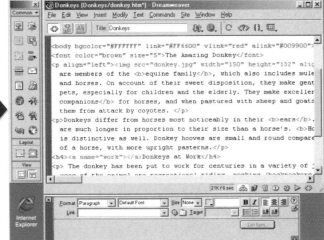

■ The Clean Up HTML dialog box appears.

4 Click the check boxes to define the information that you want to remove (☐ changes to ☑).

5 Click the check boxes to select other options (☐ changes to ☑).

6 Click **OK**.

■ Dreamweaver parses the HTML and displays the results.

7 Click **OK**.

■ The cleaned up HTML appears in the Document window.

USING THE QUICK TAG EDITOR

The Quick Tag Editor gives you easy access to HTML code without having to switch to Code View. You can open the editor when you're working inside the Document window and use it to add or modify HTML tags.

USING THE QUICK TAG EDITOR

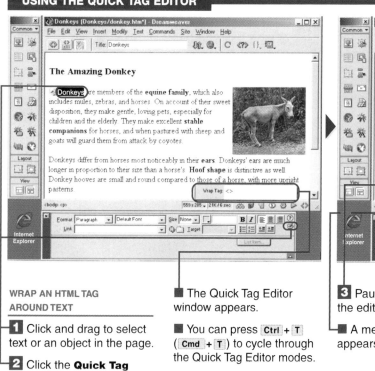

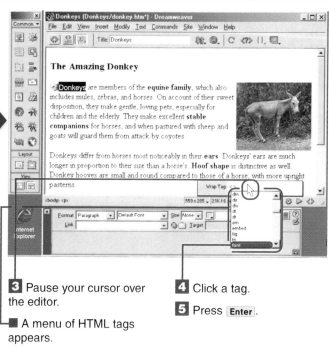

WRAP AN HTML TAG AROUND TEXT

1 Click and drag to select text or an object in the page.

2 Click the **Quick Tag** button ().

■ The Quick Tag Editor window appears.

■ You can press Ctrl + T (Cmd + T) to cycle through the Quick Tag Editor modes.

3 Pause your cursor over the editor.

■ A menu of HTML tags appears.

4 Click a tag.

5 Press Enter .

44

Does Dreamweaver fix invalid HTML?

By default, Dreamweaver rewrites some instances of invalid HTML. When you open an HTML document, Dreamweaver rewrites tags that are not nested properly, closes tags that are not allowed to remain open, and removes extra closing tags. If Dreamweaver does not recognize a tag, it highlights it in yellow and displays it in the Document window (but will not remove it). You can change this behavior by clicking **Edit**, clicking **Preferences** and then selecting **Code Rewriting**.

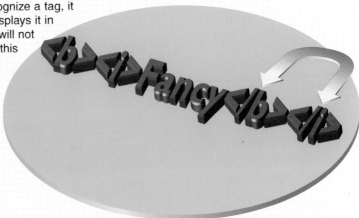

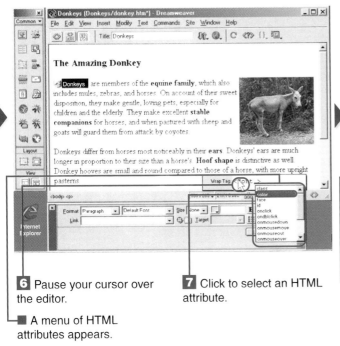

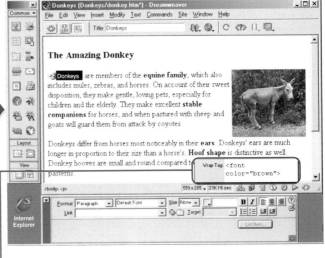

■6 Pause your cursor over the editor.

■ A menu of HTML attributes appears.

■7 Click to select an HTML attribute.

■ The attribution appears in the wrap modes.

■8 Press **Enter** (**Return**) to apply the tag and attribute.

■ To exit without applying changes, press **Esc**.

VIEW AND EDIT HEAD CONTENT

Dreamweaver gives you various ways to view, add to, and edit a Web page's head content, where special descriptive information about the page is stored.

Head Info.
Description: This travel site will help you book a vacation.
Keywords: travel, vacations, airlines, hotels.

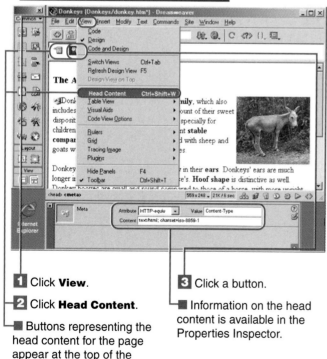

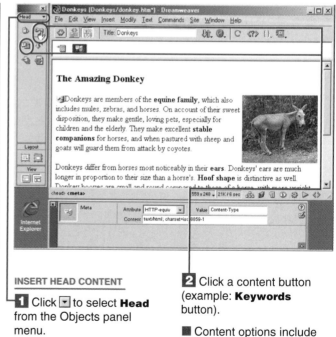

1 Click **View**.

2 Click **Head Content**.

■ Buttons representing the head content for the page appear at the top of the Document window.

3 Click a button.

■ Information on the head content is available in the Properties Inspector.

INSERT HEAD CONTENT

1 Click ▾ to select **Head** from the Objects panel menu.

2 Click a content button (example: **Keywords** button).

■ Content options include **Keywords** and **Description**.

How can I influence how my pages are ranked by search engines?

Search engines work by organizing the important information found in Web pages into a searchable database. Many search engines give greater importance to the description and keyword information that can be added to the head content of HTML documents. You can influence how search engines rank your pages by making sure you add concise descriptions and relevant keywords to the head content of each page you create.

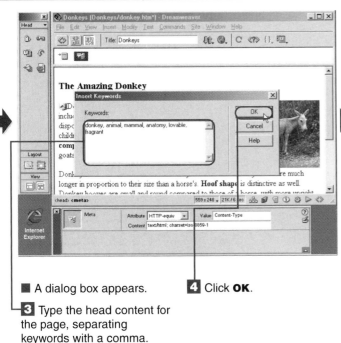

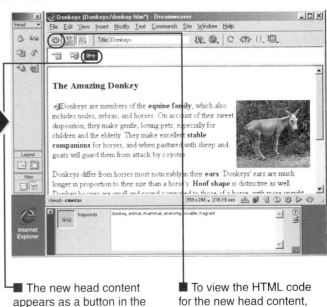

■ A dialog box appears.

3 Type the head content for the page, separating keywords with a comma.

■ If you chose **Description** in step **2**, type a sentence description for the page.

4 Click **OK**.

■ The new head content appears as a button in the head section of the Document window.

■ To view the HTML code for the new head content, click **Code View**.

USING THE REFERENCE PANEL

You can get quick access to reference information about HTML tags and their attributes via the Reference panel.

USING THE REFERENCE PANEL

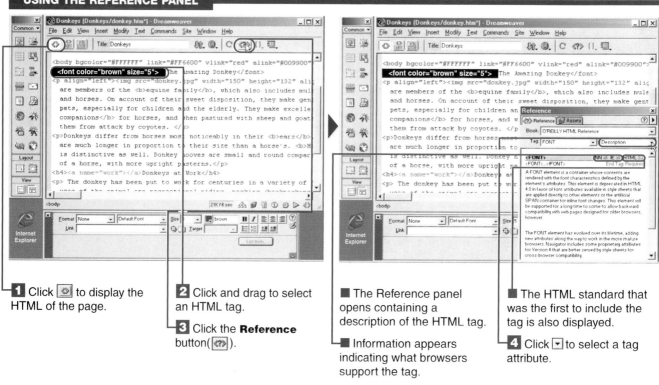

1 Click to display the HTML of the page.

2 Click and drag to select an HTML tag.

3 Click the **Reference** button (<?>).

■ The Reference panel opens containing a description of the HTML tag.

■ Information appears indicating what browsers support the tag.

■ The HTML standard that was the first to include the tag is also displayed.

4 Click ▼ to select a tag attribute.

48

Does Dreamweaver have commands for creating all the tags listed in the Reference panel?

Dreamweaver's commands allow you to create *most* of the tags listed in the Reference panel, in particular the most widely used tags. But there are tags listed that Dreamweaver doesn't offer commands for (for example, you can't insert the `<thead>` tag with any of Dreamweaver's table commands). Tags that Dreamweaver doesn't support with commands can be inserted by hand in Code View.

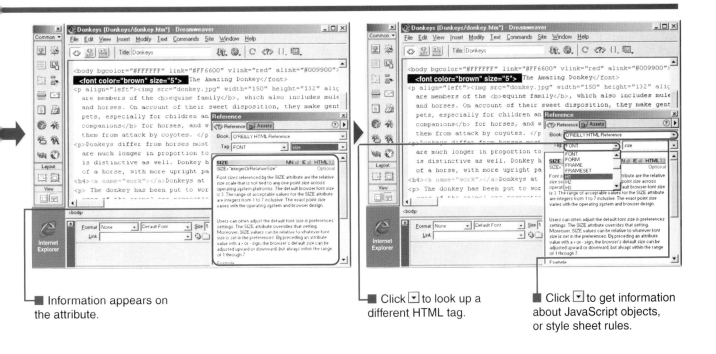

■ Information appears on the attribute.

■ Click ▼ to look up a different HTML tag.

■ Click ▼ to get information about JavaScript objects, or style sheet rules.

CHAPTER 4

Setting Up Your Web Site

You start a project in Dreamweaver by setting up a local site on your computer and then creating the first Web page of the site. This chapter shows you how.

SET UP A LOCAL SITE

Before creating your Web pages, you need to define a local site for storing the information in your site, such as your HTML documents and image files. Defining a local site allows you to manage your Web-page files in the Site window (see page 267 for more information on the Site window).

SET UP A LOCAL SITE

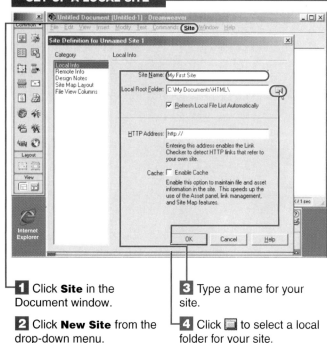

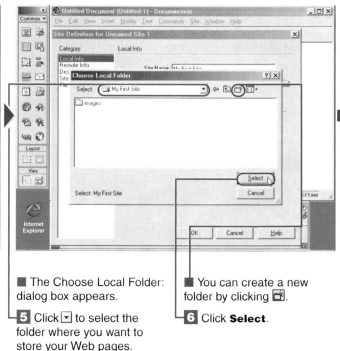

1 Click **Site** in the Document window.

2 Click **New Site** from the drop-down menu.

■ The Site Definition dialog box appears.

3 Type a name for your site.

4 Click 🔲 to select a local folder for your site.

■ The Choose Local Folder: dialog box appears.

5 Click ▼ to select the folder where you want to store your Web pages.

■ You can create a new folder by clicking 🗁.

6 Click **Select**.

52

Why is it important to keep all my Web site files in a single folder on my computer?

Keeping everything in the same folder enables you to easily transfer your site files to a Web server without changing the organization of the files (see page 268 for more information). If you do not organize your site files on the Web server the same as they are organized on your local computer, hyperlinks will not work and images will not display properly.

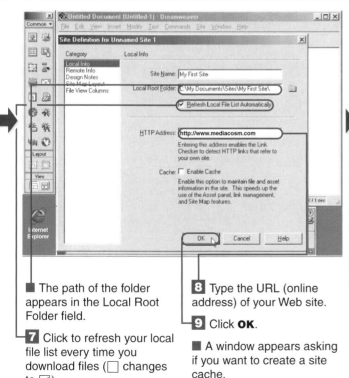

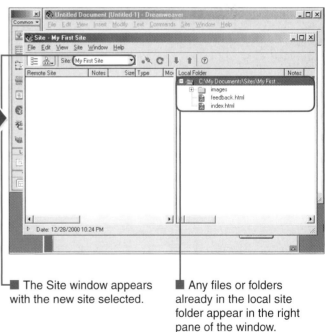

■ The path of the folder appears in the Local Root Folder field.

7 Click to refresh your local file list every time you download files (☐ changes to ✔).

8 Type the URL (online address) of your Web site.

9 Click **OK**.

■ A window appears asking if you want to create a site cache.

10 Click **Create**.

■ The Site window appears with the new site selected.

■ Any files or folders already in the local site folder appear in the right pane of the window.

OPEN A WEB PAGE

You can open an existing Web page in Dreamweaver to view and modify its structure.

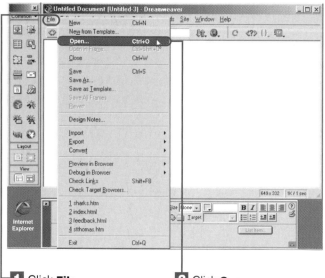

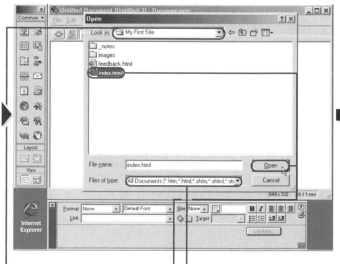

1 Click **File**.

2 Click **Open**.

■ The Open dialog box appears.

3 Click ▼ to select the folder containing the Web page.

■ You can click the **Files of type** ▼ to select a specific file type, or to limit the types of files to show in the window.

4 Click the filename.

Note: The file will probably have an .htm or .html file extension.

5 Click **Open**.

Can I open Web pages created in HTML editors other than Dreamweaver?

Yes. You can open any HTML file in Dreamweaver, no matter where it was created. You can also open non-HTML text files; however, the layout of such Web pages may look haphazard in Dreamweaver because they do not include HTML formatting.

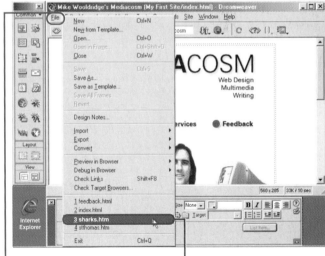

■ The file opens in a Document window.

■ You can switch between open Web pages by selecting their filenames under the Window menu.

■ Open files also appear on the Windows toolbar.

OPEN A RECENTLY OPENED PAGE

1 Click **File**.

■ A list of your last four files opened is listed.

2 Click the file you want to open.

CREATE A NEW WEB PAGE

You can open a new, blank page in Dreamweaver and then add text, images, and other elements to create a new Web page design.

CREATE A NEW WEB PAGE

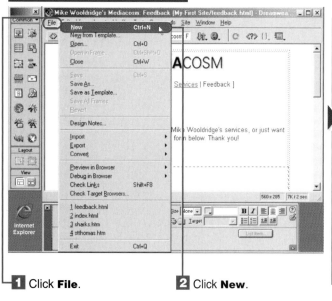

1 Click **File**.

2 Click **New**.

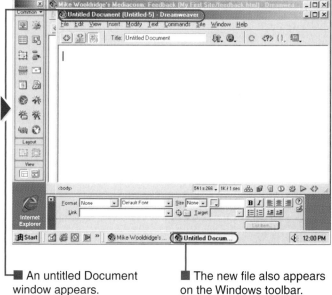

■ An untitled Document window appears.

Note: The page name and filename are untitled until you save the page. See page 58 for instructions.

■ The new file also appears on the Windows toolbar.

Adding a title to a Web page makes the page identifiable by viewers and search engines. A Web page title appears in the title bar when the page opens in a Web browser.

ADD A TITLE TO A WEB PAGE

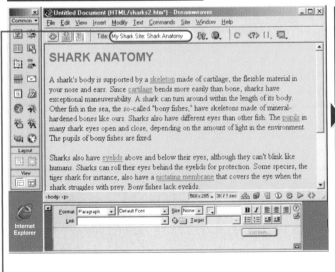

1 Type a name for your Web page.

2 Press Enter (Return).

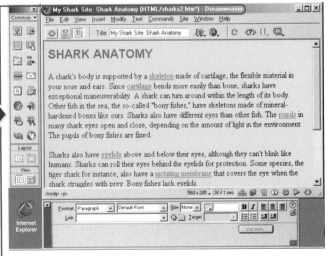

■ The title appears in the title bar of the Document window.

SAVE A WEB PAGE

You should save your Web page before closing or transferring the page to a remote site (see page 270). It is also a good idea to save all your files frequently to prevent work from being lost due to power outages or system failures.

SAVE A WEB PAGE

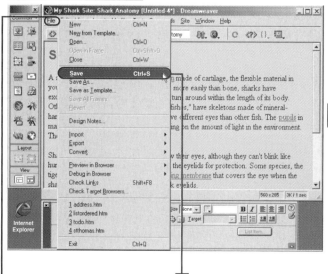

SAVE YOUR DOCUMENT

1 Click **File**.

2 Click **Save**.

■ You can click Save As to save an existing file with a new filename.

■ If you are saving a new file for the first time, the Save As dialog box appears.

3 Type a name for your Web page.

4 Click ▼ to select your local site folder.

Note: Your local site folder is where you want to save the pages and other files for your Web site. See page 52 for more information.

5 Click **Save**.

**How should I store the files for
my Web site on my computer?**

You should save all the files for
your Web site in the folder that you
defined as the local root folder
(see page 52). Keeping all the files
of the site in this folder (or in
subfolders inside this folder)
makes it easier to hyperlink
between local files, and transfer
files to a remote Web server.

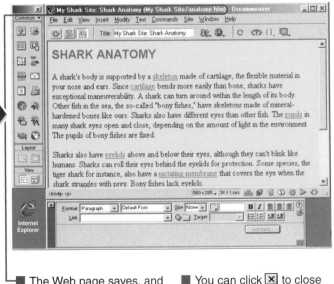

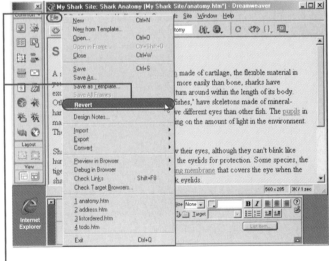

■ The Web page saves, and
the filename and path
appears in the title bar.

■ You can click ☒ to close
the page.

REVERT A PAGE

-1 Click **File**.

-2 Click **Revert**.

■ The page reverts to the
previously saved version. All
the changes made since last
saving are lost.

PREVIEW A WEB PAGE IN A BROWSER

You can see how your page will appear online by previewing it in a Web browser. The Preview in Browser command works with the Web browsers installed on your computer (Dreamweaver does not come with browser software).

PREVIEW A WEB PAGE IN A BROWSER

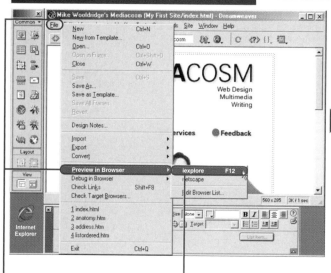

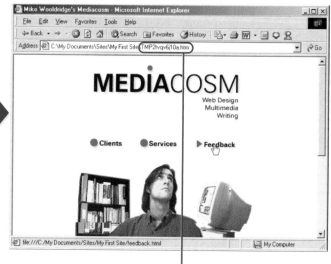

1 Click **File**.

2 Click **Preview In Browser**.

3 Click a Web browser.

■ You can also preview the page in your primary browser by pressing F12.

■ Your Web browser launches and opens the current page.

■ The file has a temporary filename for viewing in the browser.

Why does Dreamweaver create a temporary file when I preview my page?

So it can make any necessary modifications to the page so all the content appears correctly in the browser. For instance, if you defined your images using root-relative paths (paths beginning with a /), Dreamweaver needs to change those paths to document-relative paths for previewing.

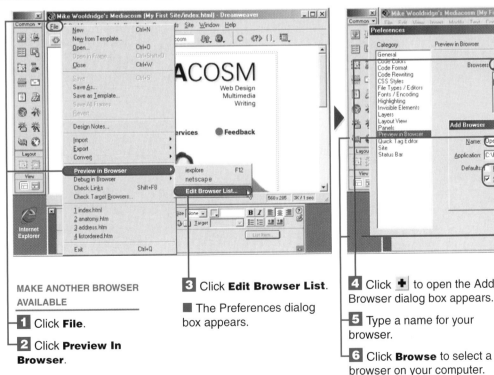

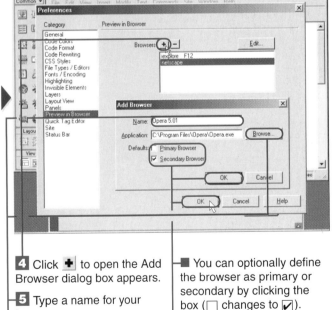

MAKE ANOTHER BROWSER AVAILABLE

1 Click **File**.

2 Click **Preview In Browser**.

3 Click **Edit Browser List**.

■ The Preferences dialog box appears.

4 Click ✚ to open the Add Browser dialog box appears.

5 Type a name for your browser.

6 Click **Browse** to select a browser on your computer.

■ You can optionally define the browser as primary or secondary by clicking the box (☐ changes to ☑).

7 Click **OK** in the Add Browser dialog box.

8 Click **OK**.

CHAPTER 5

Formatting and Styling Text

Text is the easiest type of information to add to a Web page. This chapter shows you how to create paragraphs, bulleted lists, stylized text, and more.

CREATE PARAGRAPHS

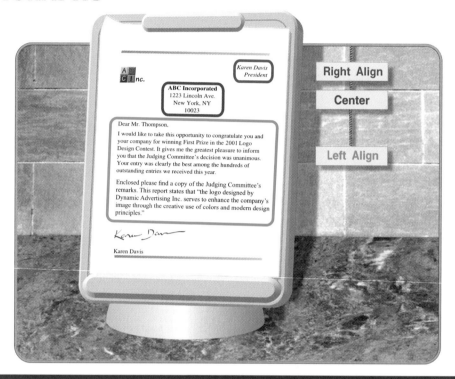

You can organize text on your Web page by creating and aligning paragraphs.

CREATE PARAGRAPHS

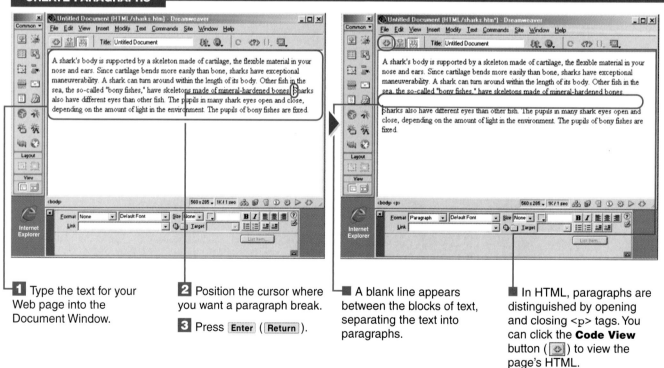

1 Type the text for your Web page into the Document Window.

2 Position the cursor where you want a paragraph break.

3 Press Enter (Return).

■ A blank line appears between the blocks of text, separating the text into paragraphs.

■ In HTML, paragraphs are distinguished by opening and closing <p> tags. You can click the **Code View** button (�) to view the page's HTML.

What controls the width of the paragraphs on my Web page?

The width of your paragraphs depends on the width of the Web browser window. When a user changes the size of the browser window, the widths of the paragraphs also change. That way, the user always sees all the text of the paragraphs.

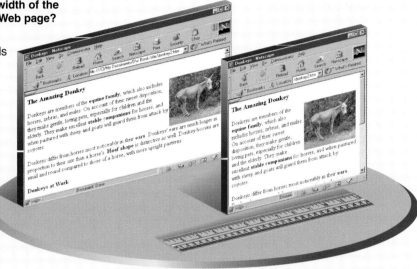

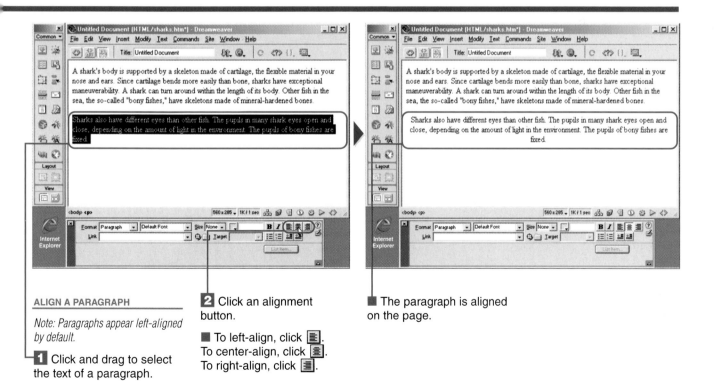

ALIGN A PARAGRAPH

Note: Paragraphs appear left-aligned by default.

1 Click and drag to select the text of a paragraph.

2 Click an alignment button.

■ To left-align, click 📄.
To center-align, click 📄.
To right-align, click 📄.

■ The paragraph is aligned on the page.

CREATE A HEADING

You can add headings to structure the text on your Web page hierarchically with titles and subtitles. You can also align your heading text.

CREATE A HEADING

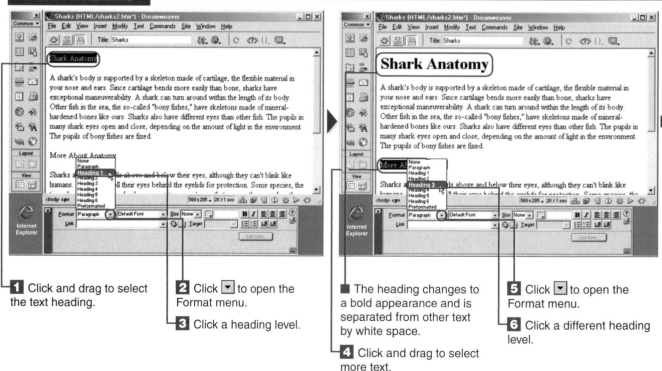

1 Click and drag to select the text heading.

2 Click ▾ to open the Format menu.

3 Click a heading level.

■ The heading changes to a bold appearance and is separated from other text by white space.

4 Click and drag to select more text.

5 Click ▾ to open the Format menu.

6 Click a different heading level.

What heading levels should I use to format my text?

Headings 1, 2, and 3 are often used for titles and subtitles. Heading 4 is similar to a bold version of default text. Headings 5 and 6 are often used for copyright and disclaimer information in page footers.

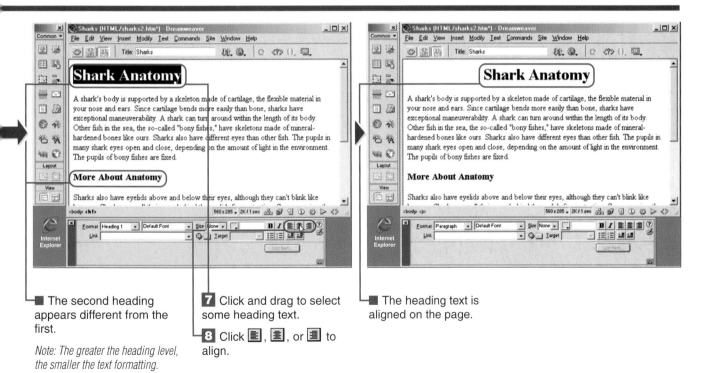

■ The second heading appears different from the first.

Note: The greater the heading level, the smaller the text formatting.

7 Click and drag to select some heading text.

8 Click 📄, 📄, or 📄 to align.

■ The heading text is aligned on the page.

CREATE LINE BREAKS

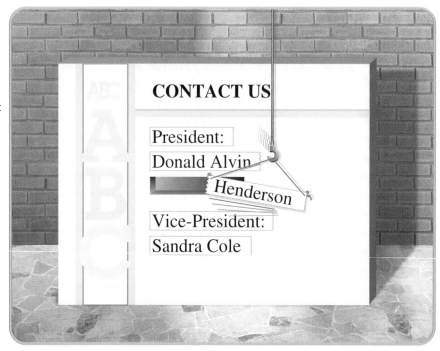

Adding line breaks to your page allows you to keep adjacent lines of related text close together.

Line breaks are an alternative to paragraph breaks, which add more space between lines of text (see page 64).

CREATE LINE BREAKS

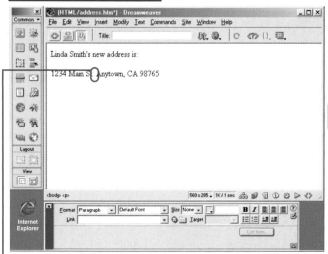

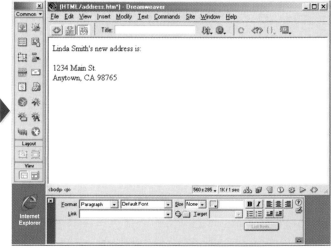

1 Click where you want the line of text to break.

2 Press Shift + Enter (Shift + Return).

■ A line break is added.

Note: You can insert multiple line breaks to add more space between lines of text.

68

INDENT PARAGRAPHS

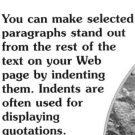

You can make selected paragraphs stand out from the rest of the text on your Web page by indenting them. Indents are often used for displaying quotations.

INDENT PARAGRAPHS

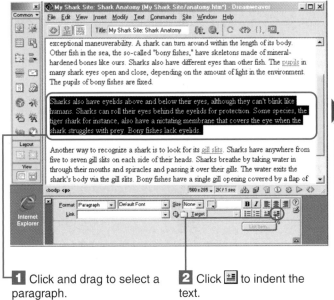

1 Click and drag to select a paragraph.

2 Click ☰ to indent the text.

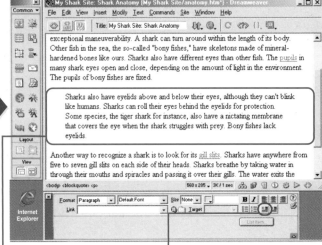

■ Additional space appears in both the left and right margins of the paragraph.

■ You can repeat steps **1** and **2** to indent a paragraph further.

■ You can outdent an indented paragraph by clicking ☰.

CREATE UNORDERED LISTS

You can organize text items into unordered lists. Unordered lists have items that are indented and bulleted.

CREATE UNORDERED LISTS

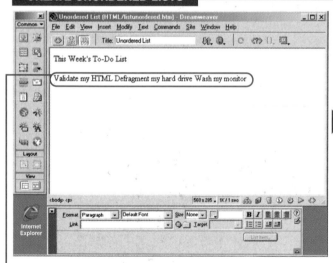

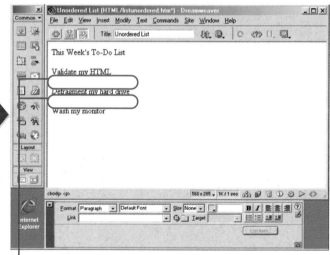

1 Type your list items into the Document window.

2 Click between the items and press `Enter` (`Return`) to place each item in a separate paragraph.

Can I modify the appearance of my unordered lists?

You can modify the style of unordered lists by highlighting an item in the list and clicking **Text**, **List**, and **Properties**. The dialog box that appears enables you to select different bullet styles for your unordered list.

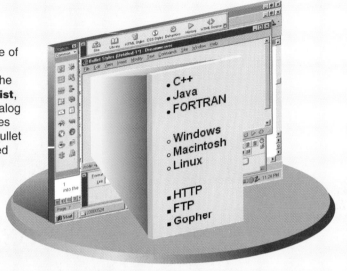

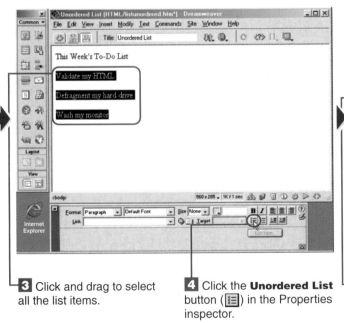

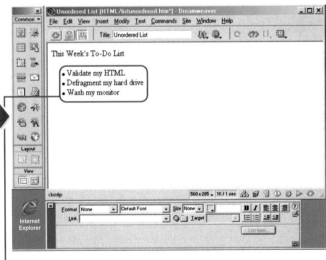

3 Click and drag to select all the list items.

4 Click the **Unordered List** button (▤) in the Properties inspector.

■ The list items appear indented and bulleted.

CREATE ORDERED LISTS

You can display step-by-step instructions on your Web page by organizing text items into an ordered list. Ordered lists have items that are indented and numbered.

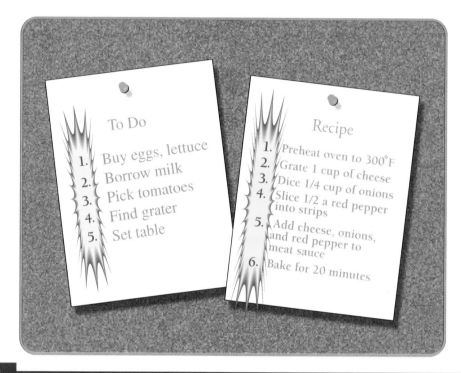

CREATE ORDERED LISTS

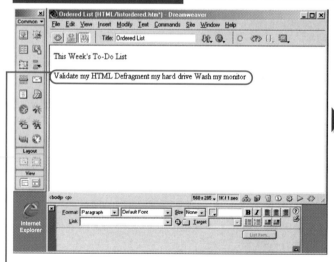

1 Type your list items into the Document window.

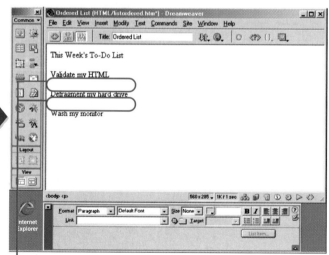

2 Click between the items and press **Enter** (**Return**) to place each item in a separate paragraph.

Can I modify the appearance of my ordered lists?

You can modify the style of ordered lists by highlighting an item in the list and clicking **Text**, **List**, and **Properties**. The dialog box that appears enables you to select different numbering schemes for your ordered list.

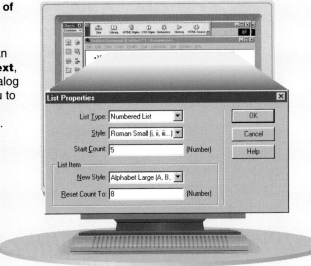

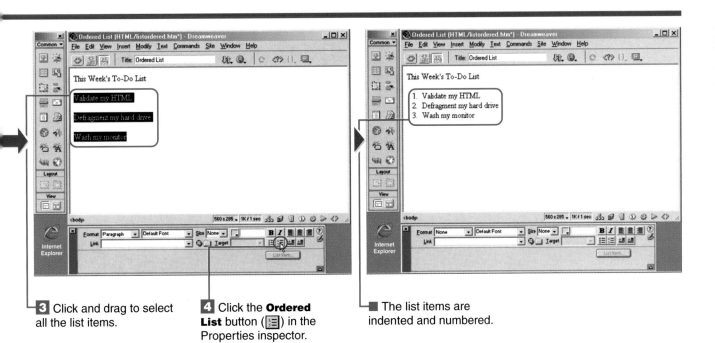

3 Click and drag to select all the list items.

4 Click the **Ordered List** button (☰) in the Properties inspector.

■ The list items are indented and numbered.

INSERT SPECIAL CHARACTERS

You can insert special characters that do not appear on your keyboard into your Web page.

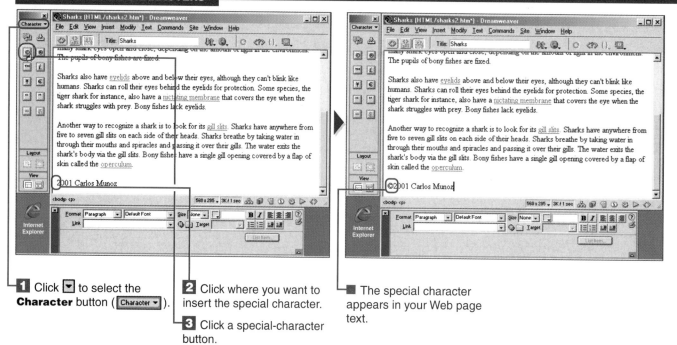

1 Click ▼ to select the **Character** button (Character ▼).

2 Click where you want to insert the special character.

3 Click a special-character button.

■ The special character appears in your Web page text.

How do I include non-English language text on my Web page?

Many European languages feature accented characters that do not appear on standard keyboards. You can insert many of these characters using the special characters tools described in this section.

Der Computer
gefällt mir

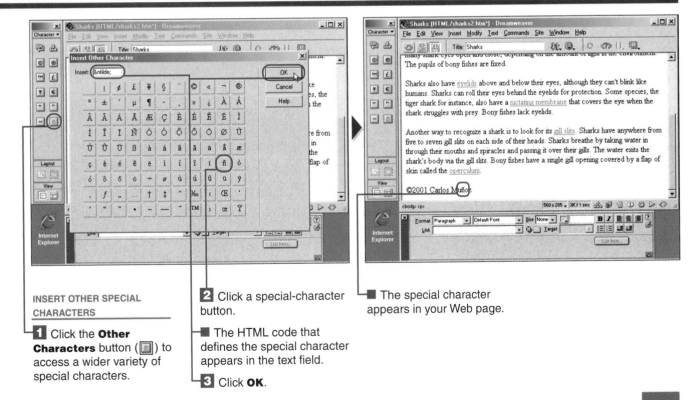

INSERT OTHER SPECIAL CHARACTERS

1 Click the **Other Characters** button (▣) to access a wider variety of special characters.

2 Click a special-character button.

■ The HTML code that defines the special character appears in the text field.

3 Click **OK**.

■ The special character appears in your Web page.

CHANGE THE FONT

To add variety or to emphasize certain elements to your Web page, you can change the font style of your text.

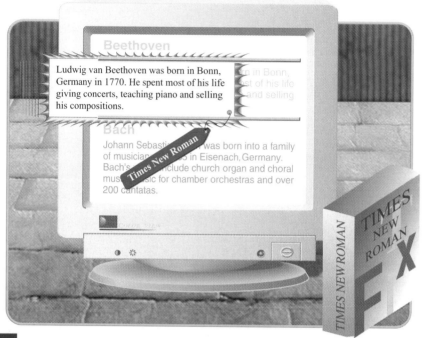

You can also customize the fonts on your Web pages by using Style Sheets (see page 218).

CHANGE THE FONT

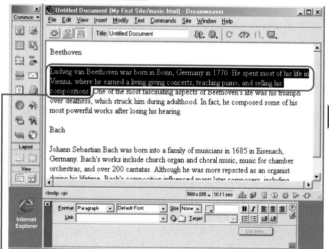

1 Click and drag to select the text.

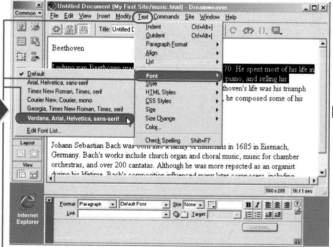

2 Click **Text**.

3 Click **Font**.

4 Click a list of fonts.

Note: A font must be installed on the user's computer to display in the browser. A list specifies alternate styles if the user does not have certain fonts installed.

How are fonts categorized?

The two most common categories of fonts are *serif* fonts and *sans-serif* fonts. Serif fonts are distinguished by the decorations on the ends of their lines. Common serif fonts include Times New Roman, Palatino, and Garamond. Sans-serif fonts lack these decorations. Common sans-serif fonts include Arial, Verdana, and Helvetica.

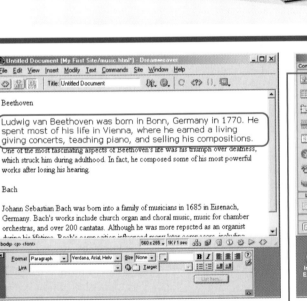

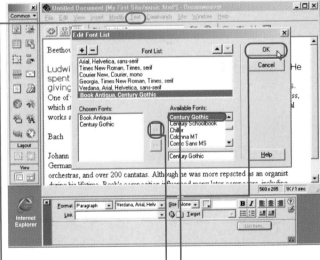

■ The text changes to the new font.

**ADD AN ENTRY TO
THE FONT MENU**

1 Repeat steps **2** and **3** on page 76 and then click **Edit Font List** from the Text submenu.

■ The fonts installed on your computer appears in the Available Fonts list.

2 Click a font.

3 Click «.

■ Repeat steps **1** to **4** to create an entry that is a list of fonts.

4 Click **OK**.

CREATE BOLD OR ITALIC TEXT

You can emphasize text on your Web page with bold or italic styles.

You can also control the style of text on your Web page using Style Sheets (see page 218).

CREATE BOLD TEXT

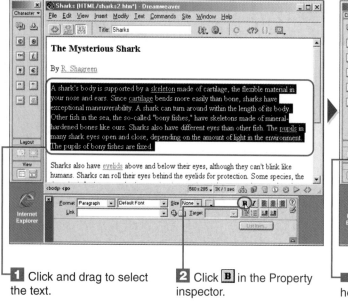

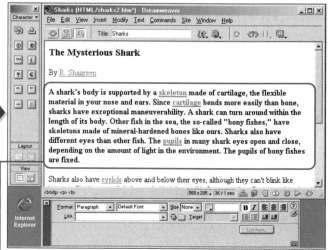

1 Click and drag to select the text.

2 Click **B** in the Property inspector.

■ The bold text has a heavier weight.

What other kinds of styles are available besides bold and italic?

You can create other styles of text besides bold and italic using commands in the **Text** and **Style** menu. The styles include Underline, Strikethrough, and Teletype (typewriter style). Many of the styles listed in the Style menu produce effects identical to bold or italic.

CREATE ITALIC TEXT

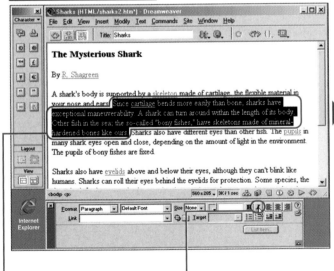

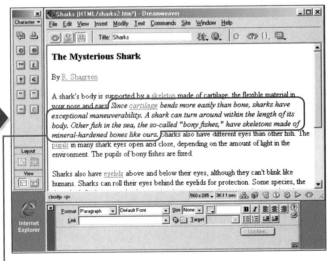

1 Click and drag to select the text.

2 Click *I* in the Property inspector.

■ The selected text is italicized.

■ You can combine text styles. For example, you can create text that is both bold and italic.

CHANGE FONT SIZE

You can emphasize or
de-emphasize sections of
text by changing the font
size. Absolute font sizes
on a Web page range
from 1 to 7.

CHANGE THE ABSOLUTE TEXT SIZE

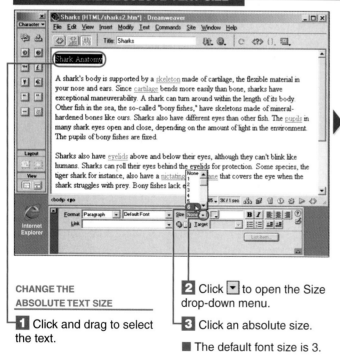

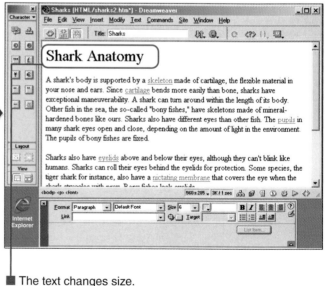

CHANGE THE
ABSOLUTE TEXT SIZE

1 Click and drag to select
the text.

2 Click ▼ to open the Size
drop-down menu.

3 Click an absolute size.

■ The default font size is 3.

■ The text changes size.

How can changing the size of text enhance my Web page?

You can experiment with the size of words to produce interesting headlines on your Web pages. You can change the size of individual characters at the beginning of text passages for a traditional effect.

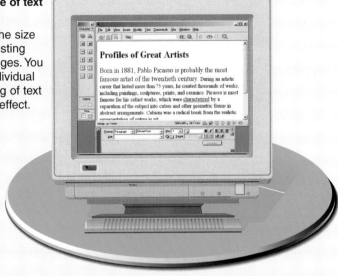

CHANGE THE RELATIVE TEXT SIZE

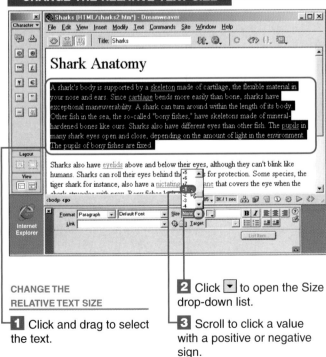

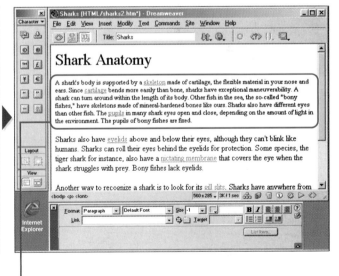

**CHANGE THE
RELATIVE TEXT SIZE**

1 Click and drag to select the text.

2 Click ▼ to open the Size drop-down list.

3 Scroll to click a value with a positive or negative sign.

■ The text changes size relative to the default size, which is 3.

Note: To adjust text size by creating a heading, see page 66.

CHANGE FONT COLOR

You can change the color of text on all or part of your Web page so that it complements the background and other page elements.

To change the background color of your Web page, see page 102.

CHANGE THE COLOR OF ALL TEXT

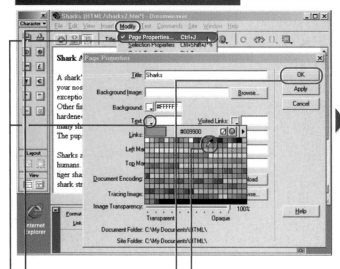

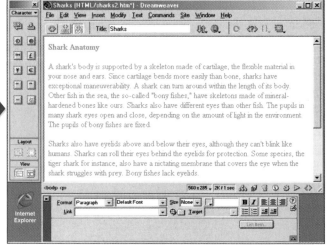

1 Click **Modify**.

2 Click **Page Properties**.

■ The Page Properties dialog box appears.

3 Click the **Text Color** button ( ).

4 Click a color from the menu by using the Eyedropper tool ( ).

5 Click **OK**.

Note: The default color of text on a Web page is black.

■ Your text appears in a new color on your Web page.

What are the letter and number combinations that appear in the color fields of Dreamweaver?

HTML represents colors using six-digit codes (called *hexadecimal codes*). Hex codes are preceded by a pound sign (#). Instead of ranging from 0 to 9, hex-code digits range from 0 to F, with A equal to 10, B equal to 11, and so on through F, which is equal to 15. The first two digits in a hex code specify the amount of red in the selected color, the second two digits specify the amount of green, and the third two digits specify the amount of blue.

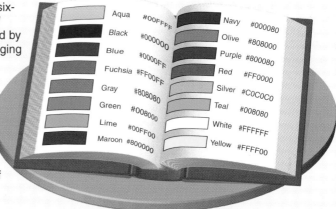

Aqua	#00FFFF
Black	#000000
Blue	#0000FF
Fuchsia	#FF00FF
Gray	#808080
Green	#008000
Lime	#00FF00
Maroon	#800000
Navy	#000080
Olive	#808000
Purple	#800080
Red	#FF0000
Silver	#C0C0C0
Teal	#008080
White	#FFFFFF
Yellow	#FFFF00

CHANGE THE COLOR OF SELECTED TEXT

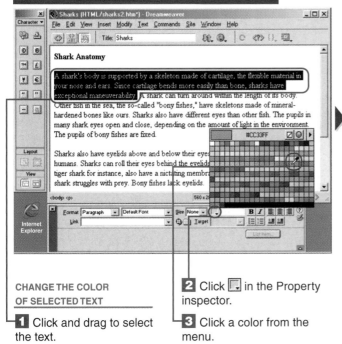

CHANGE THE COLOR OF SELECTED TEXT

1 Click and drag to select the text.

2 Click in the Property inspector.

3 Click a color from the menu.

■ The selected text appears in the new color.

You can format text using the HTML Styles panel, which allows you to apply complicated style with a single click.

APPLY HTML STYLES

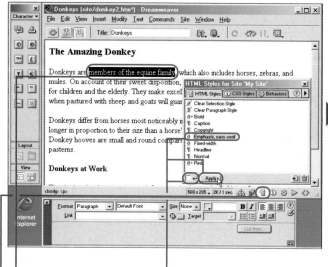

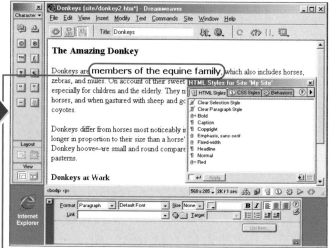

1 Click and drag to select the text you want to format in the Document window.

2 Click the **HTML Styles** button (▣).

■ You can also click **Window** and then **HTML Styles**.

■ The HTML Styles panel appears.

3 Select a style from the list.

4 Click **Apply**.

■ If the check box is selected, the style is applied automatically.

■ The text appears formatted according to the style.

Note: Dreamweaver comes with several HTML styles predefined. To add your own custom styles to the HTML Styles window, see page 85.

CREATE A NEW HTML STYLE

Dreamweaver allows you
to save time by saving
complicated text styles in
the HTML Styles panel.

CREATE A NEW HTML STYLE

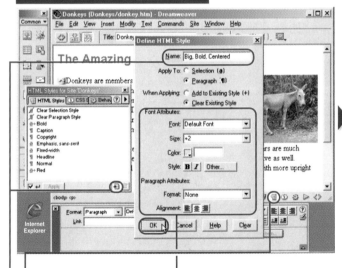

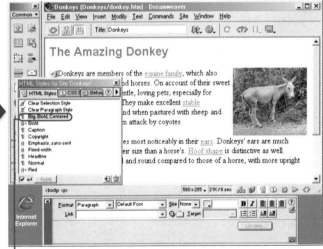

1 Click ▦ on the bottom of
the Document window.

■ The HTML Styles panel
appears.

2 Click ⊞.

3 Type the name for your
new style.

■ You can apply styles to
text or a paragraph. You
can also add new styles to
any existing styles or clear
the existing styles.

4 Select the text formatting
for your style.

5 Click **OK**.

■ The new style appears in
the HTML Styles panel.

Note: To apply a style from the
HTML Styles window, see page 84.

85

MUSIC DEPARTMENT

Many of America's most successful musicians pu[rsue] [t]hrough the reputable Boeing University Mus[ic]

Our [tale]nted staff are well known for t[he] [c]apability to help musicians take [thei]r skills to the next level.

The [Boe]ing University Band has wo[n many] national awards over th[e year]s, and performs at co[nventi]ons around the country.

If [you']re i[nteres]ted in becoming a [profe]ssional m[u]sician, or just [to learn mor]e about music, Boeing University offers the course for

CHAPTER 6

Working with Images and Graphics

You make your Web page much more interesting by adding digital photos, scanned art, and other types of images and graphics. This chapter shows you how to insert and format them.

INSERT AN IMAGE INTO A WEB PAGE

Different types of images, including clip art, digital camera images, and scanned photos, can be inserted into your Web page.

INSERT AN IMAGE INTO A WEB PAGE

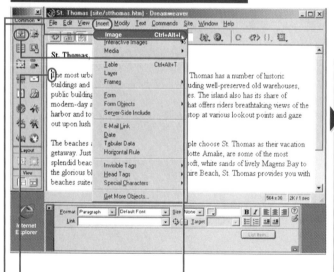

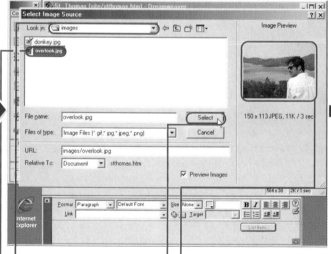

1 Position the cursor where you want to insert the image.

2 Click **Insert**.

3 Click **Image**.

■ You can also click 🖼 in the Objects panel.

■ The Select Image Source dialog box appears.

4 Click ⏷ to select the folder containing the image.

5 Click the image file that you want to insert into your Web page.

Note: Most Web image files will end in .gif (for GIF files) or .jpg (for JPEG files).

■ A preview of the image appears.

Note: If you want to insert an image that exists at an external Web address, you can type the address into the URL field.

6 Click **Select**.

What are the file formats for Web images?

The majority of the images you see on Web pages are GIF or JPEG files. Both GIF and JPEG are compressed file formats, which means they excel at storing image information in a small amount of file space. GIF is best for flat-color illustrations and other images that contain a limited number of colors (it only supports a maximum of 256 colors in an image). JPEG excels at storing photographic information (it supports millions of colors in an image). You insert GIF and JPEG files into your Web page by using the steps described on page 88.

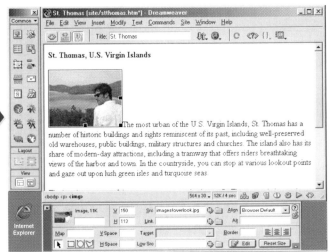

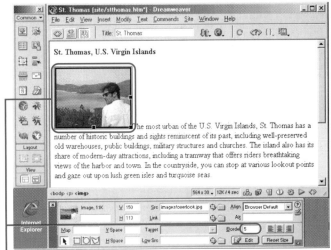

■ The image appears where you positioned your cursor in the Web page.

■ To delete an image, click the image and press Delete.

ADD A BORDER TO AN IMAGE

1 Click the image to select it.

2 Type the width (in pixels) into the Border field.

3 Press Enter (Return).

■ A border appears around the image in the same color the same as the text.

WRAP TEXT AROUND AN IMAGE

Aligning the image to one side of a Web page allows you to wrap text around it. Wrapping text around images enables you to fit more information onto the screen and gives your Web pages a more professional look.

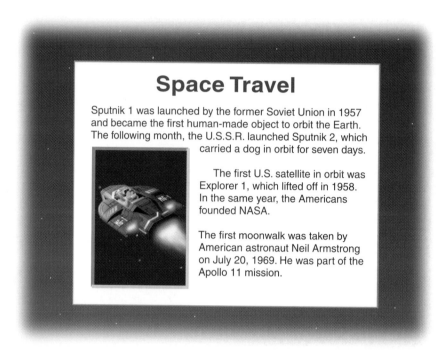

Space Travel

Sputnik 1 was launched by the former Soviet Union in 1957 and became the first human-made object to orbit the Earth. The following month, the U.S.S.R. launched Sputnik 2, which carried a dog in orbit for seven days.

The first U.S. satellite in orbit was Explorer 1, which lifted off in 1958. In the same year, the Americans founded NASA.

The first moonwalk was taken by American astronaut Neil Armstrong on July 20, 1969. He was part of the Apollo 11 mission.

WRAP TEXT AROUND AN IMAGE

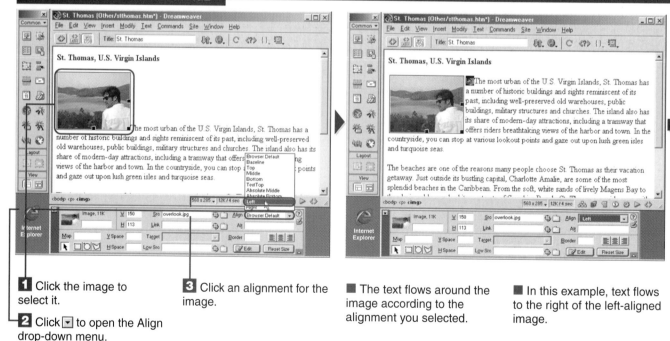

1 Click the image to select it.

2 Click ▼ to open the Align drop-down menu.

3 Click an alignment for the image.

■ The text flows around the image according to the alignment you selected.

■ In this example, text flows to the right of the left-aligned image.

How can I tell how much file space my images and text are taking up on my Web page?

The total size of your page appears in kilobytes (K) on the status bar. The total size includes the size of your HTML file, the size of your images, and the size of anything else on the page. Next to the size is the estimated download time for the page. You can specify how Dreamweaver estimates the download speed in your Preferences. (See page 30.)

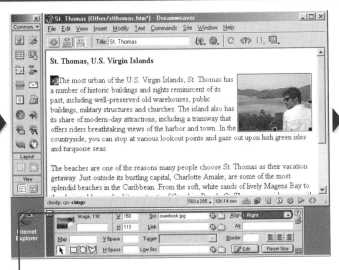

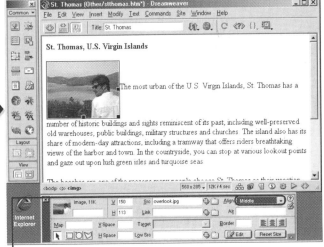

■ You can select other options from the Align drop-down menu for different wrapping effects (example: **Right Align**).

■ In this example, text flows to to the left of the right-aligned image.

■ In this example, the image has been middle-aligned on the page.

CENTER AN IMAGE

Centering an image can give a photo or banner prominence on your page.

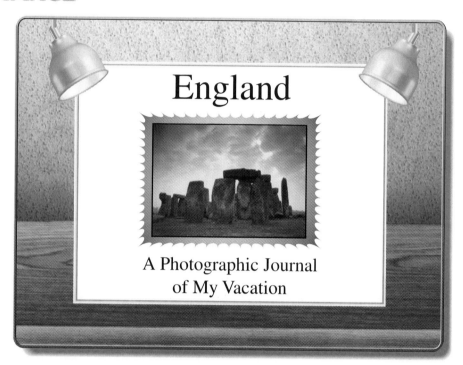

CENTER AN IMAGE

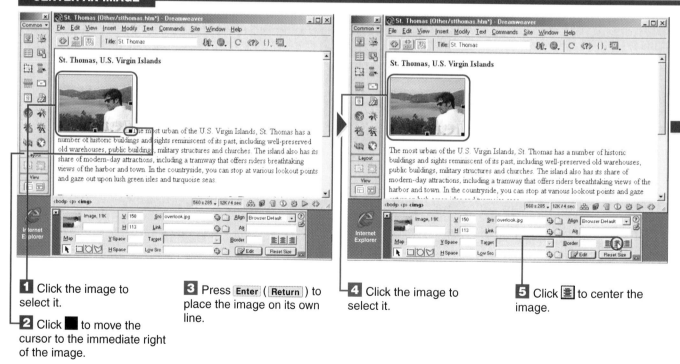

1 Click the image to select it.

2 Click ■ to move the cursor to the immediate right of the image.

3 Press Enter (Return) to place the image on its own line.

4 Click the image to select it.

5 Click 畺 to center the image.

How can I use centered images to enhance my text?

You can center small icons to divide main sections of text in your Web page. These icons serve the same purpose as horizontal rules (see page 98), but add a more sophisticated look to your pages.

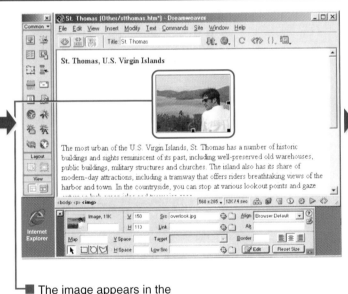

■ The image appears in the center of the page.

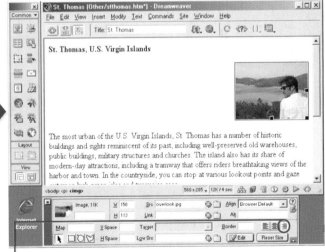

■ You can also align the image to the right side of the page by clicking 📄.

RESIZE AN IMAGE

You can change the size of an image by changing the pixel dimensions, making the image a percentage of the browser window, or clicking and dragging the corner of the image.

Pixels are the tiny, solid-color squares that make up a digital image

RESIZE AN IMAGE

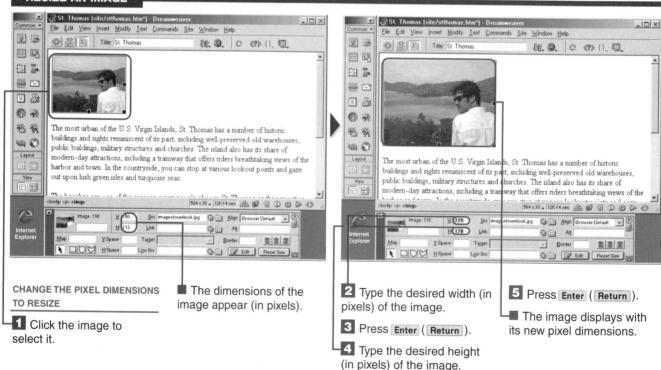

CHANGE THE PIXEL DIMENSIONS TO RESIZE

1 Click the image to select it.

■ The dimensions of the image appear (in pixels).

2 Type the desired width (in pixels) of the image.

3 Press Enter (Return).

4 Type the desired height (in pixels) of the image.

5 Press Enter (Return).

■ The image displays with its new pixel dimensions.

What is the best way to change the dimensions of a Web-page image?

The best way to change the dimensions of a Web-page image is with an image editor, which enables you to adjust the image's real height and width and save it as a new file. This maximizes the quality of the image.

Changing the dimensions of an image in Dreamweaver stretches or shrinks the original image to fit the new dimensions, but does not change the real dimensions of the file. Sometimes this results in an image on a Web page that has reduced quality compared to the original.

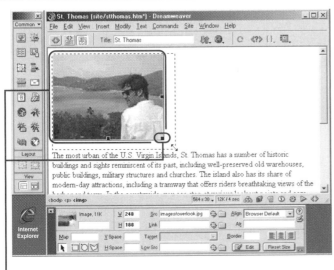

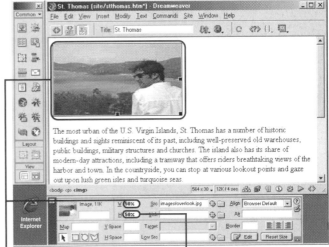

CLICK AND DRAG TO RESIZE

1 Click the image to select it.

2 Drag the handle at the edge of the image.

■ To constrain proportions, press and hold **Shift** as you drag a corner.

■ The image expands or contracts to its new dimensions.

CHANGE THE PROPORTIONAL SIZE TO RESIZE

1 Click the image to select it.

2 Type the desired percentage of the width.

3 Press **Enter** (**Return**).

4 Type the desired percentage of the height.

5 Press **Enter** (**Return**).

■ The image displays as a percentage of the browser window (not as a percentage of its original size).

ADD SPACE AROUND AN IMAGE

Adding space around an image distinguishes it from the text and other images on your Web page.

ADD SPACE AROUND AN IMAGE

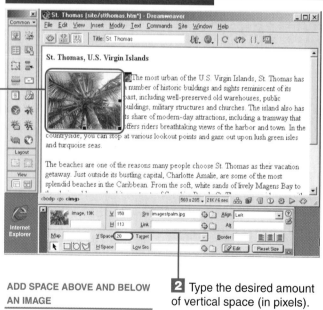

ADD SPACE ABOVE AND BELOW AN IMAGE

1 Click the image to select it.

2 Type the desired amount of vertical space (in pixels).

3 Press Enter (Return).

■ An extra space appears above and below the image.

Why should I add space around my images?

In many cases, adding space around your images enhances the appearance of your Web page. The extra space makes text easier to read and keeps adjacent images from appearing as a single image.

SUMMER VACATIONS

15 pixels

15 pixels

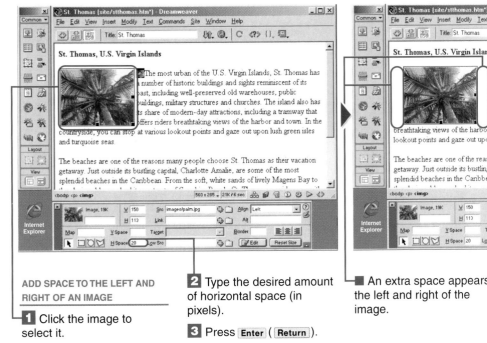

ADD SPACE TO THE LEFT AND RIGHT OF AN IMAGE

1 Click the image to select it.

2 Type the desired amount of horizontal space (in pixels).

3 Press Enter (Return).

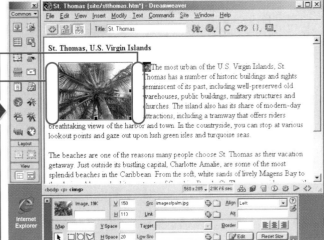

■ An extra space appears to the left and right of the image.

ADD A HORIZONTAL RULE

You can add a horizontal rule to your Web page to separate sections of content.

ADD A HORIZONTAL RULE

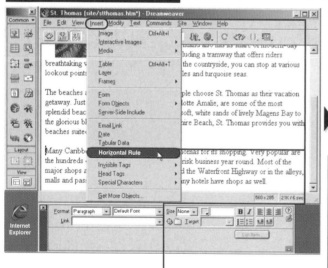

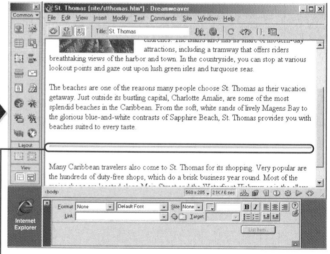

1 Position your cursor where you want to insert the horizontal rule.

2 Click **Insert**.

3 Click **Horizontal Rule**.

■ A thin horizontal line spans the entire width of the Web page.

Can I customize the color of my horizontal rule?

You can define the shading, but not the color of your horizontal rule. If you want your rules to have a particular color, you can create them as custom graphics in programs such as Macromedia Fireworks and Adobe Photoshop.

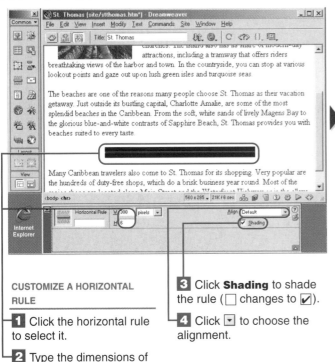

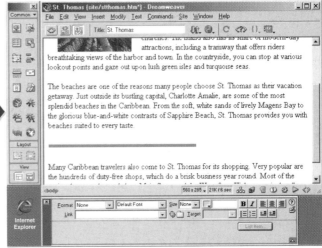

CUSTOMIZE A HORIZONTAL RULE

1 Click the horizontal rule to select it.

2 Type the dimensions of the horizontal rule (in pixels) in the W (width) and H (height) fields.

3 Click **Shading** to shade the rule (☐ changes to ☑).

4 Click ▾ to choose the alignment.

■ The horizontal rule appears with its custom style and measurements.

ADD A BACKGROUND IMAGE

You can incorporate a background image to add texture to your Web page. Background images appear beneath any text or images on your page.

ADD A BACKGROUND IMAGE

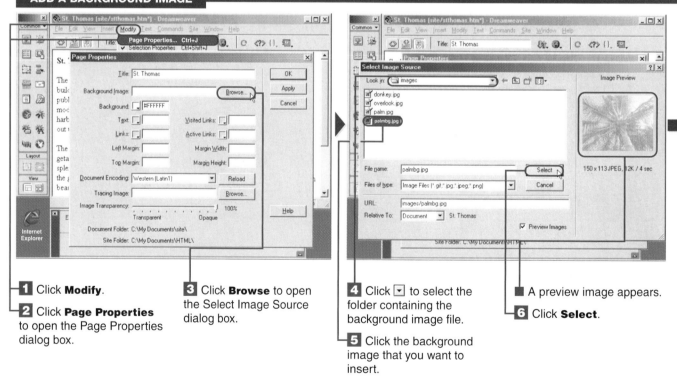

■1 Click **Modify**.

■2 Click **Page Properties** to open the Page Properties dialog box.

■3 Click **Browse** to open the Select Image Source dialog box.

■4 Click ▾ to select the folder containing the background image file.

■5 Click the background image that you want to insert.

■ A preview image appears.

■6 Click **Select**.

What types of images make good backgrounds?

Typically, images that do not clash with the text and other content in the foreground make good background images. You do not want your background image to overwhelm the rest of the page.

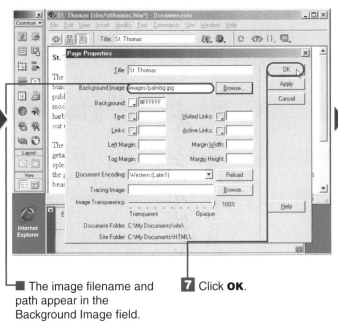

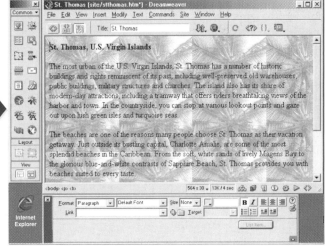

■ The image filename and path appear in the Background Image field.

7 Click **OK**.

■ The image appears as a background on the Web page.

Note: If necessary, the image tiles horizontally and vertically to fill the entire window.

CHANGE THE BACKGROUND COLOR

For variety, you can change the background color of your Web page.

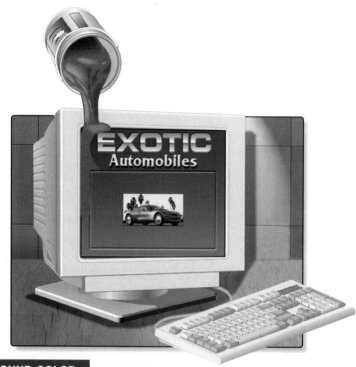

The default background color of Dreamweaver Web pages is white.

CHANGE THE BACKGROUND COLOR

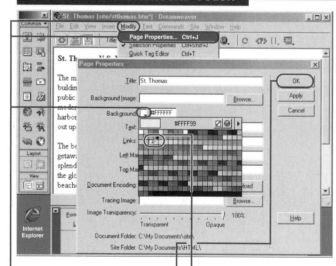

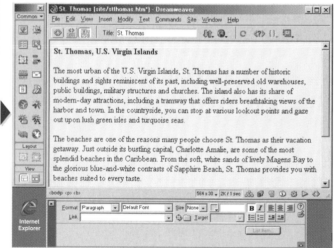

1 Click **Modify**.

2 Click **Page Properties** to open the Page Properties dialog box.

3 Click the **Background** to open the color menu.

4 Click a color from the menu using the eyedropper tool ( ).

5 Click **OK**.

■ The background of your Web page displays in the newly selected color.

Note: See page 82 for additional information on Web color.

Note: A background image will appear over any background color. See page 100 for more information.

102

You can add
alternate text for
users to read
when an image
does not appear
on your page.

Some Web
browsers cannot
display images, and
some users surf the
Web with images
turned off.

ADD ALTERNATE TEXT

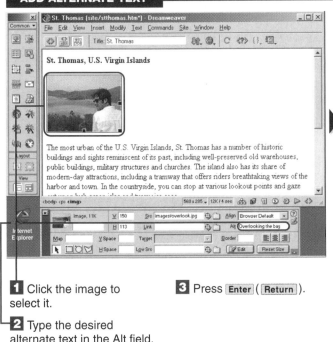

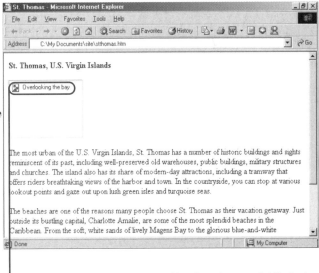

1 Click the image to
select it.

2 Type the desired
alternate text in the Alt field.

3 Press Enter (Return).

■ The alternate text appears
when the image does not
display in the browser
window.

*Note: Some browsers briefly display
alternative text when you hold your
cursor over an image.*

INSERT MULTIMEDIA

You can insert video clips and other multimedia to add life to your Web page.

INSERT MULTIMEDIA

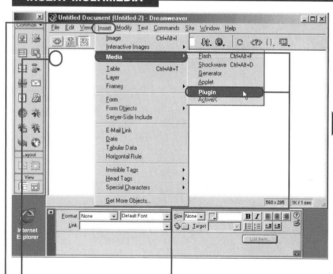

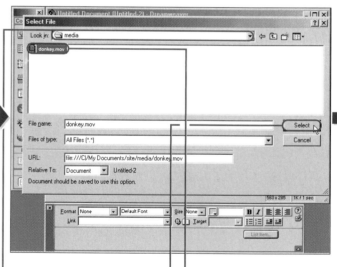

1 Position the cursor where you want to insert the multimedia in the Document window.

2 Click **Insert**.

3 Click **Media**.

4 Click **Plugin** to add a video or sound clip.

■ Many multimedia features in Web browsers are handled by special add-ons called Plugins.

■ The Select File dialog box appears.

5 Click ▣ to select the folder containing the multimedia file.

6 Click the multimedia file that you want to insert.

7 Click **Select**.

What should I consider when adding multimedia content to my site?

You can add video clips, sounds and interactive features such as Flash to jazz up a Web site. But remember that some users will not be able to view the content because their browsers do not support it and that some users are unwilling to spend the time to download and install a Plugin.

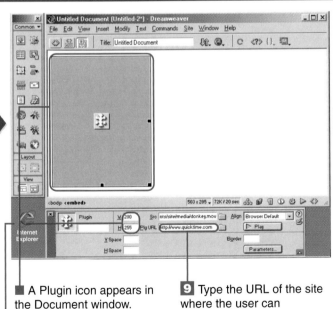

■ A Plugin icon appears in the Document window.

8 Type the dimensions of the file (in pixels) in the W (width) and H (height) fields.

9 Type the URL of the site where the user can download the Plugin.

■ If the Plugin is not installed on a user's browser, the browser will ask if the user wants to visit the site to download the Plugin.

■ You can test some multimedia files, such as QuickTime movies, in the Document window.

10 Click ▷ Play to test the multimedia file.

Microsoft FrontPage

File Edit View Insert Format Tools Table Frames Window Help

Recipes

Chicken Pasta

Stuffed Peppers

Chicken Kiev

Lasagna

Vegetable Fried Rice

Vegetable Fried Rice

Here is a great recipe that allows you to spice up your rice while making it more healthy.

- 4 tsp. olive oil
- 2 green onions, sliced in one inch pieces
- 2 cloves minced garlic
- 2 stalks sliced celery
- 2 sliced carrots
- 2 cups broccoli florets
- 1/2 red pepper (chopped)
- 1 tbsp. reduced sodium soy sauce

CHAPTER 7

Creating Hyperlinks

You can connect related information on different Web pages by creating hyperlinks. This chapter shows you how to turn both text and images into hyperlinks.

You can create a
hyperlink that allows
readers to move from
one page of your Web
site to another.

HYPERLINK TO ANOTHER PAGE IN YOUR SITE

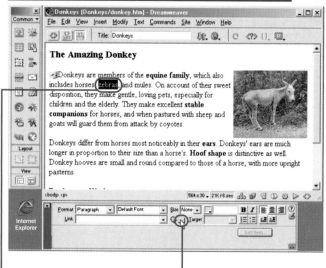

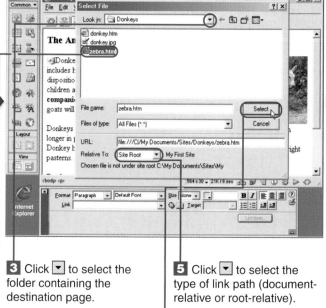

1 Click and drag to select
the text that you want to turn
into a hyperlink.

*Note: See page 112 for more
information on linking an image.*

2 Click 🔲 in the Properties
Inspector to open the Select
File dialog box.

3 Click ▼ to select the
folder containing the
destination page.

4 From the list menu, click
the HTML file to which you
want to link.

5 Click ▼ to select the
type of link path (document-
relative or root-relative).

6 Click **Select**.

How should I organize the files that make up my Web site?

You should keep the files that make up your Web site in the folder that you define as your local site folder (see page 52). This makes creating links between your pages easier and ensures that all the links work correctly when you transfer the files to a live Web server (see page 262).

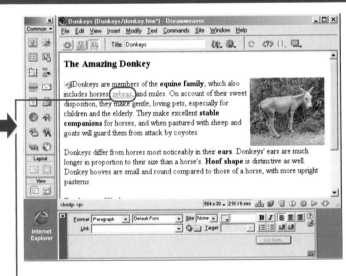

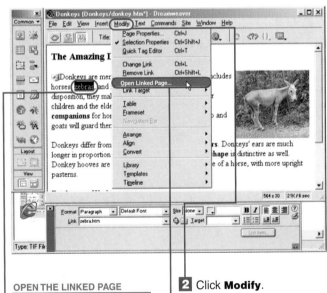

■ The new hyperlink appears in color and underlined.

■ Hyperlinks are not clickable in the Document window.

■ You can also test the link by previewing the file in a Web browser.

Note: See page 60 for instructions on previewing and testing a link.

OPEN THE LINKED PAGE

1 Click and drag to select the text of the hyperlink whose destination you want to open.

2 Click **Modify**.

3 Click **Open Linked Page**.

■ The link destination opens in a Document window.

HYPERLINK TO ANOTHER WEB SITE

You can give viewers
access to additional
information about topics
by linking to pages in
other Web sites.

HYPERLINK TO ANOTHER WEB SITE

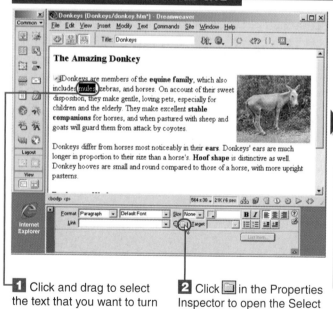

1 Click and drag to select the text that you want to turn into a hyperlink.

2 Click ▭ in the Properties Inspector to open the Select File dialog box.

3 Type the Web address of the destination page (include the **http://**) in the URL field.

4 Click **Select**.

How do I make sure my links to other Web sites always work?

You usually have no control over the Web pages on other sites to which you have linked. If you have linked to a Web page whose file is later renamed or taken offline, your viewer will receive an error message when they click the link. Maintain your site by periodically testing your links.

Other Classical Music Sites!

Here are other Web resources that I recommend:

1. **Introduction to Classical Music** ✓
2. **Composer Biographies** ✓
3. **Sound Files** ✓
4. **CD Reviews** ✓

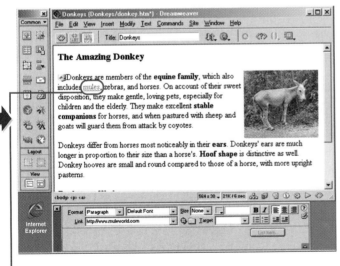

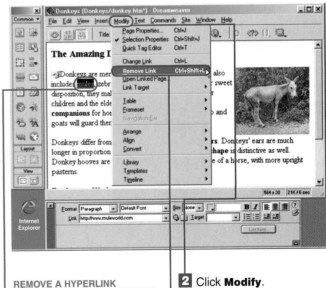

■ The new hyperlink appears colored and underlined.

■ Hyperlinks are not clickable in the Document window.

■ You can test the link by previewing the file in a Web browser.

Note: See page 60 for instructions on previewing and testing a link.

REMOVE A HYPERLINK

1 Click and drag to select the text of the hyperlink that you want to remove.

2 Click **Modify**.

3 Click **Remove Link**.

CREATE IMAGE HYPERLINKS

An image hyperlink allows users to click an image to go to another Web page.

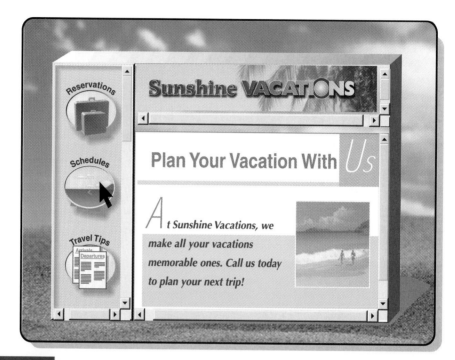

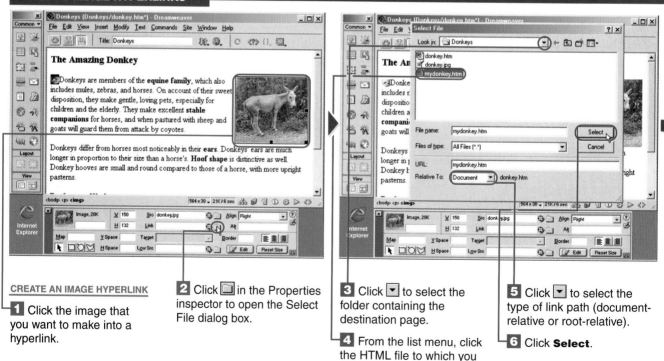

CREATE AN IMAGE HYPERLINK

1 Click the image that you want to make into a hyperlink.

2 Click ▭ in the Properties inspector to open the Select File dialog box.

3 Click ▼ to select the folder containing the destination page.

4 From the list menu, click the HTML file to which you want to link.

5 Click ▼ to select the type of link path (document-relative or root-relative).

6 Click **Select**.

How do I create a navigation bar for my Web page?

Many Web sites include a set of hyperlink buttons on the top, side, or bottom of each page. These buttons let viewers navigate to the main pages of the Web site. You can create these buttons using image-editing software such as Adobe Photoshop or Macromedia Fireworks.

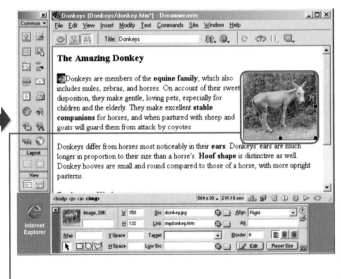

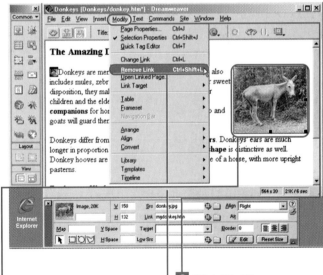

■ Your image is now a hyperlink.

■ Hyperlinks are not clickable in the Document window, but you can access the linked page via the Modify menu.

■ You can also test the link by previewing the file in a Web browser.

Note: See page 60 for instructions on previewing and testing a link.

REMOVE A HYPERLINK FROM AN IMAGE

1 Click the hyperlinked image.

2 Click **Modify**.

3 Click **Remove Link**.

■ The link destination disappears from the Property inspector.

You can create a
hyperlink to other
content on the same Web
page. Same-page
hyperlinks are useful
when a page is very
long.

HYPERLINK TO CONTENT ON THE SAME WEB PAGE

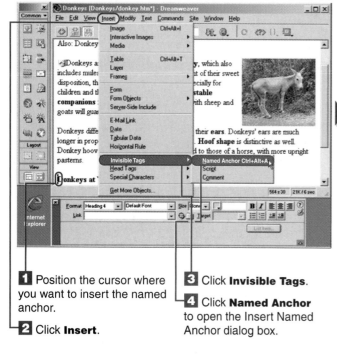

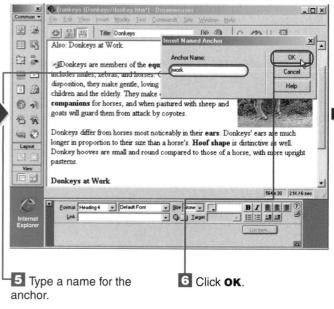

1 Position the cursor where
you want to insert the named
anchor.

2 Click **Insert**.

3 Click **Invisible Tags**.

4 Click **Named Anchor**
to open the Insert Named
Anchor dialog box.

5 Type a name for the
anchor.

6 Click **OK**.

What is an example of a useful same-page hyperlink?

If you have a Web page that is a glossary, same-page links let you link to different parts of the glossary from a hyperlink menu at the top of the page.

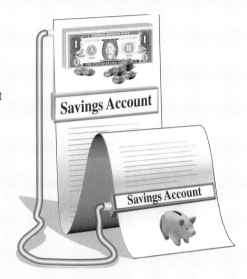

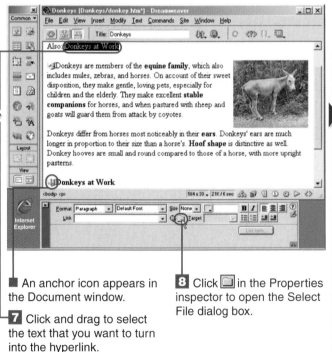

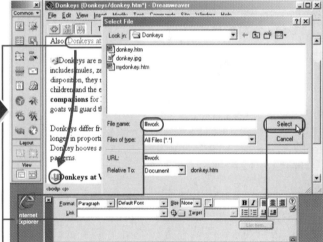

■ An anchor icon appears in the Document window.

7 Click and drag to select the text that you want to turn into the hyperlink.

8 Click ⬜ in the Properties inspector to open the Select File dialog box.

9 Type a pound sign (#) followed by the name of the anchor.

10 Click **Select**.

■ The new hyperlink links to the named anchor.

■ The new hyperlink is not clickable in the Document window.

■ You can test the link by previewing the file in a Web browser.

Note: See page 60 for instructions on previewing and testing a link.

Hyperlinks do not have to lead just to other Web pages. You can link to other file types, such as image files, word processing documents, or multimedia files.

HYPERLINK TO OTHER FILES

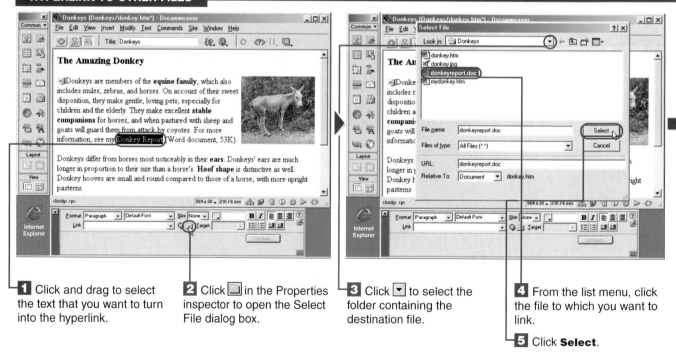

1 Click and drag to select the text that you want to turn into the hyperlink.

2 Click 🖼 in the Properties inspector to open the Select File dialog box.

3 Click ▼ to select the folder containing the destination file.

4 From the list menu, click the file to which you want to link.

5 Click **Select**.

How do users see files that are not HTML documents?

What users see when they click links to other types of files depends on how their Web browser is configured and what applications they have on their computer. For instance, if you link to a QuickTime movie, users need to have QuickTime software installed on their computer to see the movie. If a user does not have the software installed, the browser typically asks if the user wants to download the file and save it so they can view it later (after they have installed the correct software).

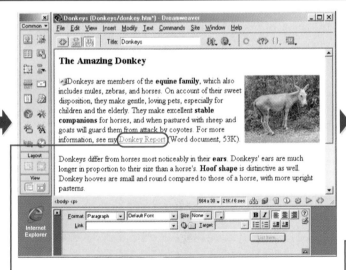

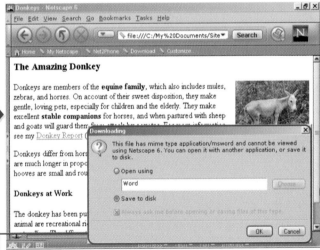

■ The new hyperlink appears in color and underlined.

■ Hyperlinks are not clickable in the Document window.

■ You can test the link by previewing the file in a Web browser.

Note: See page 60 for instructions on previewing and testing a link.

■ The particular browser is not configured to view the type of file that was linked. When you click a Web page link in a browser, an alert box appears asking whether the user wants to open the document with another application or save it.

117

CREATE MULTIPLE HYPERLINKS WITHIN AN IMAGE

To make an image serve several purposes, you can assign different hyperlinks (also called hotspots) to different parts of the image using the Dreamweaver image-mapping tools.

CREATE MULTIPLE HYPERLINKS WITHIN AN IMAGE

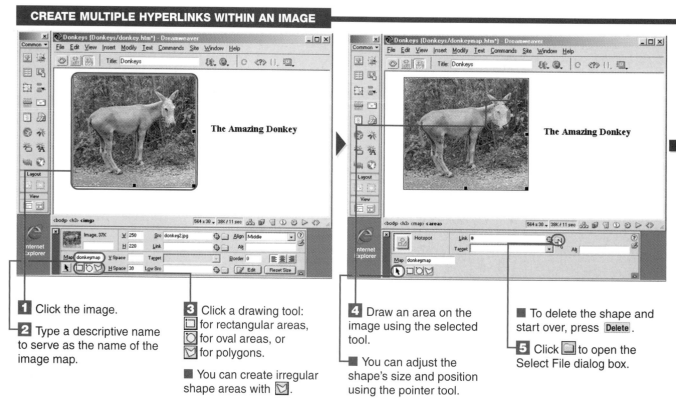

1 Click the image.

2 Type a descriptive name to serve as the name of the image map.

3 Click a drawing tool: ▢ for rectangular areas, ◯ for oval areas, or ▽ for polygons.

■ You can create irregular shape areas with ▽.

4 Draw an area on the image using the selected tool.

■ You can adjust the shape's size and position using the pointer tool.

■ To delete the shape and start over, press Delete .

5 Click ▢ to open the Select File dialog box.

How can I create an interactive map of the United States with each state having a different hyperlink?

Add a map of the U.S. to your Web page and define a hotspot over each state. (You will probably want to use the polygon tool to draw around the states.) Then assign a different hyperlink to each state.

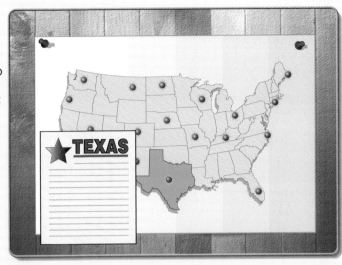

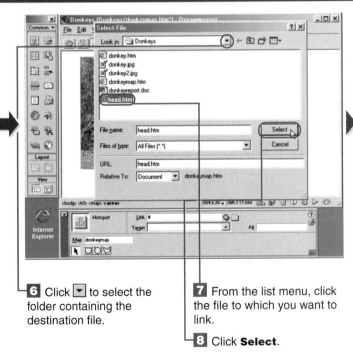

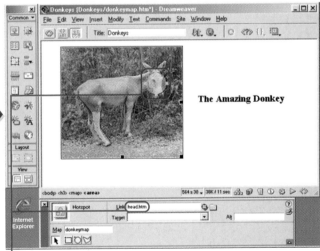

6 Click ▼ to select the folder containing the destination file.

7 From the list menu, click the file to which you want to link.

8 Click **Select**.

■ The area defined by the shape becomes a hyperlink to the selected file (example: The head area has been linked to head.htm).

■ Repeat steps **3** to **8** to add other linked areas to your image.

■ The image-map shapes will not appear when you open the page in a Web browser.

■ You can test the link by previewing the file in a Web browser.

Note: See page 60 for instructions on previewing and testing a link.

CREATE A HYPERLINK THAT OPENS A NEW WINDOW

You can create a
hyperlink that opens
a new browser
window when
clicked. The
destination page
opens in the new
window.

Opening a new
window lets you
keep a previous Web
page open on a
viewer's computer.

CREATE A HYPERLINK THAT OPENS A NEW WINDOW

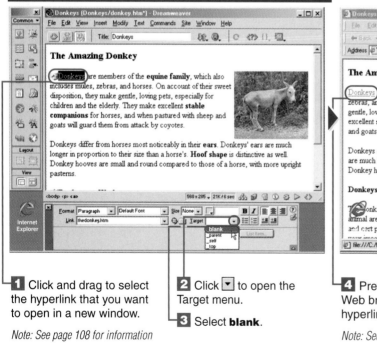

1 Click and drag to select
the hyperlink that you want
to open in a new window.

*Note: See page 108 for information
on creating a hyperlink.*

2 Click ▼ to open the
Target menu.

3 Select **blank**.

4 Preview the page in a
Web browser and click the
hyperlink.

*Note: See page 60 for instructions
on previewing a page in your Web
browser.*

■ The hyperlink destination
appears in a new window.

CREATE A LINK USING THE SITE WINDOW

You can create
hyperlinks on your
page quickly and
easily by clicking
and dragging to
the Site window.

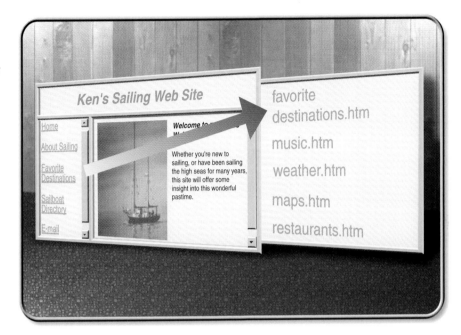

CREATE A HYPERLINK USING THE SITE WINDOW

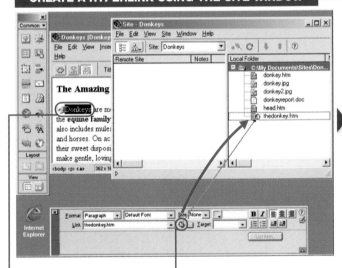

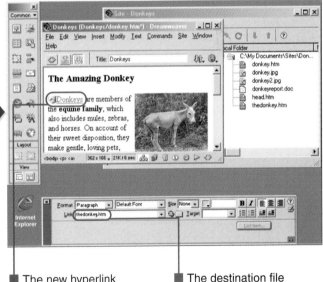

1 Arrange your workspace
making the Document and
Site windows visible.

2 Click and drag to select
the text that you want to turn
into a hyperlink.

■ Alternatively, you can
select an image to create an
image hyperlink.

3 Click and drag the **Point
to File** icon (⊕) to the
destination file in the Site
window.

■ The new hyperlink
appears in color and
underlined.

■ The destination file
displays in the Property
inspector.

CHANGE THE COLOR OF HYPERLINKS

You can change the color of the hyperlinks on your Web page to make them match the visual style of the text and images on your page.

You can change the colors of unvisited links, visited links, and active (clicked) links on your page.

CHANGE THE COLOR OF HYPERLINKS

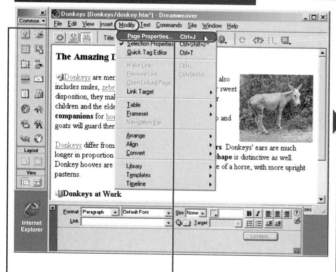

1 Click **Modify**.

2 Click **Page Properties** to open the Page Properties dialog box.

3 Click the **Links** to access a menu from which you can select a color for unvisited links.

4 Click a color from the menu using the eyedropper tool (✐).

■ The color menu closes.

■ You can click the **System Color Picker** button (◉) to select a custom color.

What color will my links appear if I do not specifically define them?

Blue is the default link color in the Dreamweaver Document window. What viewers see when the page opens in a browser depends on the browser settings. By default, most browsers display unvisited links as blue, visited links as purple, and active links as red.

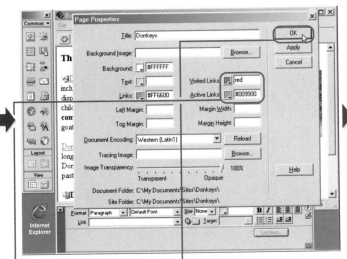

5 Click ▣ to select the colors for Visited Links and Active Links.

■ This example defines the Visited Links with a color name. You can specify common colors on your Web page with their names, instead of choosing the colors from the color menu.

6 Click **OK**.

7 Preview the page in a Web browser.

Note: See page 60 for instructions on previewing a page in your Web browser.

■ The hyperlinks display in the defined colors.

123

CHECK HYPERLINKS

You can
automatically verify
a Web page's links
and get a report
that lists any that
are broken.

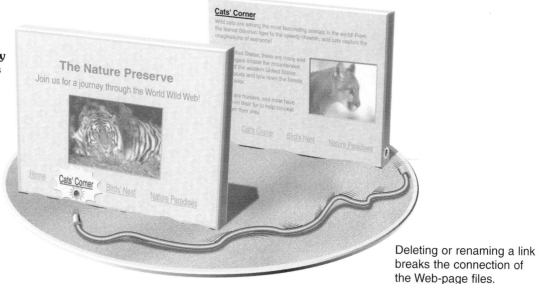

Deleting or renaming a link
breaks the connection of
the Web-page files.

CHECK HYPERLINKS

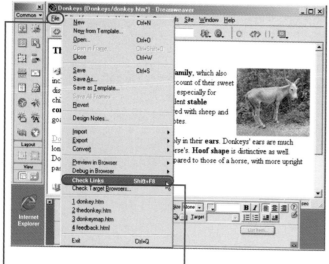

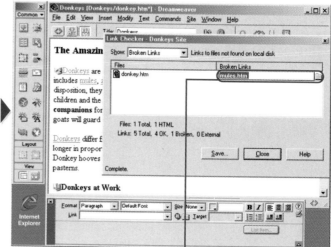

1 Open the Web page you
want to check.

2 Click **File**.

3 Click **Check Links** to
open the Link Checker
dialog box.

■ Dreamweaver checks the
local hyperlinks and lists any
broken links it finds.

*Note: Dreamweaver is unable to
verify links to Web pages on external
sites.*

■ You can edit a broken
destination file by selecting
it and editing the Broken
Links field.

■ You can also click ▣ to
select a new destination for
the link.

CREATE AN E-MAIL HYPERLINK

You can create a
hyperlink that launches
an e-mail composition
window.

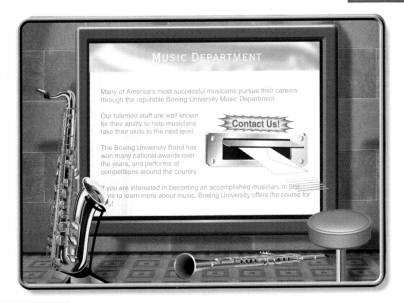

CREATE AN E-MAIL HYPERLINK

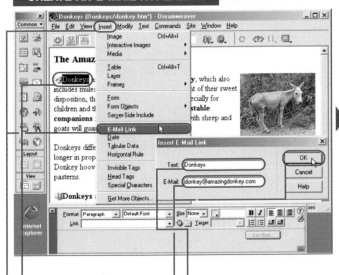

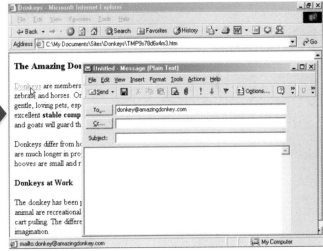

1 Click and drag to select
the text that you want to turn
into an e-mail hyperlink.

2 Click **Insert**.

3 Click **E-mail Link**.

■ The selected text appears
in the Text field of the Insert
E-Mail Link dialog box.

4 In the E-mail field, type
the e-mail address to which
you want to link.

5 Click **OK**.

6 To test the link, preview
the page in a browser.

*Note: See page 60 for instructions
on previewing a page in your Web
browser.*

■ In Web browsers that
support e-mail, clicking the
hyperlink launches an e-mail
composition window. The To:
field automatically fills with
the E-mail address you
specified in step **4**.

■ If the browser does not
have e-mail capability set up,
clicking the link has no effect.

Softball Standings

Team	Games	Wins	Losses	Ties
The Chargers	10	9	1	0
Sluggers	10	8	1	1
The Champs	10	7	2	1
The Eagles	10	5	5	0
Barry's Battalion	10	3	7	0
The Professionals	10	2	8	0
Baseball Bombers	10	1	9	0

CHAPTER 8

Creating Tables

Tables let you organize text, images, and other information into rows and columns on your Web pages. This chapter shows you how to insert and format tables.

ints

18
17
15
10
6
4
2

INSERT A TABLE INTO YOUR WEB PAGE

You can organize content into columns and rows by inserting tables into your Web page.

Softball Standings

Team	Games	Wins	Losses	Ties	Points
The Chargers	10	9	1	0	18
Sluggers	10	8	1	1	17
The Champs	10	7	2	1	15
The Eagles	10	5	5	0	10
Barry's Battalion	10	3	7	0	6
The Professionals	10	2	8	0	4
Baseball Bombers	10	1	9	0	2

INSERT A TABLE

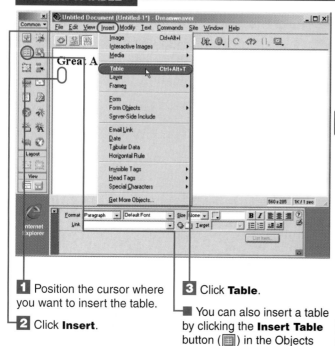

1 Position the cursor where you want to insert the table.

2 Click **Insert**.

3 Click **Table**.

■ You can also insert a table by clicking the **Insert Table** button (▦) in the Objects panel menu.

■ The Insert Table dialog box appears.

4 Type the number of rows and columns in your table.

5 Type the width of your table.

■ You can set the width in pixels or as a percentage by clicking ▼ and selecting your choice of measurements.

6 Type a border size in pixels.

7 Click **OK**.

How do I change the appearance of the content inside my table?

You can specify the size, style, and color of text inside a table the same way you do outside of a table (see pages 76 to 82). Likewise, you can control the appearance of an image inside a table the same way you can control it outside a table (see pages 92 to 94).

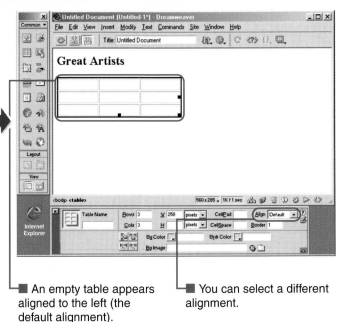

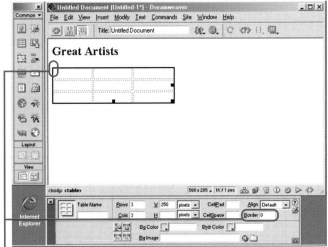

■ An empty table appears aligned to the left (the default alignment).

■ You can select a different alignment.

TURN OFF TABLE BORDERS

1 Click the upper-left corner of the table to select it.

2 Type **0** in the Border field.

3 Press Enter (Return).

■ Dashed lines define the turned off borders.

■ The dashed lines do not display when you open the page in a Web browser.

INSERT CONTENT INTO A TABLE

You can fill the cells of
your table with text,
images, form elements,
and other tables.

INSERT CONTENT INTO A TABLE

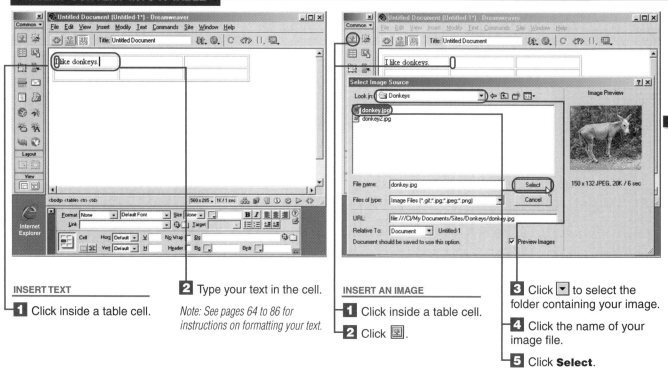

INSERT TEXT

1 Click inside a table cell.

2 Type your text in the cell.

*Note: See pages 64 to 86 for
instructions on formatting your text.*

INSERT AN IMAGE

1 Click inside a table cell.

2 Click ⊞.

3 Click ▼ to select the
folder containing your image.

4 Click the name of your
image file.

5 Click **Select**.

How can I add captions to images on my Web page?

The best way to add a caption to the top, bottom, or side of an image is by creating a two-celled table. Place the image in one cell and the caption in the other. You can then adjust the table's size and alignment to fit the captioned image in with the rest of your page's content.

Can you believe it is me?

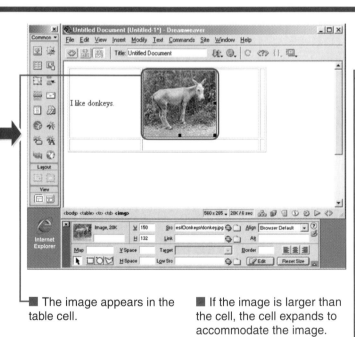

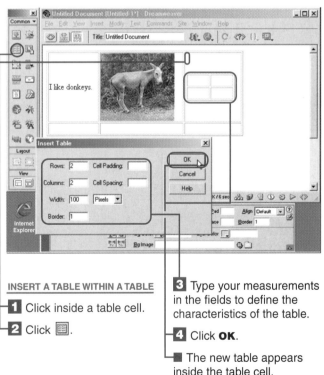

■ The image appears in the table cell.

■ If the image is larger than the cell, the cell expands to accommodate the image.

INSERT A TABLE WITHIN A TABLE

1 Click inside a table cell.

2 Click ▦.

3 Type your measurements in the fields to define the characteristics of the table.

4 Click **OK**.

■ The new table appears inside the table cell.

CHANGE THE BACKGROUND OF A TABLE

You can change the background of a table to complement the style of your Web page by changing the color or filling with an image (see pages 100 to 102).

CHANGE THE BACKGROUND COLOR OF A TABLE

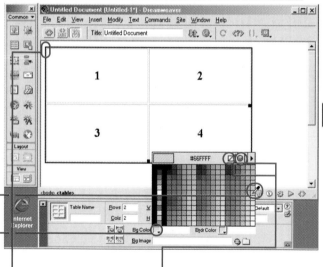

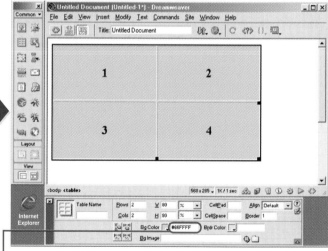

1 Click the upper-left corner of the table to select it.

2 Click **Bg Color** 🔲 to open the color menu.

3 Click a color from the menu using the eyedropper tool (🖉).

■ You can click the **System Color Picker** button (🔘) to select a custom color.

■ You can click the **Default Color** button (🔲) to specify no color.

■ The color fills the background of the table.

■ You can also type a color name or a hexadecimal color code directly.

Note: See page 82 for more information on Web color.

132

How can I change the background of a table cell?

Click inside a cell and then specify the background color using the Bg Color ⬛ or a background image by clicking ⬛.

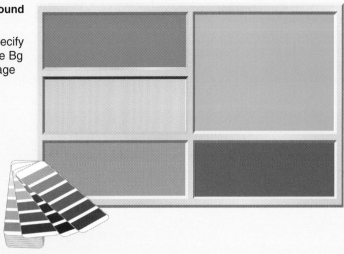

ADD A BACKGROUND IMAGE TO A TABLE

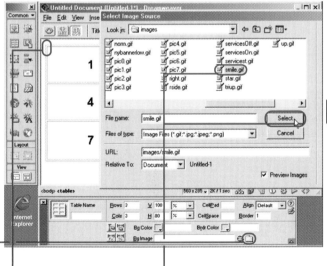

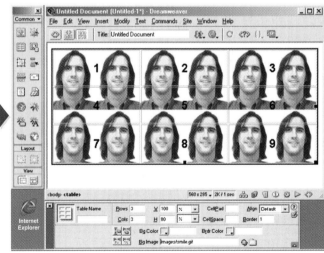

1 Click the upper-left corner of the table to select it.

2 Click ⬛ to open the Select Image Source dialog box.

3 Click an image file.

4 Click **Select**.

■ The table background fills with the image.

■ If the image is smaller than the background area, the image tiles to fill the entire table.

CHANGE THE CELL PADDING IN A TABLE

You can change the cell padding to add space between a table's content and its borders.

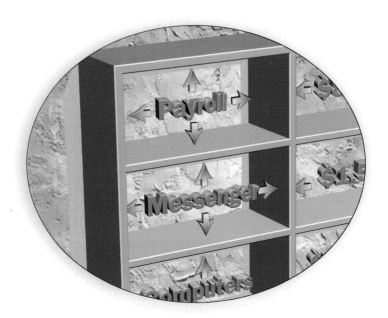

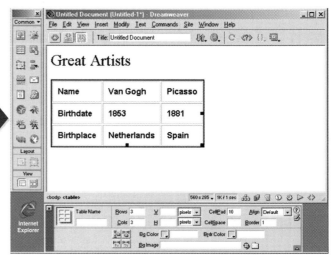

1 Click the upper-left corner of the table to select it.

2 Type the amount of padding (in pixels) in the CellPad field.

3 Press `Enter` (`Return`).

■ The space between the table content and the table borders adjusts.

Note: Adjusting the cell padding affects all the cells in a table. You cannot adjust the padding of individual cells by using the CellPad field.

You can change the cell
spacing to adjust the
width of your table
borders.

CHANGE THE CELL SPACING IN A TABLE

1 Click the upper-left corner
of the table to select it.

2 Type the amount of
spacing (in pixels) in the
CellSpace field.

■ The width of the table's
cell borders adjusts.

*Note: Adjusting the cell spacing
affects all the cell borders in the
table. You cannot adjust the spacing
of individual cell borders by using
the CellSpace field.*

CHANGE THE ALIGNMENT OF A TABLE

You can change the
alignment of a table to
center it or to wrap text
and other content
around it.

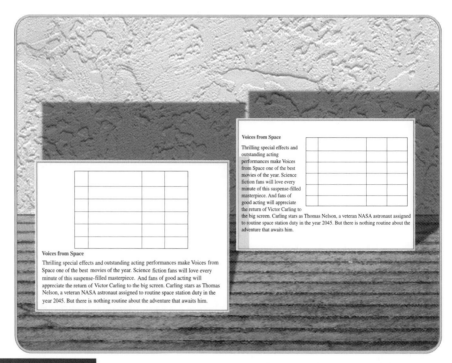

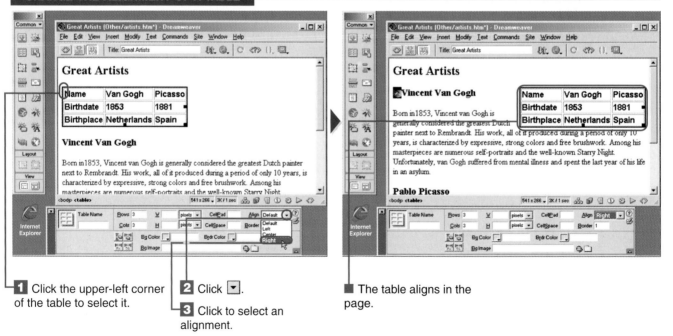

1 Click the upper-left corner
of the table to select it.

2 Click ⏷.

3 Click to select an
alignment.

■ The table aligns in the
page.

CHANGE THE ALIGNMENT OF CELL CONTENT

You can align the
content in your table
cells horizontally and
vertically.

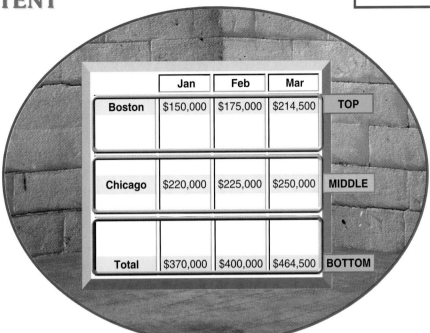

	Jan	Feb	Mar	
Boston	$150,000	$175,000	$214,500	**TOP**
Chicago	$220,000	$225,000	$250,000	**MIDDLE**
Total	$370,000	$400,000	$464,500	**BOTTOM**

CHANGE THE ALIGNMENT OF CELL CONTENT

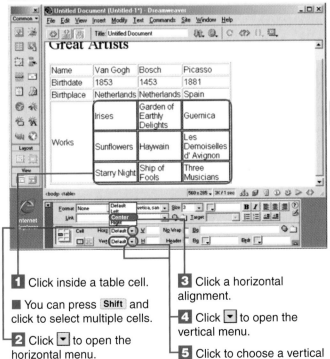

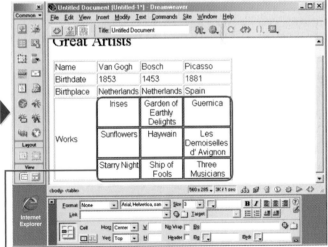

1 Click inside a table cell.

■ You can press **Shift** and click to select multiple cells.

2 Click ▼ to open the horizontal menu.

3 Click a horizontal alignment.

4 Click ▼ to open the vertical menu.

5 Click to choose a vertical alignment.

■ The content aligns inside the table cell.

Note: Nine cells have been assigned a center horizontal alignment and a top vertical alignment.

INSERT OR DELETE A ROW OR COLUMN

You can insert new rows
or columns into your
table to add table
content, or delete rows
or cells to remove
unused cells.

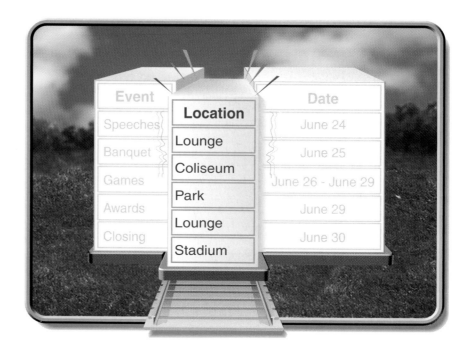

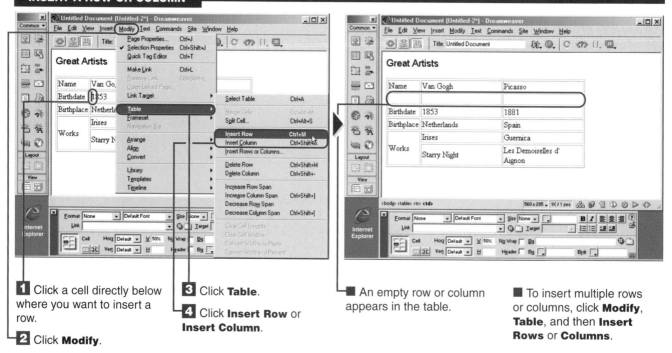

1 Click a cell directly below
where you want to insert a
row.

2 Click **Modify**.

3 Click **Table**.

4 Click **Insert Row** or
Insert Column.

■ An empty row or column
appears in the table.

■ To insert multiple rows
or columns, click **Modify**,
Table, and then **Insert
Rows** or **Columns**.

138

What happens to the content of a deleted cell?

It is deleted as well. Dreamweaver does not warn you if the cells you are deleting in a table contain content. If you accidentally remove content when deleting rows or columns, you can click **Edit** and then **Undo** to undo the last command.

DELETE A ROW OR COLUMN

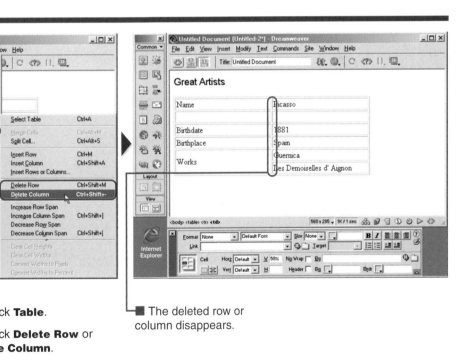

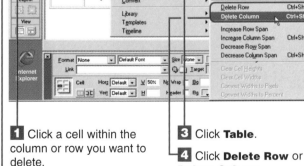

1 Click a cell within the column or row you want to delete.

2 Click **Modify**.

3 Click **Table**.

4 Click **Delete Row** or **Delete Column**.

■ The deleted row or column disappears.

SPLIT OR MERGE TABLE CELLS

You can create a more elaborate arrangement of cells in a table by splitting or merging its cells.

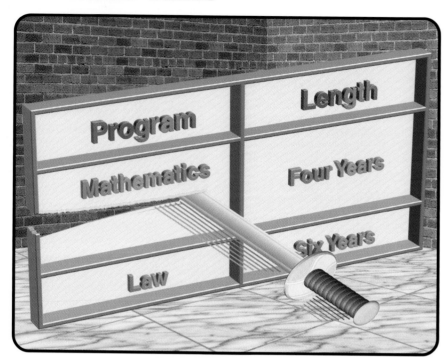

SPLIT A TABLE CELL

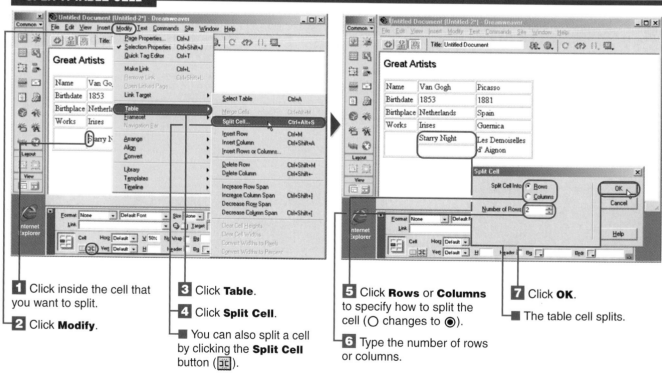

1 Click inside the cell that you want to split.

2 Click **Modify**.

3 Click **Table**.

4 Click **Split Cell**.

■ You can also split a cell by clicking the **Split Cell** button (🔲).

5 Click **Rows** or **Columns** to specify how to split the cell (○ changes to ◉).

6 Type the number of rows or columns.

7 Click **OK**.

■ The table cell splits.

Can I merge any combination of table cells?

No. The cells must have a rectangular arrangement. For instance, you can merge all the cells in a two-row-by-two-column table. But you cannot select three cells that form an L shape and merge them into one.

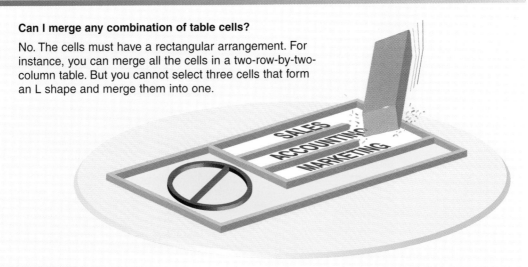

MERGE TABLE CELLS

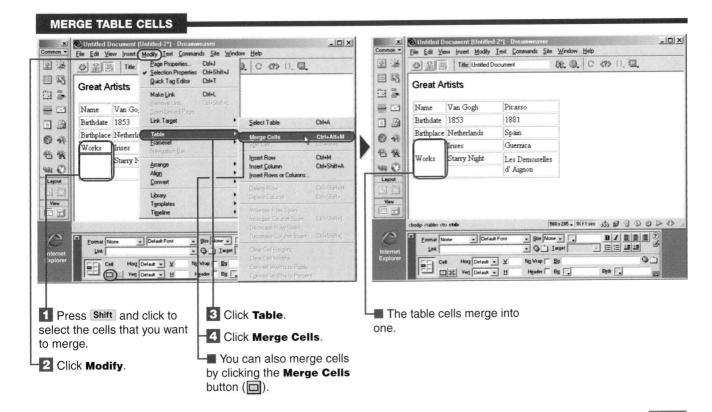

1 Press **Shift** and click to select the cells that you want to merge.

2 Click **Modify**.

3 Click **Table**.

4 Click **Merge Cells**.

■ You can also merge cells by clicking the **Merge Cells** button (▣).

■ The table cells merge into one.

CHANGE THE DIMENSIONS OF A TABLE

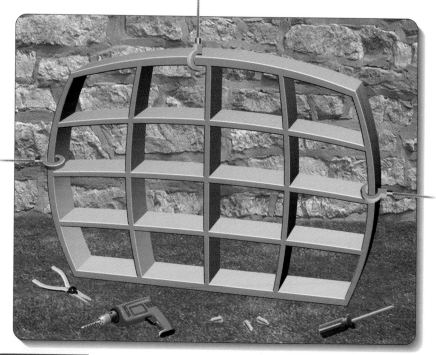

You can change the dimensions of your table to better fit it into your Web page.

CHANGE THE DIMENSIONS OF A TABLE

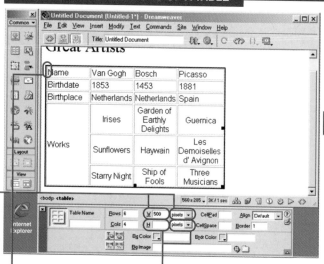

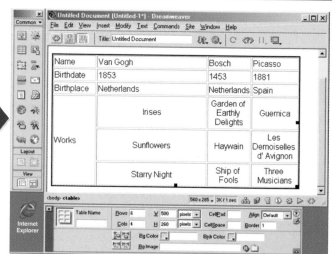

1 Click the upper-left corner of the table to select it.

2 Type the new width.

3 Click ▼ to select the width setting as pixels or a percentage.

4 Type the new height.

5 Click ▼ to select the height setting as pixels or a percentage.

6 Press [Enter] ([Return]).

■ The table readjusts to its new dimensions.

Note: Table dimensions may be constrained by content. Dreamweaver cannot shrink a table smaller than the size of the content it contains.

You can change the dimensions of individual table cells to better organize the content in your table.

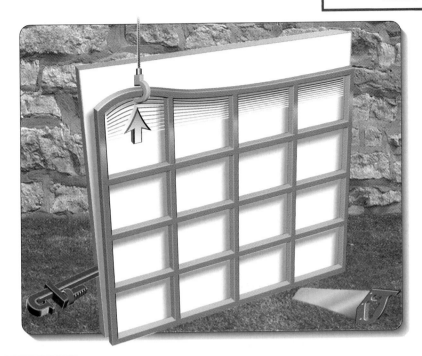

CHANGE THE DIMENSIONS OF A CELL

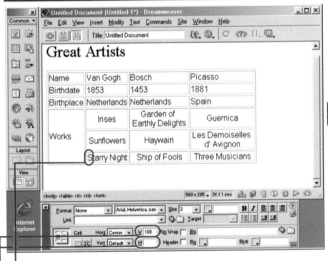

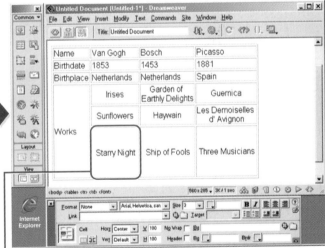

1 Click the cell you want to change.

2 Type the new width (in pixels).

3 Type the new height (in pixels).

■ You can also express your cell dimensions as a percentage of the table size (example: **40%**).

4 Press Enter (Return).

■ The cell readjusts to its new dimensions. The neighboring cells readjust as well.

Note: Cell dimensions may be constrained by content. Dreamweaver cannot shrink a cell smaller than the size of the content it contains.

CREATE A LAYOUT TABLE

Layout Table

You can easily create tables that determine the layout of content in a Web page. Tables used for layout typically take up the entire dimensions of the page and have their borders turned off.

CREATE A LAYOUT TABLE

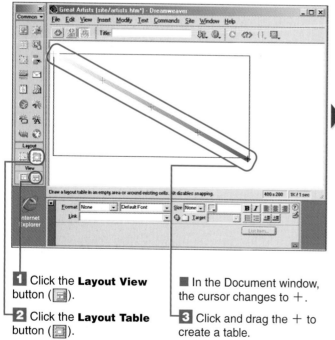

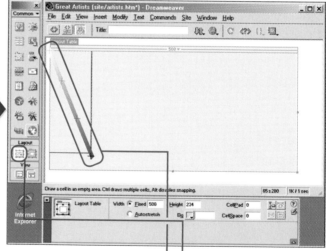

1 Click the **Layout View** button (▣).

2 Click the **Layout Table** button (▣).

■ In the Document window, the cursor changes to +.

3 Click and drag the + to create a table.

■ The outline of a table appears.

■ To add content to your table in Layout View, you must first create layout cells in your table.

4 Click the **Layout Cell** button (▣).

5 Click and drag inside the table to create a Layout Cell.

What can I do that will help me draw my layout table cells precisely?

Turn on the grid feature by clicking **View**, **Grid**, and then **Show Grid**. To customize the grid, click **Edit Grid** under the Grid submenu. Options include changing the grid square size and specifying that table and cell edges snap to the grid edges when they are near them.

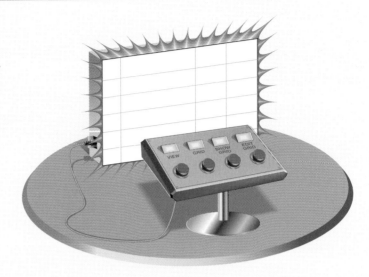

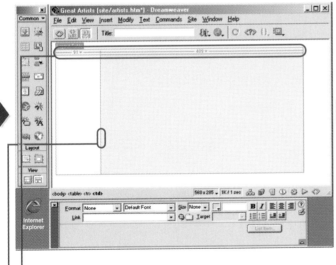

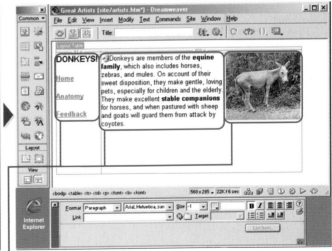

■ The sizes of the table columns appear at the top in pixels.

■ You can adjust the size and position of a cell by clicking and dragging its edge.

Note: See page 146 for information on rearranging a layout table.

■ You can click 🖼 again to draw more cells.

6 Insert content into your cells.

Note: You can insert content in Layout View the same way you do in Standard View. See page 130.

■ To change the properties of a table cell, click the cell's edge and make changes in the Property inspector.

REARRANGE A LAYOUT TABLE

You can easily change the size and the arrangement of a table's cells in Layout View.

REARRANGE A LAYOUT TABLE

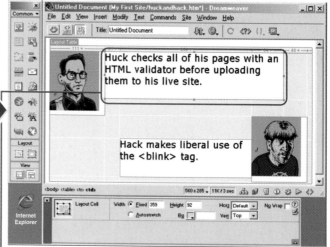

CHANGE THE SIZE OF A CELL

1 Click the edge of a layout cell.

2 Click and drag a side or corner handle.

■ The layout cell resizes.

■ You cannot overlap other layout cells that you have defined.

How do I delete a layout cell or table?

Click the edge of the cell, and then press Delete. Dreamweaver will replace the space with gray, non-editable cells. Similarly, you can delete a layout table by clicking the table's top tab and pressing Delete.

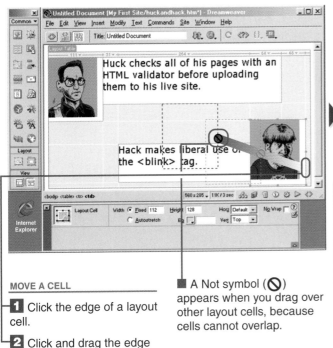

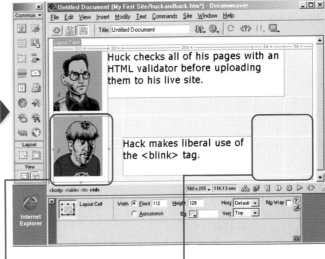

MOVE A CELL

1 Click the edge of a layout cell.

2 Click and drag the edge of the cell (do not click and drag a handle).

■ A Not symbol (⊘) appears when you drag over other layout cells, because cells cannot overlap.

3 Move the layout cell into its new position and release the mouse.

■ Undefined cells in the table adjust their sizes to make room for the cell's new position.

ADJUST THE WIDTH OF A LAYOUT TABLE

By resizing the browser window, you can specify how a layout table's width behaves when the browser window is resized.

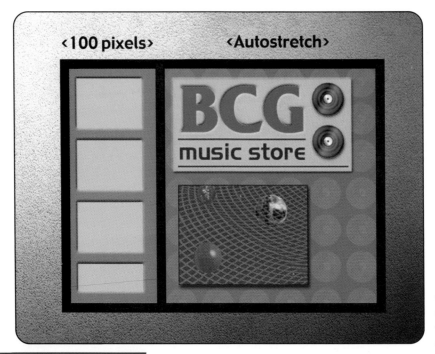

<100 pixels>   <Autostretch>

You can define the table columns as fixed-width or as autostretch.

ADJUST THE WIDTH OF A LAYOUT TABLE

CREATE A FIXED-WIDTH COLUMN

■1 Click a column heading.

■ A drop-down menu appears.

■2 Click **Add Spacer Image**.

■ If your site lacks a spacer image file that it can reference, a dialog box will appear asking if you want to create one. Click **OK** to create a spacer and close the dialog box.

■3 To see where the spacer was added, click 🔲 to view the source code.

■ In the HTML code, you can find where the spacer image has been added.

■ Fixed-width columns appear with a distinct heading style.

148

What is a spacer image?

A spacer image is a transparent GIF image file that is 1x1 pixel in size. Dreamweaver inserts these images into tables then uses HTML code to stretch them to specific sizes to keep table cells at fixed widths.

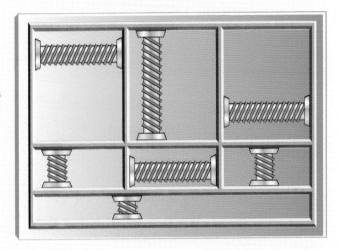

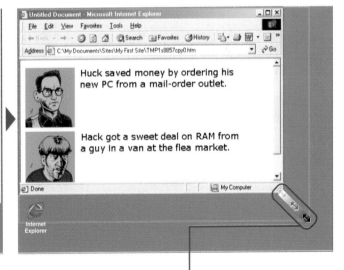

CREATE AN AUTOSTRETCH COLUMN

1 Click a column heading.

■ A drop-down menu appears.

2 Click **Make Column Autostretch**.

■ Dreamweaver writes HTML code that stretches the column to take up any available horizontal space in the browser window.

3 Preview the page in a Web browser.

Note: See page 60 for details on previewing Web pages in a browser.

■ To see the autostretch effect, click and drag the lower-corner of the browser window.

FORMS

What is your age?
- 18-29 30-39 40-49 50-over

Do you visit Web sites dealing with:
- Hobbies Work Travel Studie

Would you recomme
- Yes No

Do you visit Web sites often?
- Every day 3-4 times a week 1-2 times a week

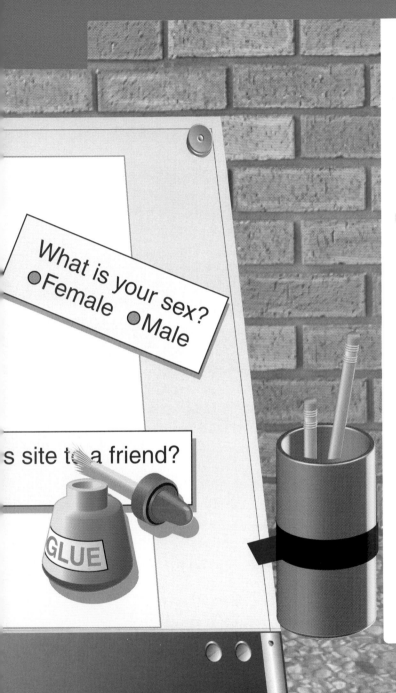

CHAPTER 9

Creating Forms

You can enable your site visitors to send you information by creating forms on your Web pages. This chapter shows you how to create forms with different types of fields, buttons, and menus.

INTRODUCTION TO FORMS

Adding forms to your Web site makes it more interactive, enabling viewers to enter and submit information to you through your Web pages.

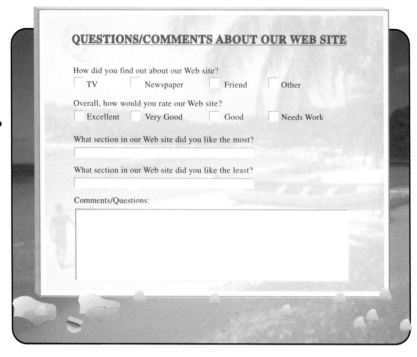

QUESTIONS/COMMENTS ABOUT OUR WEB SITE

How did you find out about our Web site?
☐ TV ☐ Newspaper ☐ Friend ☐ Other

Overall, how would you rate our Web site?
☐ Excellent ☐ Very Good ☐ Good ☐ Needs Work

What section in our Web site did you like the most?

What section in our Web site did you like the least?

Comments/Questions:

Every form works in conjunction with a separate program called a *form handler,* which processes the form information.

Create a Form

You can construct a form by inserting text fields, pull-down menus, check boxes, and other interactive elements into your page. You can also assign the Web address of a form handler to the form so that the information can be processed. Visitors to your Web page fill the form out and send the information to the form handler by clicking a "submit" button.

Process Form Information

The *form handler,* also known as a CGI script, is the program that processes the form information and does something useful with it, such as forwarding the information to an e-mail address or entering it into a database. Many ready-made form handlers are available free on the Web. Your Internet service provider may also have forms available for you to use with your site.

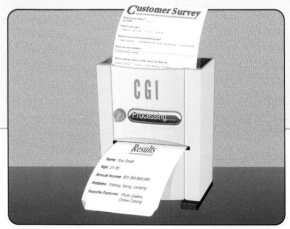

SET UP A FORM

You set up a form on your Web page by first creating a container that holds the text fields, menus, and other form elements. This container gets assigned the Web address of the form handler — the program that processes the submitted form.

SET UP A FORM

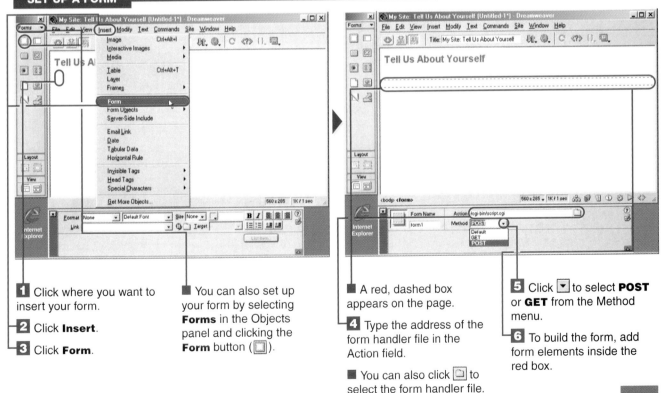

1 Click where you want to insert your form.

2 Click **Insert**.

3 Click **Form**.

■ You can also set up your form by selecting **Forms** in the Objects panel and clicking the **Form** button (▢).

■ A red, dashed box appears on the page.

4 Type the address of the form handler file in the Action field.

■ You can also click ▢ to select the form handler file.

5 Click ▾ to select **POST** or **GET** from the Method menu.

6 To build the form, add form elements inside the red box.

ADD A TEXT FIELD TO A FORM

You can add a text field to enable viewers to submit text through your form. Text fields are probably the most common form elements, enabling users to enter names, addresses, brief answers to questions, and other short pieces of text.

ADD A TEXT FIELD TO A FORM

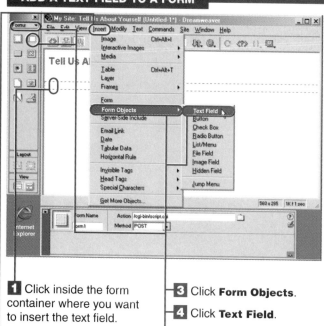

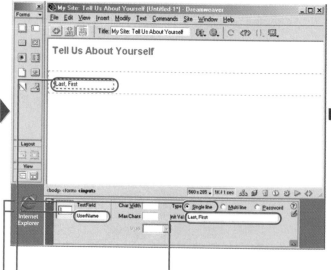

1 Click inside the form container where you want to insert the text field.

Note: See page 153 to set up a form.

2 Click **Insert**.

3 Click **Form Objects**.

4 Click **Text Field**.

■ You can also create a text field by selecting **Forms** in the Objects panel and clicking the **Insert Text Field** button (▣).

■ A text field appears in your form.

■ The Single line radio button is selected by default.

5 Type a name in the text field.

■ This name lets the browser distinguish the field from other form elements.

6 Type the optional initial value for the text field.

■ This value appears in the form when the Web page is viewed in a browser.

Can I define the style of text that appears in the text field?

No. The browser determines what style of text appears in the form fields. However, you can customize the style of the text labels that you place beside the text fields, just as you can other Web page text.

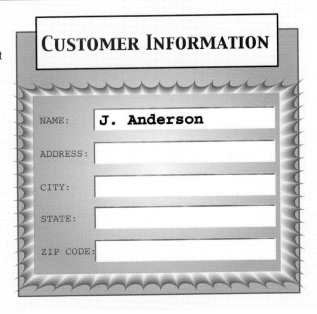

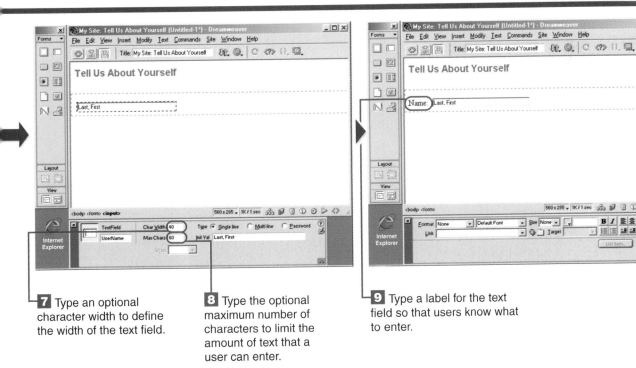

7 Type an optional character width to define the width of the text field.

8 Type the optional maximum number of characters to limit the amount of text that a user can enter.

9 Type a label for the text field so that users know what to enter.

ADD A MULTILINE TEXT FIELD TO A FORM

Multiline text fields enable viewers to submit large amounts of text in a form. These can be useful if you want to allow viewers to send you lengthy comments about your site, or cut and paste large amounts of text — for example, a résumé — into a form.

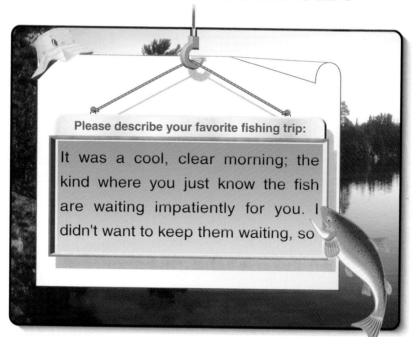

Please describe your favorite fishing trip:

It was a cool, clear morning; the kind where you just know the fish are waiting impatiently for you. I didn't want to keep them waiting, so

ADD A MULTILINE TEXT FIELD TO A FORM

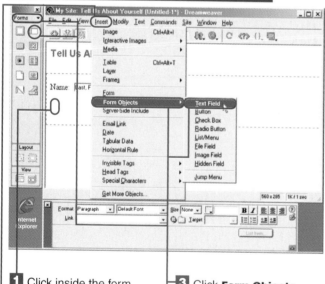

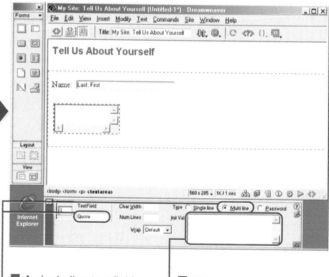

1 Click inside the form container where you want to insert a multiline text field.

Note: See page 153 to set up a form.

2 Click **Insert**.

3 Click **Form Objects**.

4 Click **Text Field**.

■ You can also select **Forms** in the Objects panel and click the **Insert Text Field** button (▣).

■ A single-line text field appears in your form.

5 Click **Multi line** (○ changes to ◉).

6 Type a name in for your multiline text field.

■ This name lets the browser distinguish the field from other elements.

■ You can enter an optional initial value for the multiline text field. The initial value appears in the multiline text field when you view the Web page in a browser.

Why is it important to define the wrap attribute of a multiline text field?

In some Web browsers, text typed into a multiline text field does not automatically wrap when it reaches the right edge of the field, which can be annoying for the user. Specifying Virtual or Physical in the Wrap menu ensures that text automatically wraps in a multiline text field.

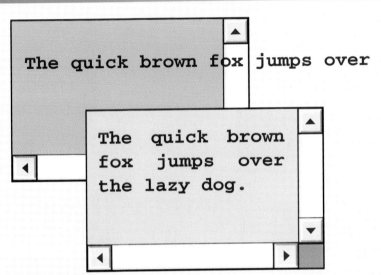

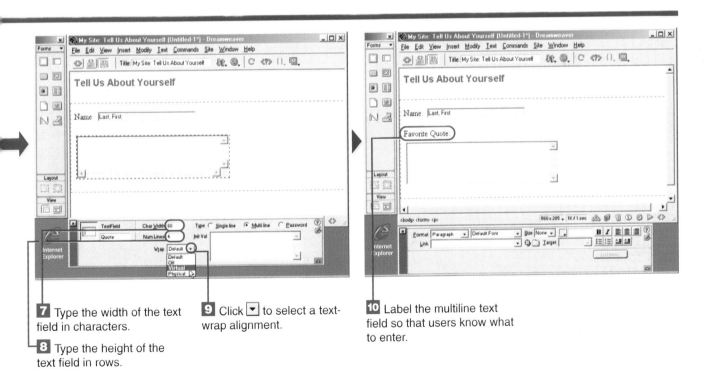

7 Type the width of the text field in characters.

8 Type the height of the text field in rows.

9 Click ▼ to select a text-wrap alignment.

10 Label the multiline text field so that users know what to enter.

ADD A PASSWORD FIELD TO A FORM

A password field is similar to a text field, except the text in the field is hidden as the user enters it. The characters display as asterisks or bullets, depending on the type of operating system being used to view the page.

ADD A PASSWORD FIELD TO A FORM

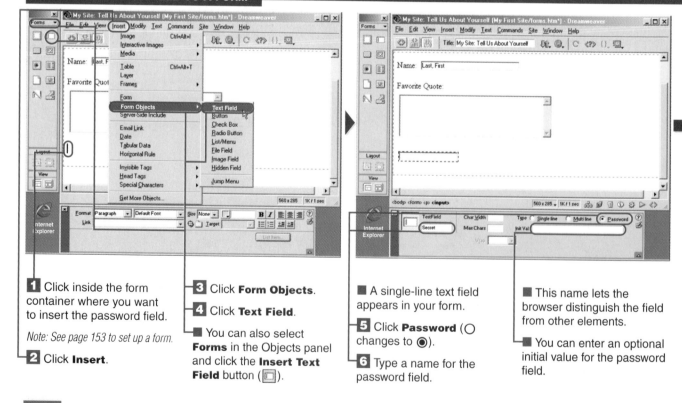

1 Click inside the form container where you want to insert the password field.

Note: See page 153 to set up a form.

2 Click **Insert**.

3 Click **Form Objects**.

4 Click **Text Field**.

■ You can also select **Forms** in the Objects panel and click the **Insert Text Field** button (□).

■ A single-line text field appears in your form.

5 Click **Password** (○ changes to ●).

6 Type a name for the password field.

■ This name lets the browser distinguish the field from other elements.

■ You can enter an optional initial value for the password field.

Does using a password field protect the entered information as it is transmitted over the Internet?

No. The browser sends the password field information to the form handler as plain text, just like it does everything else in the form. The password field does not protect your information from someone intercepting it as it travels between the user's computer and the form handler.

Credit Card - 0011 1234 5678 8765

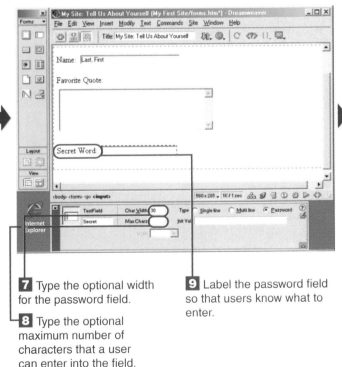

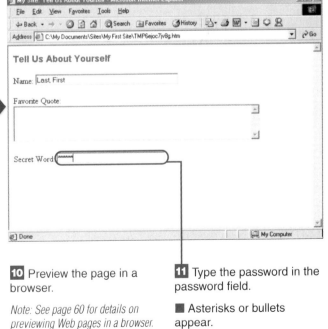

7 Type the optional width for the password field.

8 Type the optional maximum number of characters that a user can enter into the field.

9 Label the password field so that users know what to enter.

10 Preview the page in a browser.

Note: See page 60 for details on previewing Web pages in a browser.

11 Type the password in the password field.

■ Asterisks or bullets appear.

ADD CHECK BOXES TO A FORM

Check boxes enable you to present multiple options in a form, and allow the user to select one, several, or none of the options.

ADD CHECK BOXES TO A FORM

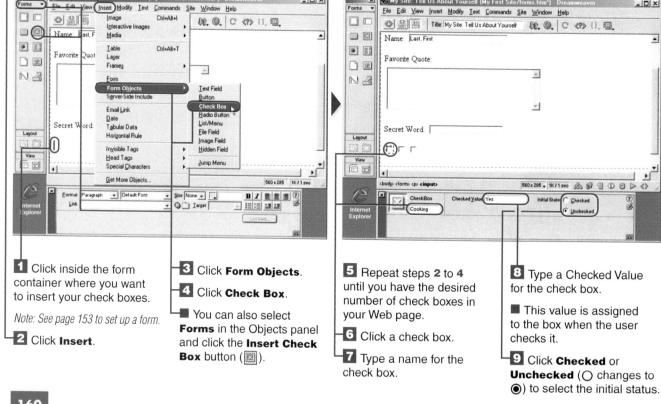

1 Click inside the form container where you want to insert your check boxes.

Note: See page 153 to set up a form.

2 Click **Insert**.

3 Click **Form Objects**.

4 Click **Check Box**.

■ You can also select **Forms** in the Objects panel and click the **Insert Check Box** button (▩).

5 Repeat steps **2** to **4** until you have the desired number of check boxes in your Web page.

6 Click a check box.

7 Type a name for the check box.

8 Type a Checked Value for the check box.

■ This value is assigned to the box when the user checks it.

9 Click **Checked** or **Unchecked** (○ changes to ◉) to select the initial status.

Can I have several different groups of check boxes in the same form?

Yes. How you organize the check boxes in a form — in one group, several groups, or each check box by itself — is up to you. Because each box has a unique name, the visual organization of the boxes does not matter to the form handler.

Favorite Food:
- ☐ **Lasagna**
- ☐ **Steak**
- ☐ **Spaghetti**
- ☐ **Hamburgers**

Favorite Drink:
- ☐ **Fruit Juice**
- ☐ **Soft Drinks**
- ☐ **Lemonade**
- ☐ **Iced T**

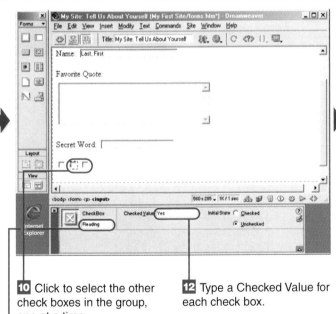

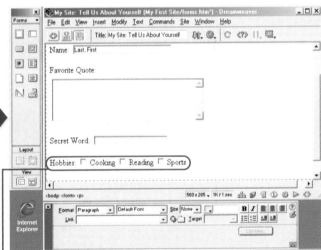

10 Click to select the other check boxes in the group, one at a time.

11 Type a different name for each check box.

12 Type a Checked Value for each check box.

■ You can enter the same checked value for all the boxes.

13 Label the check boxes so that users can identify what to check.

ADD RADIO BUTTONS TO A FORM

You can let users select one option from a set of several options by adding a set of radio buttons to your form. With radio buttons, a user cannot select more that one option from a set.

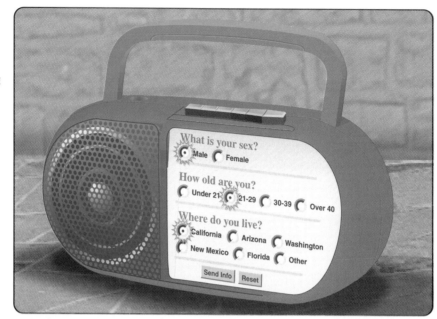

ADD RADIO BUTTONS TO A FORM

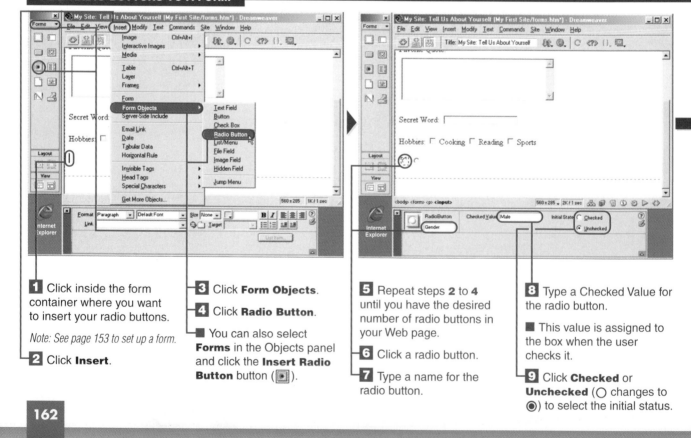

1 Click inside the form container where you want to insert your radio buttons.

Note: See page 153 to set up a form.

2 Click **Insert**.

3 Click **Form Objects**.

4 Click **Radio Button**.

■ You can also select **Forms** in the Objects panel and click the **Insert Radio Button** button (■).

5 Repeat steps **2** to **4** until you have the desired number of radio buttons in your Web page.

6 Click a radio button.

7 Type a name for the radio button.

8 Type a Checked Value for the radio button.

■ This value is assigned to the box when the user checks it.

9 Click **Checked** or **Unchecked** (○ changes to ◉) to select the initial status.

What happens if I give each radio button in a set a different name?

If you do this, a user can select more than one button in the set at a time, and once a button is selected, the user can not deselect it. This defeats the purpose of radio buttons.

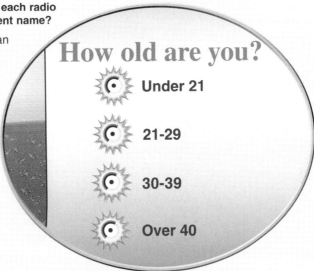

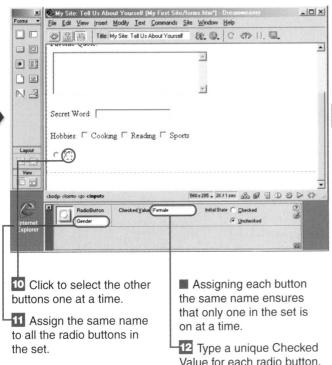

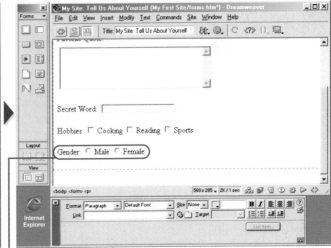

10 Click to select the other buttons one at a time.

11 Assign the same name to all the radio buttons in the set.

■ Assigning each button the same name ensures that only one in the set is on at a time.

12 Type a unique Checked Value for each radio button.

13 Label the radio buttons so that users can identify what to select.

ADD A MENU TO A FORM

A menu allows users to choose one option from a list of options. Because it hides the information until a user clicks it, a menu allows you to put a long list of options in a small amount of space.

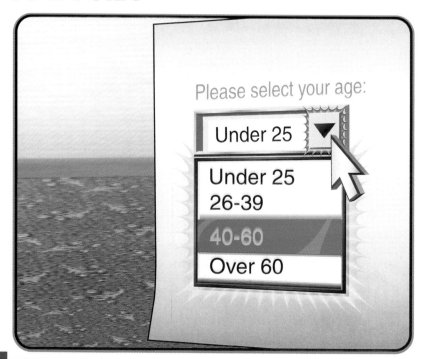

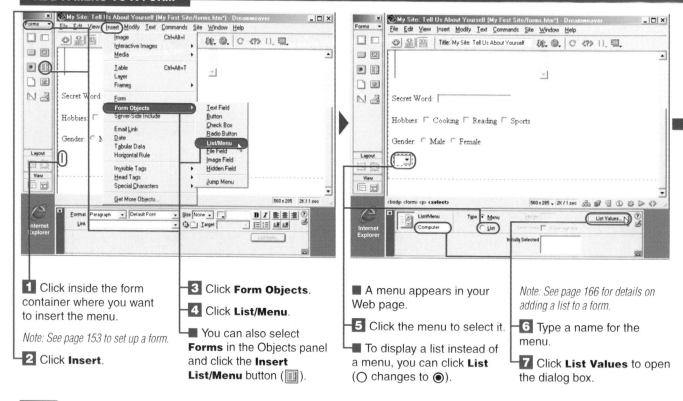

1 Click inside the form container where you want to insert the menu.

Note: See page 153 to set up a form.

2 Click **Insert**.

3 Click **Form Objects**.

4 Click **List/Menu**.

■ You can also select **Forms** in the Objects panel and click the **Insert List/Menu** button (▦).

■ A menu appears in your Web page.

5 Click the menu to select it.

■ To display a list instead of a menu, you can click **List** (○ changes to ●).

Note: See page 166 for details on adding a list to a form.

6 Type a name for the menu.

7 Click **List Values** to open the dialog box.

164

What determines the width of a menu?

The widest item determines the width of the menu. To change the width, you can change the width of your item descriptions.

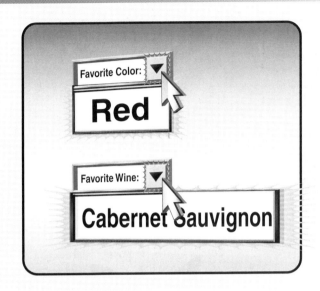

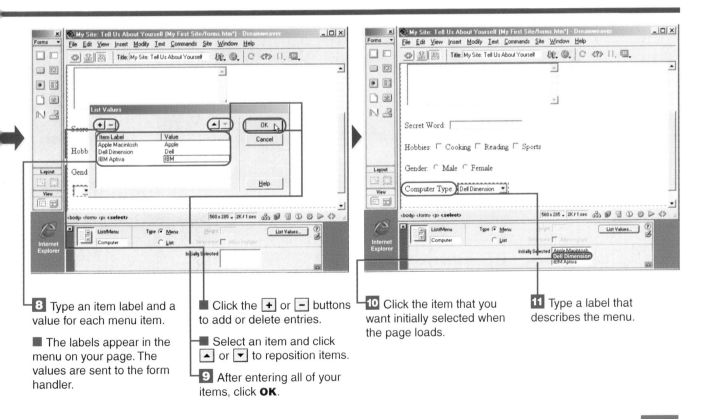

■8 Type an item label and a value for each menu item.

■ The labels appear in the menu on your page. The values are sent to the form handler.

■ Click the + or – buttons to add or delete entries.

■ Select an item and click ▲ or ▼ to reposition items.

■9 After entering all of your items, click **OK**.

■10 Click the item that you want initially selected when the page loads.

■11 Type a label that describes the menu.

ADD A LIST TO A FORM

A list allows a user to choose one option from a list of options. You can also create a list that allows a user to choose multiple options from your list.

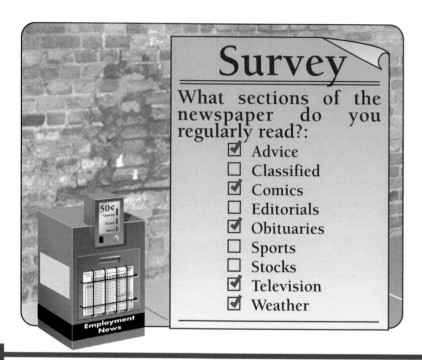

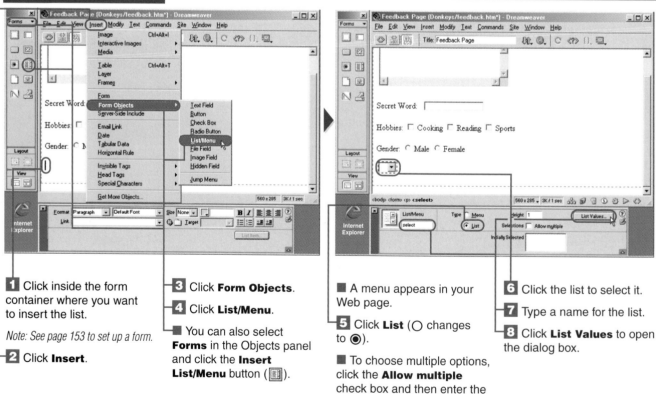

1 Click inside the form container where you want to insert the list.

Note: See page 153 to set up a form.

2 Click **Insert**.

3 Click **Form Objects**.

4 Click **List/Menu**.

■ You can also select **Forms** in the Objects panel and click the **Insert List/Menu** button (▦).

■ A menu appears in your Web page.

5 Click **List** (○ changes to ◉).

■ To choose multiple options, click the **Allow multiple** check box and then enter the number of preferences in the **Height** field.

6 Click the list to select it.

7 Type a name for the list.

8 Click **List Values** to open the dialog box.

When should I use a list instead of check boxes?

Both elements can let your viewers choose several
options from a set of options
in your form. Lists let you
combine your set of options
into a relatively small space;
check boxes let your viewers
have a clearer view of all the
options that are available.
The best choice depends on
the type of information
you are presenting
and the space
available.

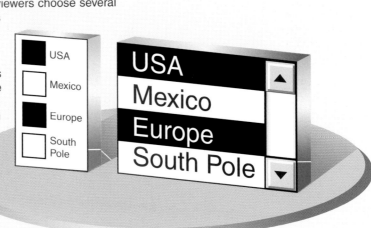

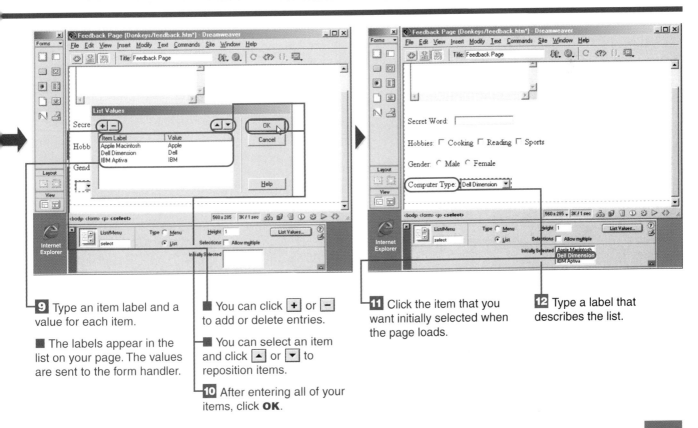

9 Type an item label and a
value for each item.

■ The labels appear in the
list on your page. The values
are sent to the form handler.

■ You can click ⊞ or ⊟
to add or delete entries.

■ You can select an item
and click ▲ or ▼ to
reposition items.

10 After entering all of your
items, click **OK**.

11 Click the item that you
want initially selected when
the page loads.

12 Type a label that
describes the list.

CREATE A JUMP MENU

A *jump menu* lets users
easily navigate to other
Web pages using the
menu form object.
Dreamweaver uses
JavaScript to make the
jump menu work.

Breaking News

Interesting Discussions

Low-Priced Books

CREATE A JUMP MENU

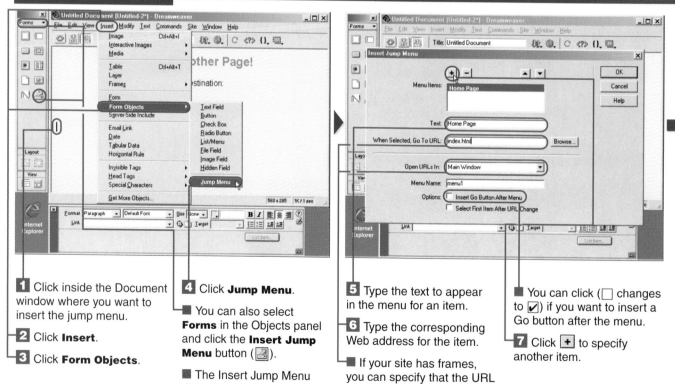

1 Click inside the Document
window where you want to
insert the jump menu.

2 Click **Insert**.

3 Click **Form Objects**.

4 Click **Jump Menu**.

■ You can also select
Forms in the Objects panel
and click the **Insert Jump
Menu** button (🖾).

■ The Insert Jump Menu
dialog box appears.

5 Type the text to appear
in the menu for an item.

6 Type the corresponding
Web address for the item.

■ If your site has frames,
you can specify that the URL
opens in a particular frame.

■ You can click (☐ changes
to ☑) if you want to insert a
Go button after the menu.

7 Click ➕ to specify
another item.

Does a jump menu require a form handler?

No. For a jump menu, JavaScript code processes the menu information instead of a form handler. If you view the code used to display a jump menu, you may notice that the `<form>` tag is missing the `action` attribute that usually specifies the form handler.

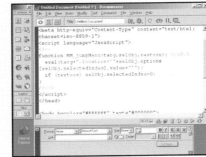

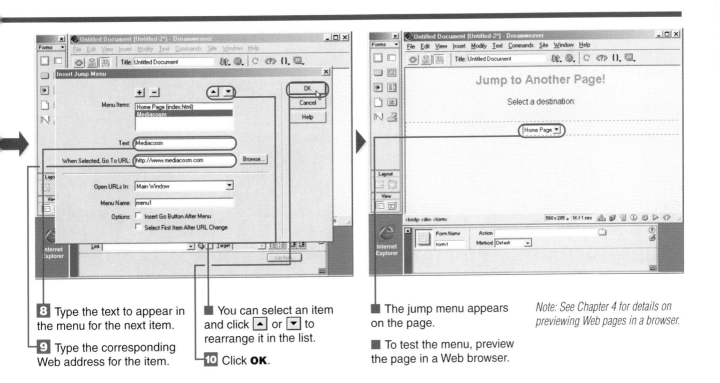

8 Type the text to appear in the menu for the next item.

9 Type the corresponding Web address for the item.

■ You can select an item and click ▲ or ▼ to rearrange it in the list.

10 Click **OK**.

■ The jump menu appears on the page.

■ To test the menu, preview the page in a Web browser.

Note: See Chapter 4 for details on previewing Web pages in a browser.

169

ADD A SUBMIT BUTTON TO A FORM

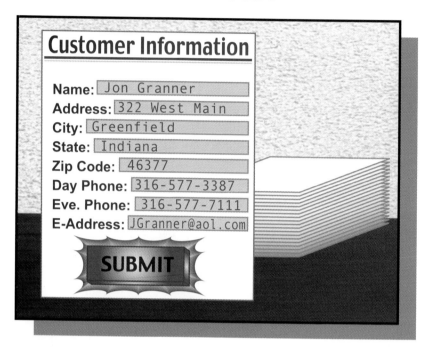

You can add a button that enables users to submit information in a form, sending it to the specified form handler. To specify a form handler, see "Set Up a Form."

Customer Information

Name: Jon Granner
Address: 322 West Main
City: Greenfield
State: Indiana
Zip Code: 46377
Day Phone: 316-577-3387
Eve. Phone: 316-577-7111
E-Address: JGranner@aol.com

SUBMIT

ADD A SUBMIT BUTTON TO A FORM

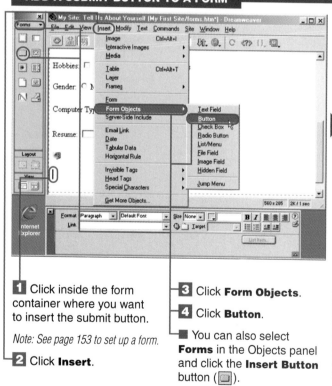

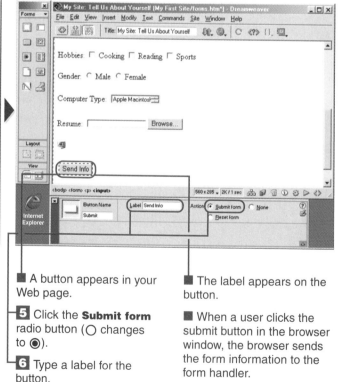

1 Click inside the form container where you want to insert the submit button.

Note: See page 153 to set up a form.

2 Click **Insert**.

3 Click **Form Objects**.

4 Click **Button**.

■ You can also select **Forms** in the Objects panel and click the **Insert Button** button (▭).

■ A button appears in your Web page.

5 Click the **Submit form** radio button (○ changes to ⊙).

6 Type a label for the button.

■ The label appears on the button.

■ When a user clicks the submit button in the browser window, the browser sends the form information to the form handler.

You can add a button that
enables users to reset all
elements of a form to their
initial values. This allows users
to erase their form entries so
they can start over again.

ADD A RESET BUTTON TO A FORM

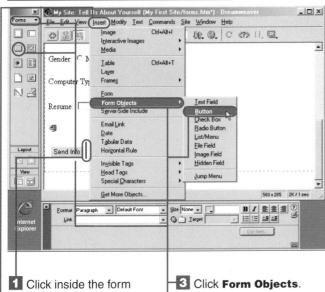

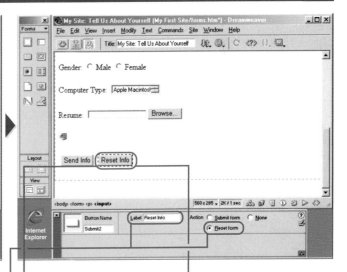

1 Click inside the form
container where you want
to insert the reset button.

Note: See page 153 to set up a form.

2 Click **Insert**.

3 Click **Form Objects**.

4 Click **Button**.

■ You can also select
Forms in the Objects panel
and click the **Insert Button**
button (▢).

■ A button appears in your
Web page.

5 Click the **Reset form**
radio button (○ changes
to ◉).

6 Type a label for the
button.

■ The label appears on the
button.

■ When a user clicks the
reset button, the browser
resets the form to its initial
values.

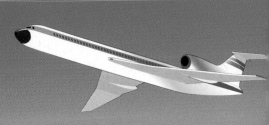

ABC Travel

Reservations

Schedules

Travel Tips
Arrivals
Departures

CHAPTER 10

Creating Frames

You can divide the site window into multiple panes by creating frames. This chapter shows you how to manipulate frames when organizing the information on your pages.

INTRODUCTION TO FRAMES

Frames allow you to divide your Web page into several smaller windows, then display a different Web page in each window.

You can put a list of navigation links in one frame of your site, and have the links open their destination pages in a larger content frame.

Setting Up Frames

You create a framed Web site in Dreamweaver by dividing the Document window horizontally or vertically one or more times. You can then use the Property inspector to load a Web page into each frame. The overall organization of frames in your site is controlled by a separate HTML document called a *frameset page*.

How Frames Work

Frames on a page operate independently of one another. As you scroll through the content of one frame, the content of the other frames remains fixed. You can create hyperlinks in one frame that open pages in other frames.

You can split a
Document
window vertically
to create a
frameset with left
and right frames,
or split it
horizontally to
create a frameset
with top and
bottom frames.

You can also choose a
predefined frameset for
your site. See page 176.

DIVIDE A PAGE INTO FRAMES

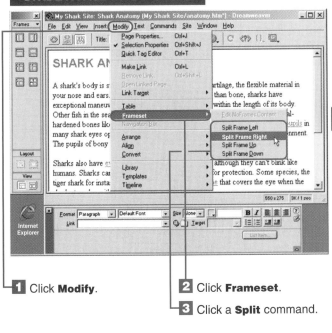

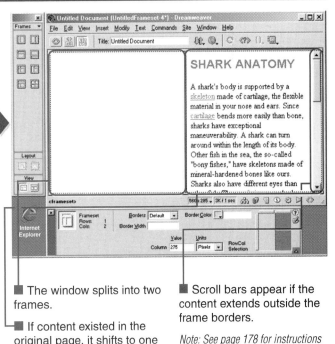

1 Click **Modify**.

2 Click **Frameset**.

3 Click a **Split** command.

■ The window splits into two
frames.

■ If content existed in the
original page, it shifts to one
of the new frames.

■ Scroll bars appear if the
content extends outside the
frame borders.

*Note: See page 178 for instructions
on how to add content to a new
frame.*

INSERT A PREDEFINED FRAMESET

You can easily create popular frame styles using the predefined framesets located in the Objects panel.

If you do not want to use one of Dreamweaver's framesets, you can divide the window manually. See page 175.

INSERT A PREDEFINED FRAMESET

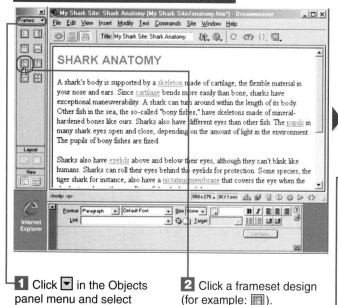

1 Click ▾ in the Objects panel menu and select **Frames**.

2 Click a frameset design (for example: ▦).

■ Dreamweaver applies the frameset to your page.

■ If content existed in the original page, it shifts to one of the new frames.

■ Scroll bars appear if the content extends outside the frame borders.

Note: See page 178 for instructions on how to add content to a new frame.

You can subdivide a frame of an existing frameset to create nested frames. Nested frames allow you to organize the information in your site in a more complex way.

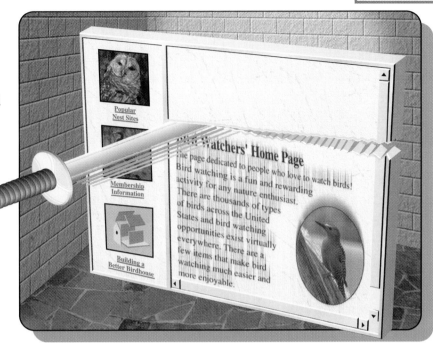

NEST FRAMES

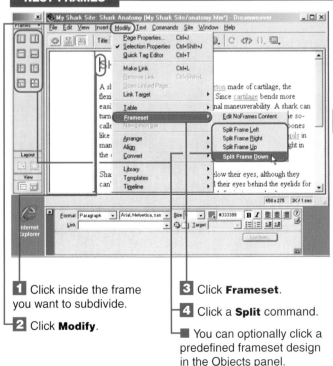

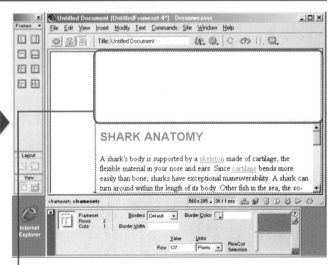

1 Click inside the frame you want to subdivide.

2 Click **Modify**.

3 Click **Frameset**.

4 Click a **Split** command.

■ You can optionally click a predefined frameset design in the Objects panel.

■ Dreamweaver splits the selected frame into two frames, creating a nested frameset.

Note: See page 178 for instructions on how to add content to a new frame.

■ You can continue to split your frames into more frames.

ADD CONTENT TO A FRAME

You can add content to a frame by inserting an existing HTML document into the frame. You can also add content by typing text or inserting elements such as images and tables, just as you would in an unframed page.

ADD CONTENT TO A FRAME

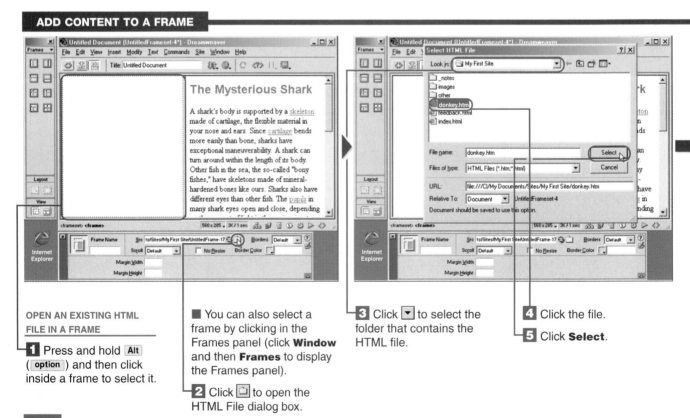

OPEN AN EXISTING HTML FILE IN A FRAME

1 Press and hold Alt (option) and then click inside a frame to select it.

■ You can also select a frame by clicking in the Frames panel (click **Window** and then **Frames** to display the Frames panel).

2 Click 🗀 to open the HTML File dialog box.

3 Click ▼ to select the folder that contains the HTML file.

4 Click the file.

5 Click **Select**.

Can I load a page from the Web into a frame on my Web site?

Yes. You can insert an external Web-page address into the URL field in the Select HTML File dialog box (see steps **3** to **5** on page 178). Because Dreamweaver cannot display external files, the Web page will not appear in the Document window. However, it will appear if you preview your site in a Web browser. See page 60 for instructions on how to preview a Web page in your browser.

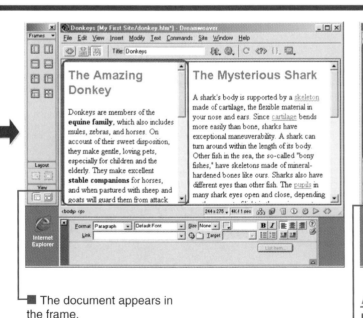

■ The document appears in the frame.

ADD NEW CONTENT TO A FRAME

■1 Click inside the frame.

■2 Type the text you want to display.

■ You can click buttons in the Objects panel to add images, tables, and other elements.

Note: See page 23 for more information on using the Objects panel.

SAVE A FRAMED SITE

Saving your framed site requires you to save the HTML documents that appear in the frames as well as the frameset that defines how the frames are organized.

You need to save all of the documents before you can upload your site.

SAVE A FRAMED SITE

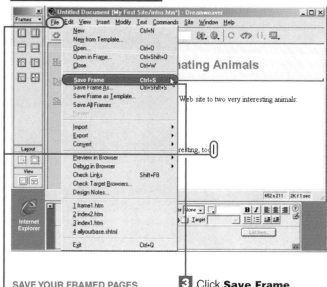

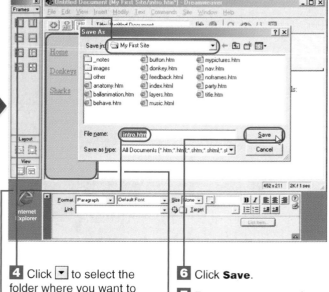

SAVE YOUR FRAMED PAGES

1 Click inside the frame you want to save.

2 Click **File**.

3 Click **Save Frame**.

Note: The Save Frame appears gray if the current frame has already been saved.

■ The Save As dialog box appears.

4 Click ▼ to select the folder where you want to save the framed page.

5 Type a name for the page with an **.htm** or **.html** file extension.

6 Click **Save**.

7 Repeat steps **1** to **6** for the other framed pages in your document.

8 Save each page as a different filename.

Is there a shortcut for saving all the pages of my framed site?

Yes. You can click **File** and then **Save All Frames**. This will save all the framed pages and framesets that make up your site. This is definitely a time saver!

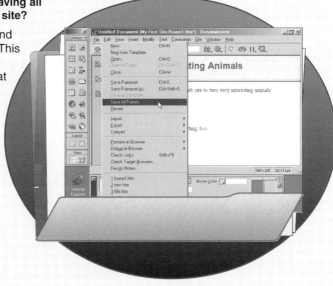

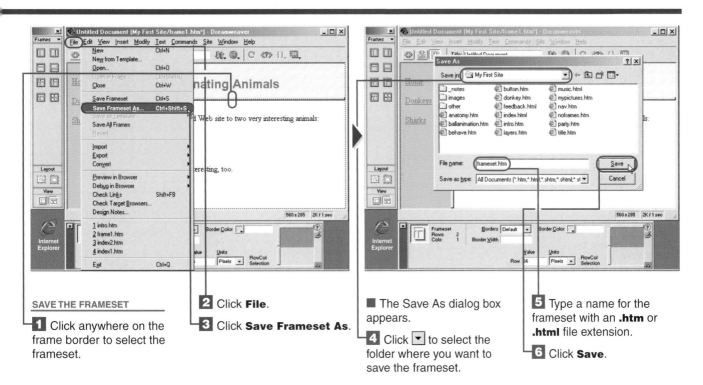

SAVE THE FRAMESET

1 Click anywhere on the frame border to select the frameset.

2 Click **File**.

3 Click **Save Frameset As**.

■ The Save As dialog box appears.

4 Click ▼ to select the folder where you want to save the frameset.

5 Type a name for the frameset with an **.htm** or **.html** file extension.

6 Click **Save**.

DELETE A FRAME

You can delete a frame if you want to make your frameset less complicated.

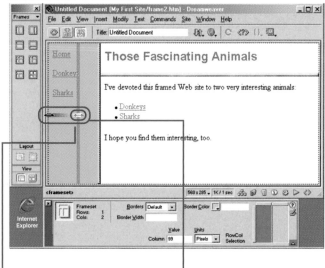

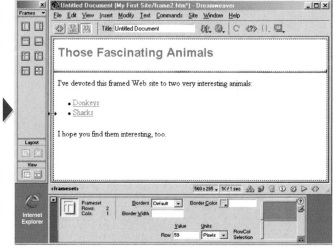

1 Position the mouse over the border of the frame you want to delete (⟨ changes to ↔).

2 Click and drag the border to the edge of the window.

■ Dreamweaver deletes the frame.

To create hyperlinks
that can work
between your frames,
you need to give
your frames names.
The name tells where
the hyperlink
destination should
open in the frameset.

NAME A FRAME

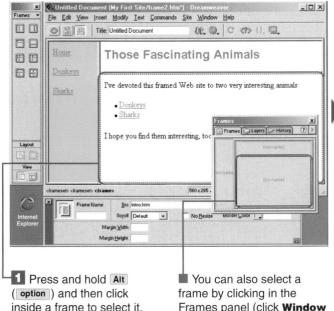

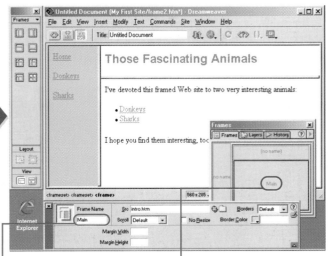

1 Press and hold **Alt**
(**option**) and then click
inside a frame to select it.

■ You can also select a
frame by clicking in the
Frames panel (click **Window**
and then **Frames** to display
the panel).

2 Type a name for the
frame.

3 Press **Enter** (**Return**).

■ The name of the frame
appears in the Frames
panel.

HYPERLINK TO A FRAME

You can create a hyperlink that opens a page in a different frame. You will want to do this for frames that contain navigation hyperlinks.

For more information about hyperlinking, see pages 110 to 129.

HYPERLINK TO A FRAME

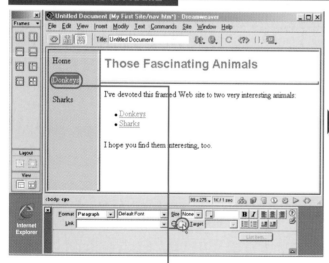

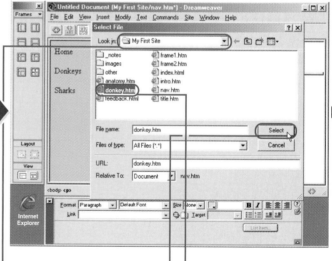

1 Name the frames of your frameset.

Note: See page 183 for instructions on how to name a frame.

2 Click and drag to select the text or image that you want to turn into a hyperlink.

3 Click 🗀 to open the Select File dialog box.

4 Click ▼ to select the folder containing the destination file.

5 Click the destination file.

6 Click **Select**.

What happens if I select _top for my hyperlink target?

Selecting _top, instead of a frame name, opens the hyperlink destination on top of any existing framesets. This action takes the user out of an existing frameset in a site.

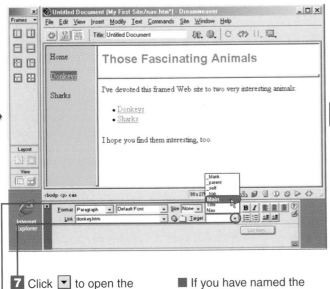

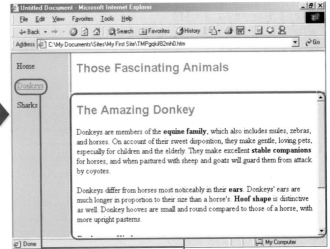

7 Click ▾ to open the Target menu.

8 Click to select a frame where the target file will open.

■ If you have named the frame, it appears in the menu.

9 Preview the page in a Web browser.

Note: See page 60 for instructions on how to preview a Web page in your browser.

■ When you open the framed page in a Web browser and click the hyperlink, the destination page opens inside the targeted frame.

CHANGE THE DIMENSIONS OF A FRAME

You can change the dimensions of a frame to attractively and efficiently display the information inside it.

CHANGE THE DIMENSIONS OF A FRAME

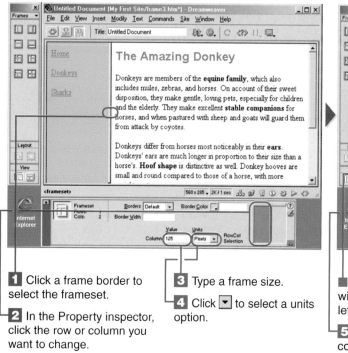

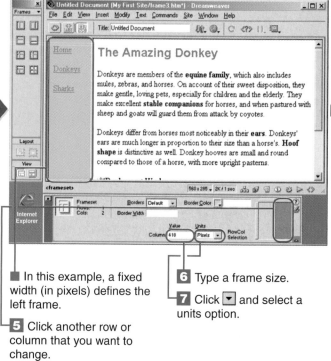

1 Click a frame border to select the frameset.

2 In the Property inspector, click the row or column you want to change.

3 Type a frame size.

4 Click ⬛ to select a units option.

◼ In this example, a fixed width (in pixels) defines the left frame.

5 Click another row or column that you want to change.

6 Type a frame size.

7 Click ⬛ and select a units option.

Is there a shortcut for changing the dimensions of frames?

Yes. You can click and drag a frame border to adjust the dimensions of a frame quickly. The values in the Property inspector will change as you drag.

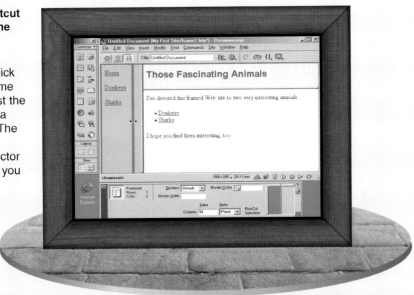

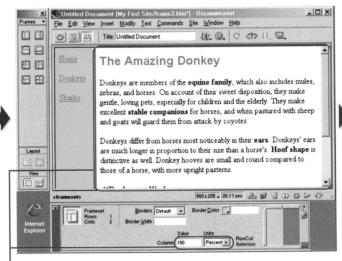

■ A percentage width defines the right frame. The right frame takes up the remaining space in the browser window.

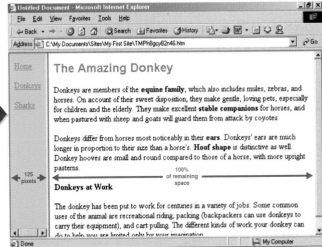

8 Preview the page in a Web browser.

Note: See page 60 for instructions on how to preview a Web page in your browser.

■ The frameset displays as it was defined in Dreamweaver.

FORMAT FRAME BORDERS

You can modify the appearance of your frame borders to make them complement the style of your Web-site content. You can specify that borders be turned on or off, and you can set the color and width of your borders.

FORMAT FRAME BORDERS

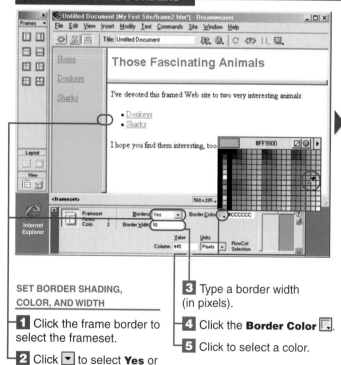

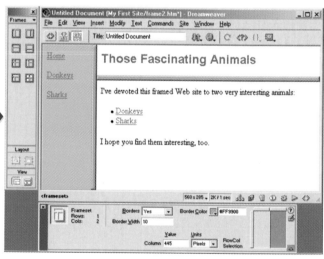

SET BORDER SHADING, COLOR, AND WIDTH

1 Click the frame border to select the frameset.

2 Click ▼ to select **Yes** or **Default** to keep the borders.

3 Type a border width (in pixels).

4 Click the **Border Color** ▣.

5 Click to select a color.

■ The frame border appears at the specified settings.

Why would I want to make my frame borders invisible?

Turning borders off can disguise the fact that you are using frames in the first place. If you want to further disguise your frames, you can set the pages inside your frames to the same background color (see page 102).

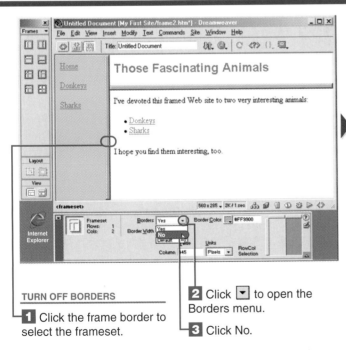

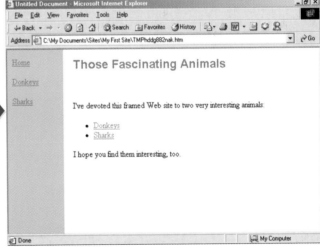

TURN OFF BORDERS

1 Click the frame border to select the frameset.

2 Click ▼ to open the Borders menu.

3 Click No.

4 Preview the page in a Web browser.

Note: See page 60 for instructions on how to preview the Web page in a browser.

■ The frame border does not appear.

CONTROL SCROLL BARS IN FRAMES

You can control whether or not scroll bars will appear in your frames. Hiding scroll bars allows you to have more control over the presentation of your site, but may also prevent some users from seeing all of your site content.

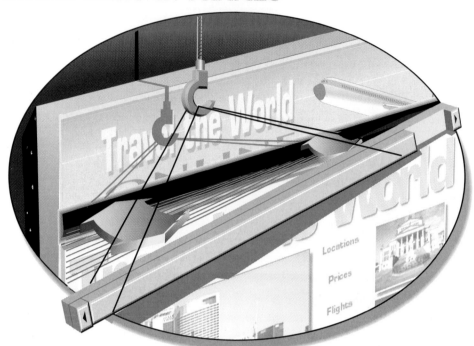

CONTROL SCROLL BARS IN FRAMES

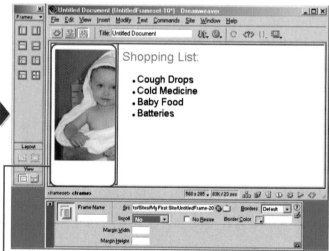

Note: The default behavior in Dreamweaver displays scroll bars only when they are needed.

■ **1** Press and hold **Alt** (**option**) and then click inside a frame to select it.

■ **2** Click ▾ to open the Scroll menu.

■ **3** Click a scroll setting.

■ The frame appears with the new setting.

■ In this example, scroll bars are turned off in the left frame. There is now no way for the user to access all of the content of the frame.

190

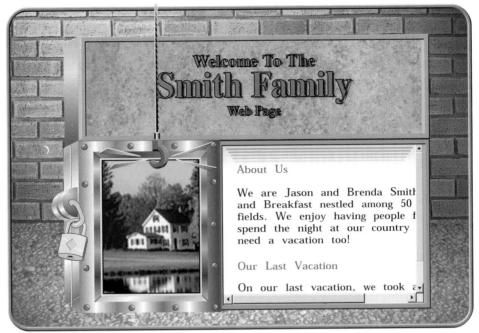

The default behavior for most browsers allows users to resize frames by clicking and dragging frame borders.

You can prevent users from resizing the frames of a site and protect the presentation of content.

CONTROL RESIZING IN FRAMES

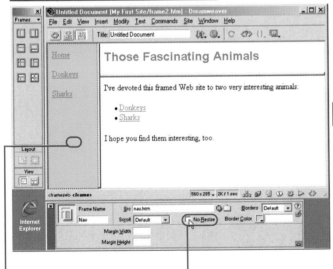

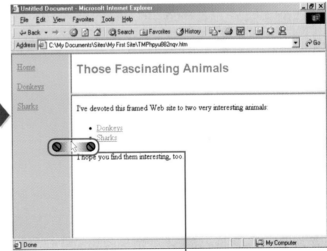

1 Press and hold `Alt` (`option`) and then click in a frame to select it.

2 Click the **No Resize** check box (☐ changes to ☑).

3 Preview the page in a Web browser.

Note: See page 60 for instructions on how to preview the Web page in a browser.

4 Click and drag the border.

■ The browser prevents you from resizing the frame.

ADD NOFRAMES CONTENT

Because not every user
has a browser that
displays frames, you can
provide content that
displays instead of
frames when these
frames-challenged users
view your Web site.

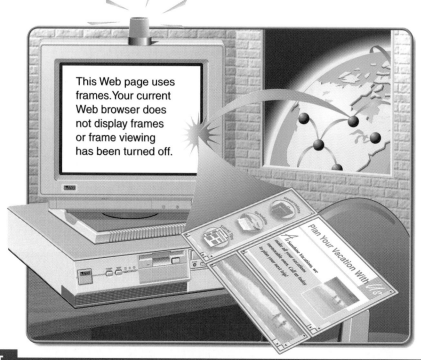

This Web page uses
frames. Your current
Web browser does
not display frames
or frame viewing
has been turned off.

ADD NOFRAMES CONTENT

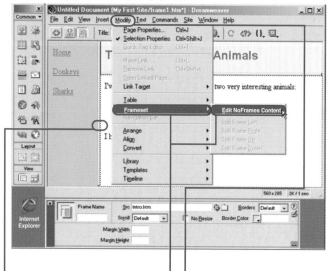

1 Click the frame border to
select the frameset.

*Note: You must select the outermost
frameset in a Document window that
has nested framesets.*

2 Click **Modify**.

3 Click **Frameset**.

4 Click **Edit NoFrames
Content**.

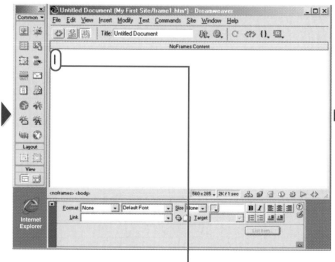

■ Dreamweaver displays a
blank NoFrames content
window.

5 Click inside the window
to add the content you want
to display.

What kinds of users are unable to view frames?

Users with text-based (nongraphical) browsers are usually unable to view frames, as are users with older versions of graphical browsers.

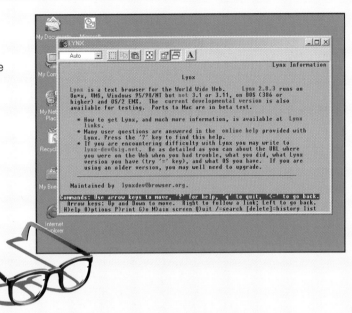

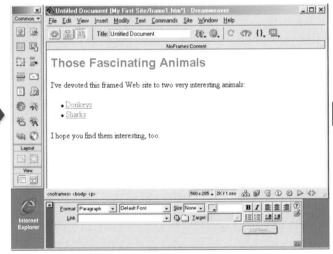

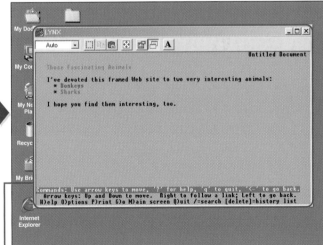

■ A browser that cannot display frames will display the NoFrames content when your framed site is opened.

6 Open your framed site in a text-based browser, or any other browser that cannot display frames.

■ The NoFrames content appears.

CHAPTER 11

Using Library Items and Templates

You can save time by storing frequently used Web-page elements and layouts as library items and templates. This chapter shows you how to use these features to your advantage.

INTRODUCTION TO LIBRARY ITEMS AND TEMPLATES

Library items and templates let you avoid repetitive work by storing copies of page elements and layouts that you frequently use. You can access the library items and templates that you create for your site by accessing the Assets panel.

Library Items

You can define parts of your Web pages that are repeated in your site as *library items,* so you do not have to create them from scratch repeatedly. Each time you need a library item, you can just insert it from your library. If you ever make changes to a library item, Dreamweaver automatically updates all instances of the item across your Web site. Good candidates for library items include advertising banners, company slogans, and any other feature that appears many times across a site.

Templates

You can define commonly used Web page layouts as *templates* to save you time as you build your pages. Templates can also help you maintain a consistent page design throughout a site. After you make changes to a template, Dreamweaver automatically updates all the pages of your site that are based on that template. If you use just a few page layouts across all the pages in your site, consider defining those layouts as templates.

You can access the
library and templates of
a site by using
commands in the
Window menu. You can
also access them via the
Assets panel.

VIEW LIBRARY ITEMS AND TEMPLATES

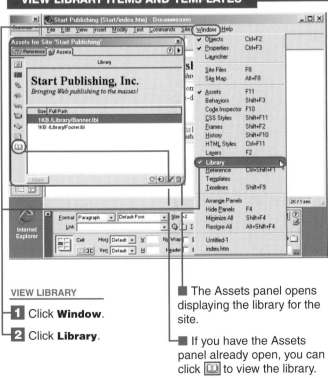

VIEW LIBRARY

1 Click **Window**.

2 Click **Library**.

■ The Assets panel opens
displaying the library for the
site.

■ If you have the Assets
panel already open, you can
click ▦ to view the library.

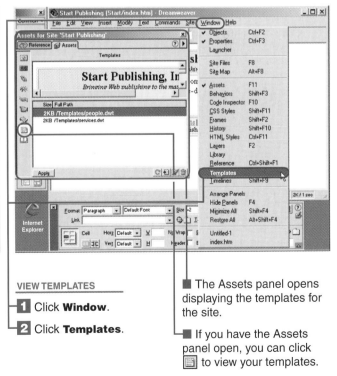

VIEW TEMPLATES

1 Click **Window**.

2 Click **Templates**.

■ The Assets panel opens
displaying the templates for
the site.

■ If you have the Assets
panel open, you can click
▤ to view your templates.

CREATE A LIBRARY ITEM

You can define text, images, and other Dreamweaver objects that you want to appear frequently in your Web site as library items. Library items enable you to insert such page elements quickly without having to re-create them from scratch every time.

If you edit a library item, Dreamweaver can automatically update each instance of the item throughout your site.

CREATE A LIBRARY ITEM

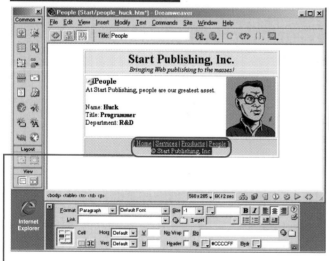

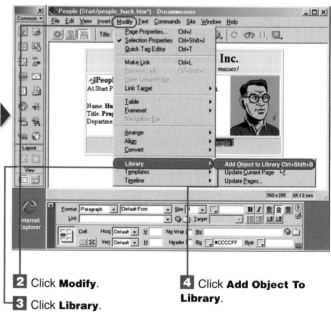

1 Click and drag to select the part of your page that you want to define as a library item.

Note: To create library items for your Web pages, you must define a local site. See page 52 for instructions on setting up a local site.

■ You can create Library items from any elements that appear in the body of an HTML document. These elements include text, images, tables, forms, layers, and multimedia.

2 Click **Modify**.

3 Click **Library**.

4 Click **Add Object To Library**.

What page elements should I consider defining as library items?

Anything that appears multiple times in a Web site is a good candidate to become a library item. These elements include headers, footers, navigational menus, contact information, and disclaimers.

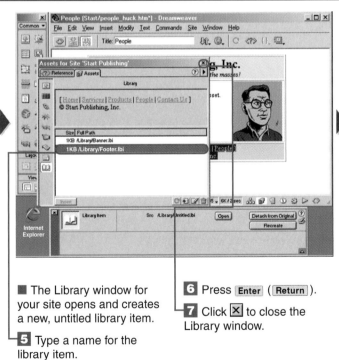

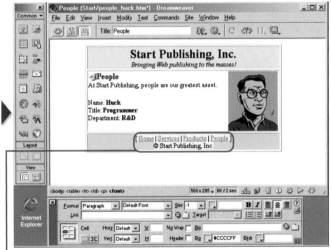

■ The Library window for your site opens and creates a new, untitled library item.

5 Type a name for the library item.

6 Press `Enter` (`Return`).

7 Click ✕ to close the Library window.

■ Yellow highlighting appears around the new library item.

■ Defining an element as a library item prevents you from editing it in the Document window.

Note: See page 202 to edit library items.

INSERT A LIBRARY ITEM

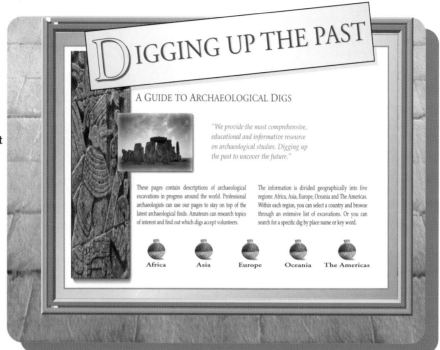

Inserting an element onto your page from the library saves you from having to create it from scratch. It also ensures that the element is identical to other instances of that library item in your site.

A GUIDE TO ARCHAEOLOGICAL DIGS

"We provide the most comprehensive, educational and informative resource on archaeological studies. Digging up the past to uncover the future."

These pages contain descriptions of archaeological excavations in progress around the world. Professional archaeologists can use our pages to stay on top of the latest archaeological finds. Amateurs can research topics of interest and find out which digs accept volunteers.

The information is divided geographically into five regions: Africa, Asia, Europe, Oceania and The Americas. Within each region, you can select a country and browse through an extensive list of excavations. Or you can search for a specific dig by place name or key word.

Africa   Asia   Europe   Oceania   The Americas

INSERT A LIBRARY ITEM

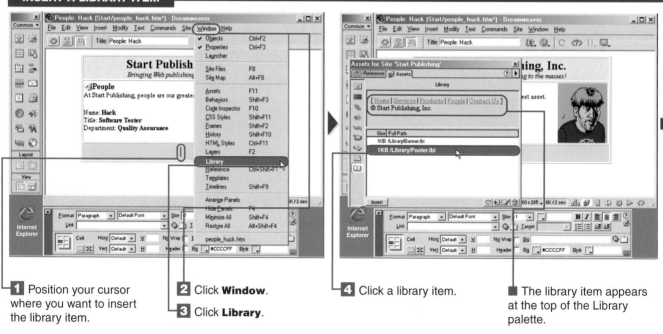

1 Position your cursor where you want to insert the library item.

2 Click **Window**.

3 Click **Library**.

4 Click a library item.

■ The library item appears at the top of the Library palette.

How do I edit a library item that has been inserted into a page?

Instances of library items in your pages are locked, and cannot be edited. To edit a library item, you need to edit the original version of that item from the library. You can also detach an instance of a library item from the library for editing, but then the instance is no longer a part of the library. (See pages 202 to 205.)

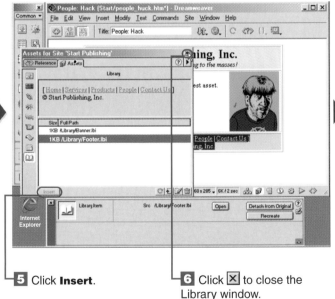

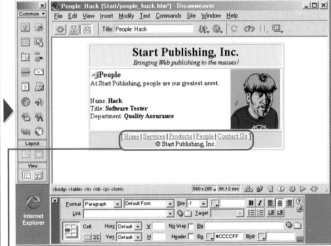

5 Click **Insert**.

6 Click ⊠ to close the Library window.

■ Dreamweaver inserts the library item, which is highlighted in yellow, in the Document window.

You can edit a
library item and
then automatically
update all the
pages in your site
that feature that
item. This feature
can save you time
when maintaining a
Web site.

You can also edit a
specific instance of a
library item on a page.
See page 204.

EDIT A LIBRARY ITEM AND UPDATE YOUR WEB SITE

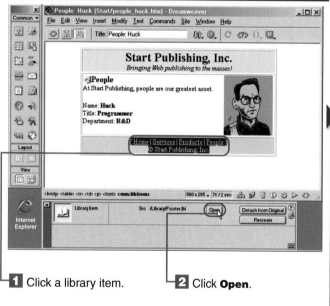

1 Click a library item.

2 Click **Open**.

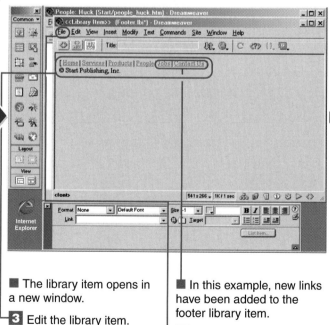

■ The library item opens in
a new window.

3 Edit the library item.

■ In this example, new links
have been added to the
footer library item.

4 Click **File**.

5 Click **Save**.

What will my pages look like after I have edited a library item and updated my site?

All the pages in your site that contain an instance of the library item will have those instances replaced with the edited version. By using the library feature, you can make a change to a single library item and have hundreds of Web pages updated automatically.

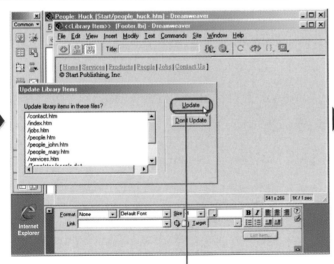

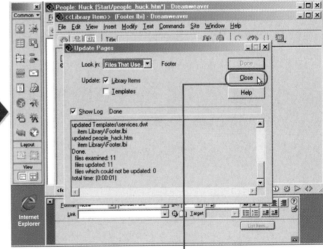

■ An alert box asks if you want to update all the instances of the library item in the site.

6 Click **Update**.

■ A dialog box shows the progress of the updates.

7 After Dreamweaver finishes updating the site, click **Close**.

DETACH LIBRARY CONTENT FOR EDITING

You can detach an instance of a library item from the library and then edit it just like regular content.

DETACH LIBRARY CONTENT FOR EDITING

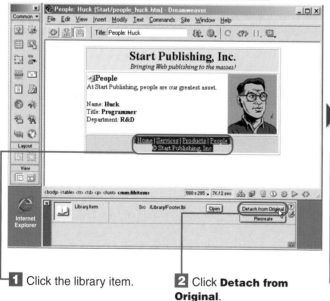

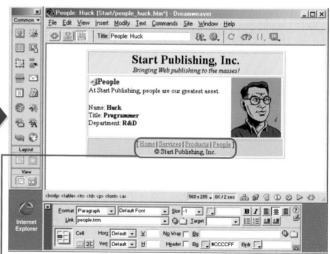

1 Click the library item.

2 Click **Detach from Original**.

■ The element is no longer a library item and no longer has the distinctive highlighting.

204

Why might I use the Detach from Original command on a regular basis?

You might use it if you are using library items as templates for specific design elements on your pages. For instance, if you need numerous captioned images in your Web site, you can create a library item that has a two-cell table with a generic image and caption. To place an image and caption, you insert the library item and then detach the item from the library to make it editable. You can then replace the generic image and caption with appropriate content.

3 Edit the content.

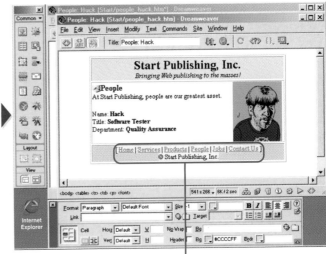

4 Open another page that has the library item.

■ Editing the detached library item on the other page has no effect on the existing library items.

CREATE A TEMPLATE

To help you save time, you can create generic template pages to use as starting points for new pages.

Our Little Angel
Watch as he grows!

The most recent cute thing he did!

The latest photo!

Click here to see delivery room photos!

Click here for colleges we're considering!

CREATE A TEMPLATE

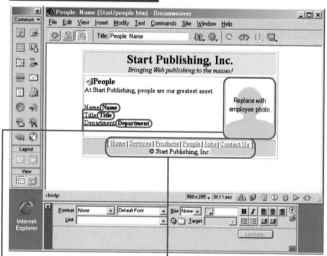

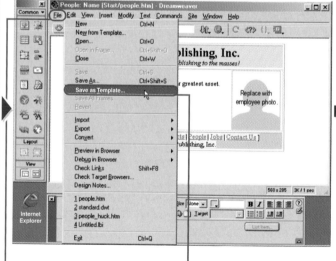

1 Create the page that will serve as a template.

■ You can add generic placeholders where information will change from page to page.

Note: To create templates for your Web pages, you must already have defined a local site. See page 52 for instructions on setting up a local site.

■ In this example, the template includes a library item.

2 Click **File**.

3 Click **Save As Template**.

What are the different types of content in a template?

A template contains two types of content: editable and locked. After you create a new Web page based on a template, you can only change the parts of the new page that are defined as editable. To change locked content, you must edit the original template.

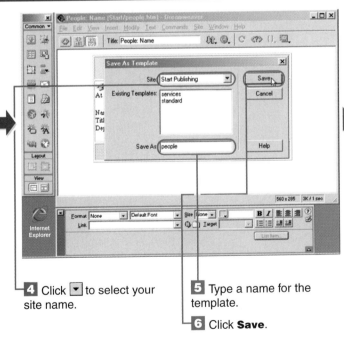

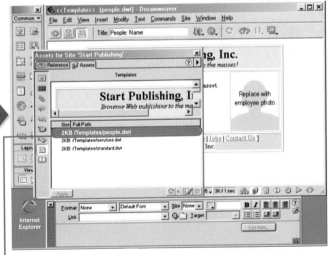

4 Click ▼ to select your site name.

5 Type a name for the template.

6 Click **Save**.

■ Dreamweaver saves the page with a `.dwt` extension in the Templates folder.

Note: To make the template functional, you must define the editable regions where you want to be able to modify content. See page 208 for instructions.

SET A TEMPLATE'S EDITABLE REGIONS

After you create a Web-page template, you must define which regions of the template are editable. These regions are changeable in a page according to its template design.

SET A TEMPLATE'S EDITABLE REGIONS

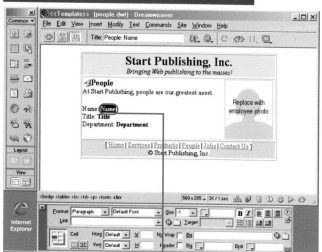

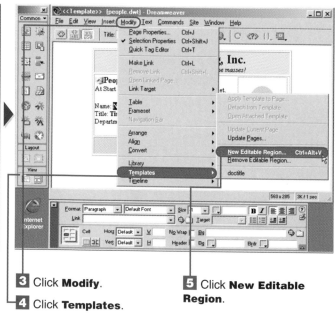

1 Open the template.

■ You can also open templates from the Assets panel by clicking **Window**, **Templates**, and then double-clicking the template file to open it.

■ You can also click **File**, **Open**, and then open the template from inside the Templates folder.

2 Click and drag to select the element that you want to define as editable.

3 Click **Modify**.

4 Click **Templates**.

5 Click **New Editable Region**.

**What parts of a template
should be defined as editable?**

You should define any part that
needs to be changed from page
to page as editable. Generally,
variable areas in the page body
are defined as editable while
site navigation, disclaimers, and
copyright information are kept
locked.

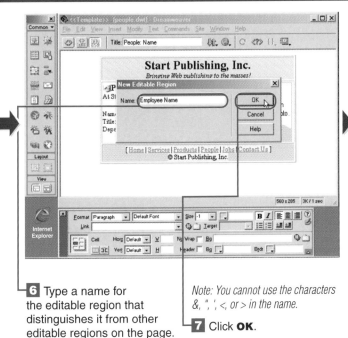

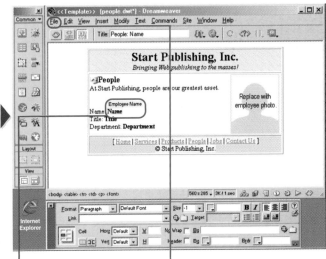

6 Type a name for
the editable region that
distinguishes it from other
editable regions on the page.

*Note: You cannot use the characters
&, ", ', <, or > in the name.*

7 Click **OK**.

■ The editable region is
highlighted in light blue on
the page. A tab denotes its
name.

*Note: See page 30 for instructions
on changing the highlighting color
for editable text in Preferences.*

8 Repeat steps 1 to 7 for
all the regions on the page
that you want to be editable
in the template.

9 Click **File**.

10 Click **Save**.

CREATE A PAGE BY USING A TEMPLATE

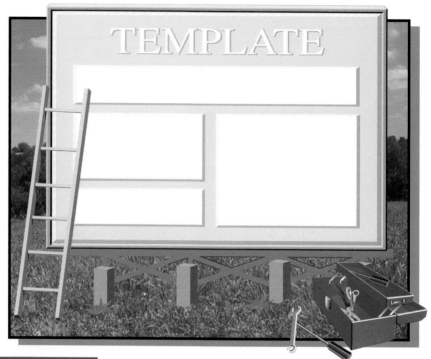

You can create a new Web page based on a template that you have already defined. This step saves you from having to build all the generic elements that appear on many of your pages from scratch.

CREATE A PAGE BY USING A TEMPLATE

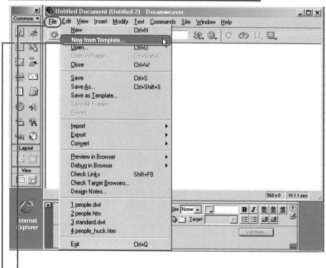

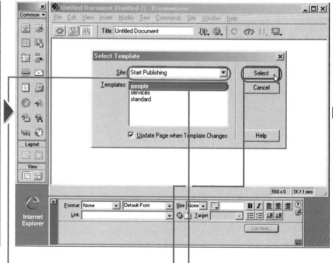

1 Click **File**.

2 Click **New from Template**.

■ You can also apply a template to an existing page by clicking **Modify**, **Templates**, and then **Apply Template to Page**.

3 Click ▾ to select your site.

4 Click a template.

5 Click **Select**.

How do I detach a page from a template?

Click **Modify**, **Templates**, and then select the **Detach from Template** command from the submenu. The page becomes a regular document with previously locked regions now fully editable. The page will no longer be updated when the original template is updated.

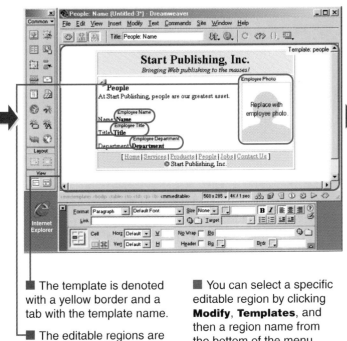

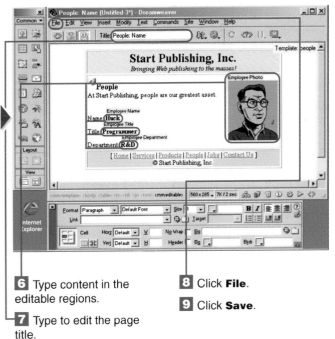

■ The template is denoted with a yellow border and a tab with the template name.

■ The editable regions are highlighted in blue.

■ You can select a specific editable region by clicking **Modify**, **Templates**, and then a region name from the bottom of the menu that appears.

6 Type content in the editable regions.

7 Type to edit the page title.

8 Click **File**.

9 Click **Save**.

EDIT A TEMPLATE AND UPDATE YOUR WEB SITE

You can make changes to an original template file and then have Dreamweaver update other pages that were based on that template. This enables you to make changes to the page design of your site in seconds.

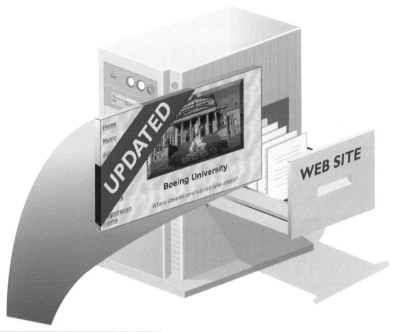

EDIT A TEMPLATE AND UPDATE YOUR WEB SITE

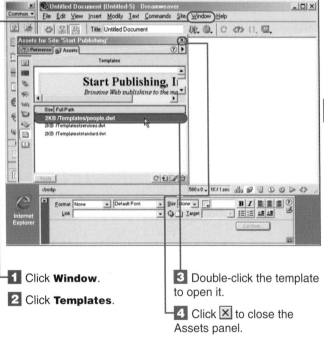

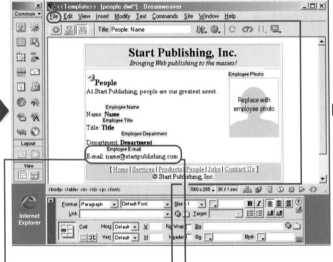

1 Click **Window**.

2 Click **Templates**.

3 Double-click the template to open it.

4 Click ⊠ to close the Assets panel.

5 Edit the template.

■ Editing a template includes adding, modifying, or deleting editable or locked content on the page.

Note: See page 208 for information about editable regions.

■ In this example, an e-mail entry has been added to a template. The E-mail: label is noneditable; the E-mail that is hightlighted in blue and tabbed is editable.

6 Click **File**.

7 Click **Save**.

How does Dreamweaver store page templates?

Dreamweaver stores page templates in a folder called *Templates* inside the local site folder. You can open templates by clicking **File**, **Open**, the **Templates** folder, and then opening a file. (You can also open templates from inside the Assets panel.)

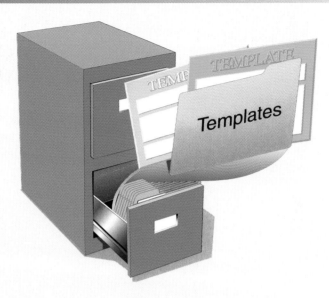

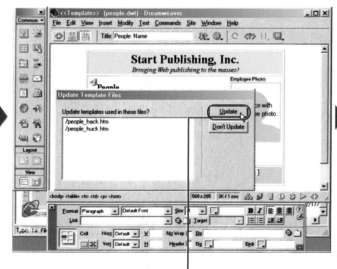

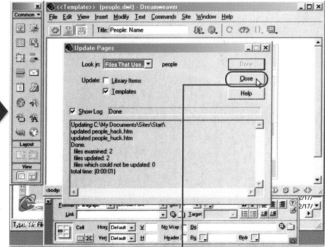

■ An alert box appears asking if you want to update all the pages that are based on the template.

8 Click **Update**.

■ A dialog box shows the progress of the updates.

9 After Dreamweaver finishes updating the site, click **Close**.

SUNSHINE VACATIONS

Here at Sunshine Vacations, we are commited to making your vacation or business trip a memorable one! We provide the best rates available for flights, accommodations and rental cars and important advice about what to see and do at your destination city.

Kick back, relax and enjoy the peace of mind that comes with knowing Sunshine Vacations is available 24 hours a day should you need our assistance.

STYLE SHEET

FANCY HEADLINE

BORDERED IMAGE

BOLD PARAGRAPH

BORDERED

CHAPTER 12

Implementing Style Sheets and Layers

This chapter shows you how to apply complex formatting to your page text using style sheets. It also shows you how to position page elements precisely using layers.

INTRODUCTION TO STYLE SHEETS

You can apply many different types of formatting to your Web pages with *style sheets* (also known as Cascading Style Sheets, or CSS).

Format Text

A separate standard from HTML, style sheets let you format fonts, adjust character, paragraph, and margin spacing, customize the look of hyperlinks, tailor the colors on your page, and more.

Position Web Page Elements

You can use style sheets to position images, text, and other elements precisely on your Web page, something that is not possible with HTML. Layers in Dreamweaver offers a user-friendly way to apply style sheet positioning capabilities.

Use Style Sheets Instead of HTML

You can perform many of the HTML-based formatting features discussed on pages 64 to 86. You can also use Style sheets to apply more elaborate formatting to your pages than is possible with regular HTML.

Embedded Style Sheets

A style sheet that is saved inside a particular Web page is an *embedded style sheet*. Embedded style sheet rules apply only to the page in which they are embedded.

External Style Sheets

You can save style sheets as separate files; these external style sheets exist independently of your HTML pages. Different Web pages can access a common set of style rules by linking to the same external style sheet.

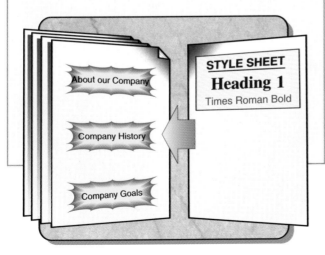

Style Sheets and Browsers

Some older browsers support style sheet standards partly, or not at all. You should test pages that use style sheets on different browsers before you place the pages live, to ensure that content displays as you expect it.

Microsoft Internet Explorer

Netscape Communicator

CUSTOMIZE AN HTML TAG

You can use style sheets to customize the style that is applied by an HTML tag. This capability gives you control over how HTML makes the text and other content on your page appear.

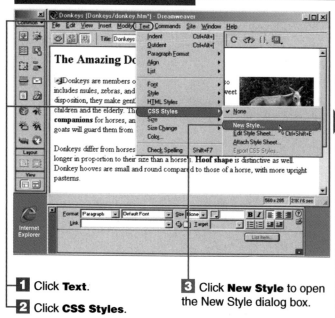

1 Click **Text**.

2 Click **CSS Styles**.

3 Click **New Style** to open the New Style dialog box.

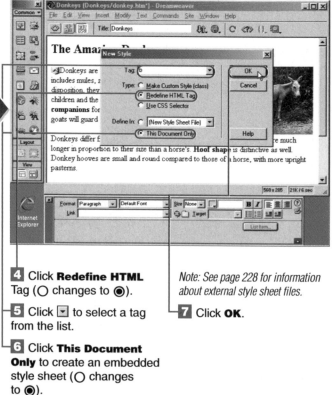

4 Click **Redefine HTML** Tag (○ changes to ●).

5 Click ▼ to select a tag from the list.

6 Click **This Document Only** to create an embedded style sheet (○ changes to ●).

Note: See page 228 for information about external style sheet files.

7 Click **OK**.

**How do I edit the style that
I have applied to a tag?**

Click **Text**, **CSS Styles**,
and then **Edit Style Sheet**.
A dialog box displays the
current customized tags
and style-sheet classes.
Click the tag and then click
Edit.

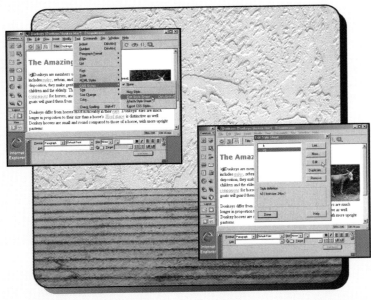

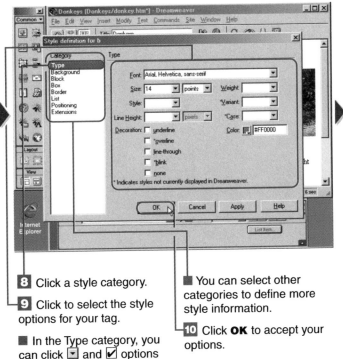

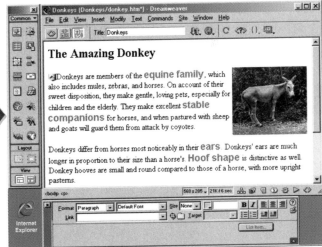

■8 Click a style category.

■9 Click to select the style
options for your tag.

■ In the Type category, you
can click ▼ and ☑ options
to customize font
characteristics.

■ You can select other
categories to define more
style information.

■10 Click **OK** to accept your
options.

■ Dreamweaver adds the
new style to any content
formatted with the redefined
tag (example: **<b> tag**).

■ You can also apply the
style by formatting new
content with the tag.

CREATE A CLASS

You can define specific
style attributes as a style
sheet *class*. You can
then apply that class to
elements on your Web
page.

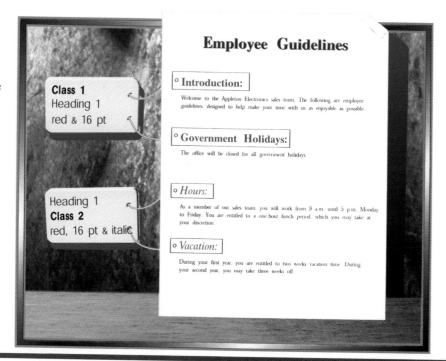

Class 1
Heading 1
red & 16 pt

Heading 1
Class 2
red, 16 pt & italic

Employee Guidelines

○ Introduction:

Welcome to the Appleton Electronics sales team. The following are employee guidelines, designed to help make your time with us as enjoyable as possible.

○ Government Holidays:

The office will be closed for all government holidays.

○ *Hours:*

As a member of our sales team, you will work from 9 a.m. until 5 p.m. Monday to Friday. You are entitled to a one hour lunch period, which you may take at your discretion.

○ *Vacation:*

During your first year, you are entitled to two weeks vacation time. During your second year, you may take three weeks off.

CREATE A CLASS

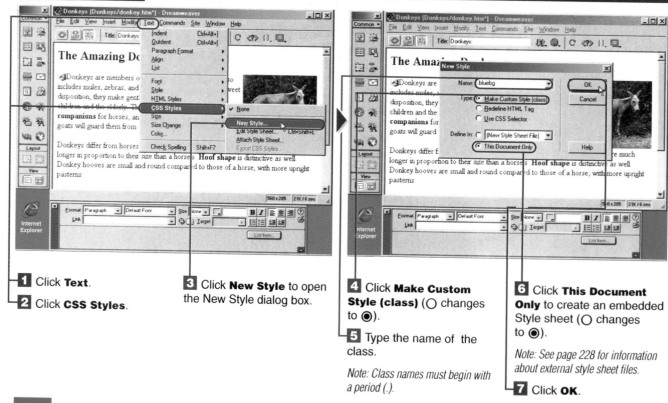

1 Click **Text**.

2 Click **CSS Styles**.

3 Click **New Style** to open
the New Style dialog box.

4 Click **Make Custom
Style (class)** (○ changes
to ◉).

5 Type the name of the
class.

*Note: Class names must begin with
a period (.).*

6 Click **This Document
Only** to create an embedded
Style sheet (○ changes
to ◉).

*Note: See page 228 for information
about external style sheet files.*

7 Click **OK**.

How does customizing an HTML tag differ from creating a class?

Customizing an HTML tag links style rules to a specific tag. The new style affects every instance of that tag on your Web page. If you customize your paragraph tags as red using style sheets, every paragraph in your page will be red. Classes let you define custom styles that are independent of specific HTML tags. You can apply a class that turns text green to a paragraph, an H3 heading, or another text-based tag.

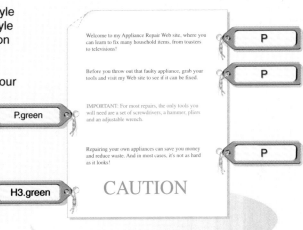

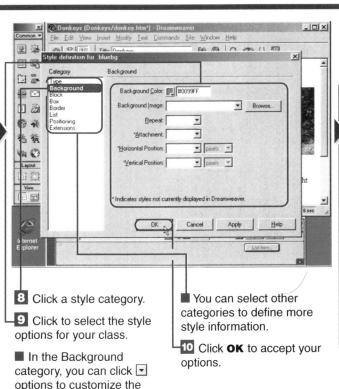

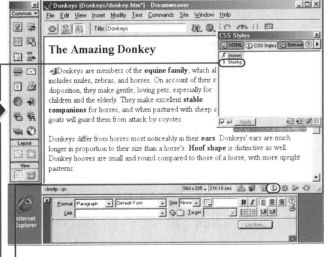

8 Click a style category.

9 Click to select the style options for your class.

■ In the Background category, you can click ▾ options to customize the appearance and positioning of the background.

■ You can select other categories to define more style information.

10 Click **OK** to accept your options.

11 Click the **CSS Styles** button (▣) to open the CSS Styles panel.

■ The new class appears in the panel.

■ The new class has no effect on your content until you apply it.

Note: See page 222 for instructions on applying a class.

APPLY A CLASS

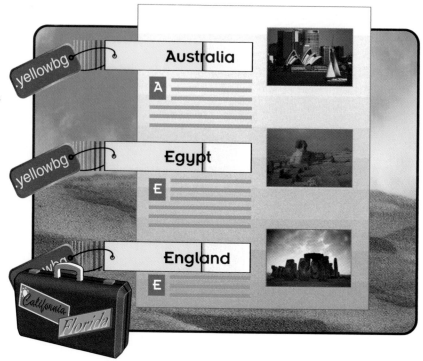

You can apply a style-sheet class to elements on your Web page. This enables you to change the color, font, size, background, and other characteristics of content on your page.

APPLY A CLASS

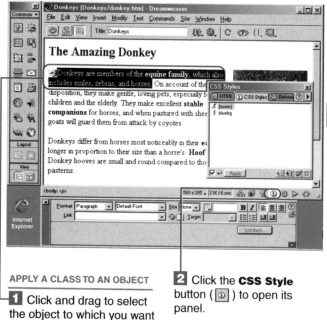

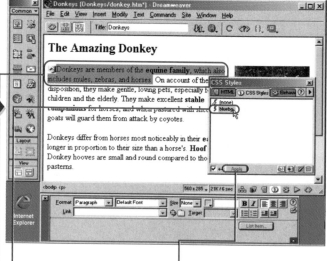

APPLY A CLASS TO AN OBJECT

1 Click and drag to select the object to which you want to apply the class.

2 Click the **CSS Style** button (⬛) to open its panel.

3 Click a class.

■ Dreamweaver applies the style-sheet class to the selected content in the Document window.

■ If the Apply check box is unchecked, you can click the **Apply** button to apply the selected class.

Does Dreamweaver display all the styles that I apply to my pages?

Dreamweaver can display only a subset of the style rules that it lets you define. Style rules that are marked with an * in the Style Definitions dialog box cannot be displayed. You need to open the page in a style-sheet-capable browser to view these styles. Some of the styles that Dreamweaver cannot display include borders, word and letter spacing, and list characteristics.

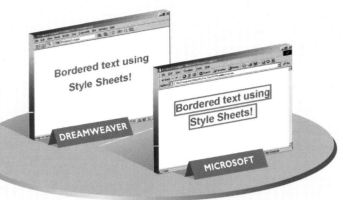

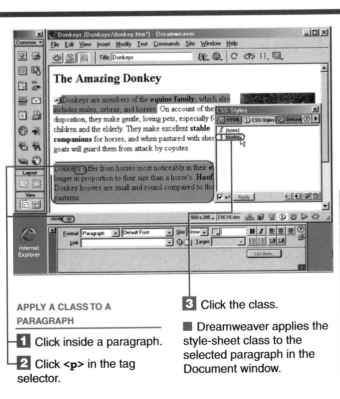

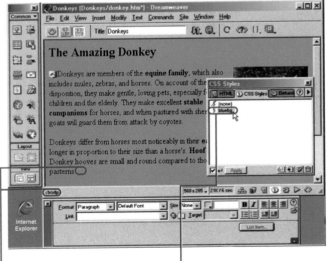

APPLY A CLASS TO A PARAGRAPH

-1 Click inside a paragraph.

-2 Click **<p>** in the tag selector.

3 Click the class.

■ Dreamweaver applies the style-sheet class to the selected paragraph in the Document window.

APPLY A CLASS TO THE ENTIRE BODY OF A PAGE

-1 Click inside the Document window.

-2 Click **<body>** in the tag selector.

3 Click the class.

■ Dreamweaver applies the style-sheet class to entire body of the page in the Document window.

EDIT A STYLE SHEET CLASS

You can edit the style rules of a class. This will change all the instances where you have applied the class on your pages.

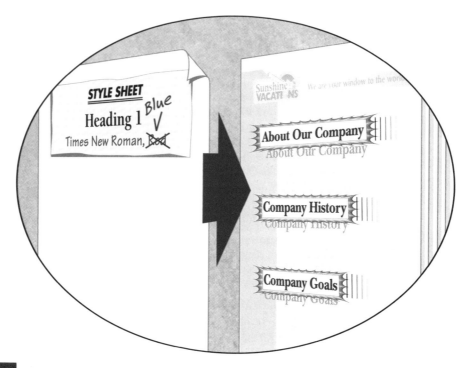

EDIT A STYLE SHEET CLASS

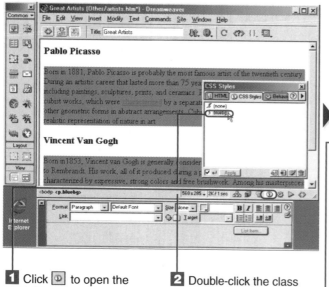

1 Click 🔲 to open the CSS Styles panel.

■ The CSS Styles panel displays the classes available to that page.

2 Double-click the class you want to edit.

3 Click a style category.

4 Edit the style definitions in the dialog box.

■ In this example, the background color has been changed to a different shade of blue.

224

What are some type-based features that I can apply with style sheets that I cannot with HTML?

Style sheets let you specify a numeric value for font weight, enabling you to apply varying degrees of boldness (instead of just a single boldness setting as with HTML). This works only with certain fonts. You can also define type size in absolute units (pixels, points, picas, in, cm, or mm) or relative units (ems, exs, or percentage). HTML offers no such choices of units.

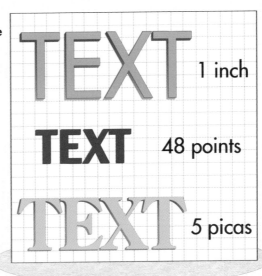

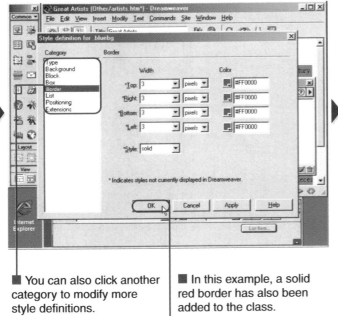

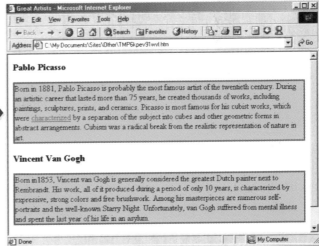

■ You can also click another category to modify more style definitions.

■ In this example, a solid red border has also been added to the class.

5 Click **OK**.

6 Preview the page in a Web browser.

Note: See page 60 for instructions on previewing pages in Web browsers.

■ The page appears with the edited class applied.

Note: Dreamweaver cannot display some style definitions, for example, border styles. Therefore you must open the page in a Web browser to see the full effect of your edits.

USING CSS SELECTORS TO MODIFY LINKS

You can use style-sheet *selectors* to customize the links on your page. Selectors let you customize your links in ways that you cannot with HTML.

USING CSS SELECTORS TO MODIFY LINKS

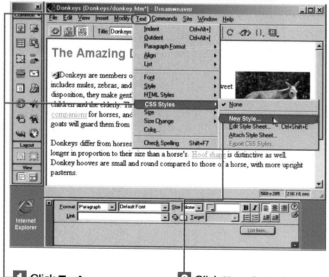

1 Click **Text**.

2 Click **CSS Styles**.

3 Click **New Style** to open the New Style dialog box.

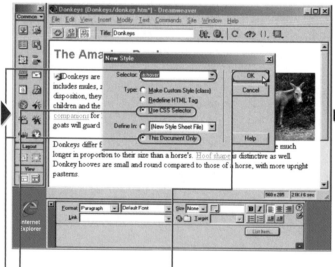

4 Click **Use CSS Selector** (○ changes to ◉).

5 Click ▼ to select a selector.

6 Click **This Document Only** to create an embedded style sheet (○ changes to ◉).

Note: See page 228 for information about external style sheet files.

7 Click **OK**.

How can I make my links looked like they have been marked with highlighter pen?

Define a bright background color for your links under the Background category in the Style Definition box.

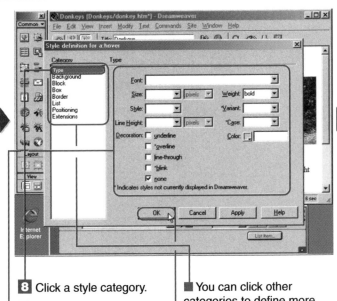

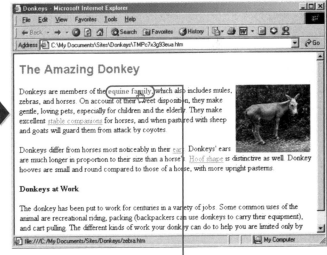

■8 Click a style category.

■9 Click to select the style options for your link.

■ In the Type category, you can click 🔽 and ☑ options to change the characteristics of your text links.

■ You can click other categories to define more style information.

■10 Click **OK** to accept your options.

■11 Preview the page in a Web browser

Note: See page 60 for instructions on previewing pages in Web browsers.

■ Because this exercise defined the a:hover selector, the style of the links change when the cursor is placed over them.

■ In this example, the underlining disappears and the text becomes bold.

CREATE AN EXTERNAL STYLE SHEET

External style sheets enable you to define a set of style-sheet rules and apply them to many different pages — even pages on different Web sites. This capability lets you keep a consistent look and feel across many pages and streamline style updates.

CREATE AN EXTERNAL STYLE SHEET

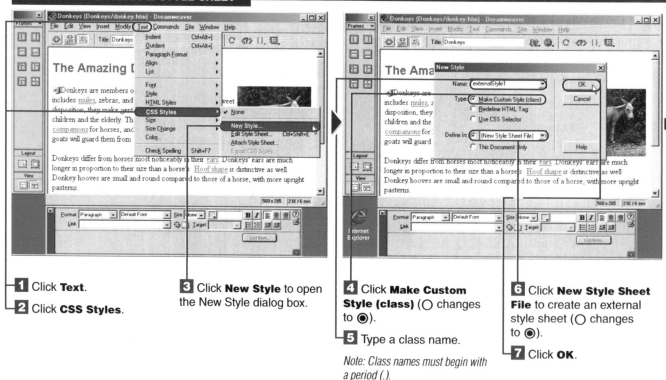

1 Click **Text**.

2 Click **CSS Styles**.

3 Click **New Style** to open the New Style dialog box.

4 Click **Make Custom Style (class)** (○ changes to ◉).

5 Type a class name.

Note: Class names must begin with a period (.).

6 Click **New Style Sheet File** to create an external style sheet (○ changes to ◉).

7 Click **OK**.

How do I attach an external style sheet to a Web page?

Open the Web page to where you want to attach the style sheet and click **Text**, **CSS Styles**, and **Attach Style Sheet**. A dialog box appears allowing you to select and attach a style sheet file. Once the style sheet is attached, the styles from it appear in the CSS Styles panel.

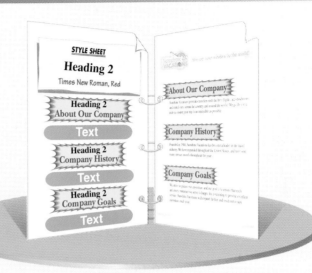

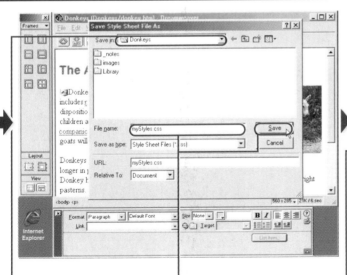

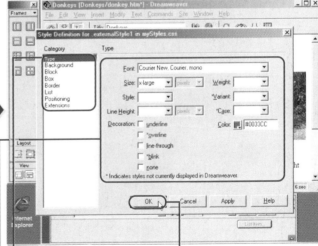

8 Click ▼ to select where you want to store the external style sheet.

■ You should store the external style sheet somewhere inside your local site folder.

Note: See page 52 for information on defining a local site.

9 Name the style sheet file with a **.css** extension.

10 Click **Save**.

11 Click a style category.

12 Click to select the style options for your style sheet.

■ In the Type category, you can click ▼ and ☑ options to change characteristics of your text links.

13 Click **OK** to accept your options.

■ You can repeat steps **1** to **6** (selecting the file you just created in step **6**) and steps **11** to **13** to add more style rules to the external style sheet.

CREATE A LAYER

Layers let you create rectangular areas that float above the other content on your page. You can fill these areas with different types of content and position them precisely in the browser window.

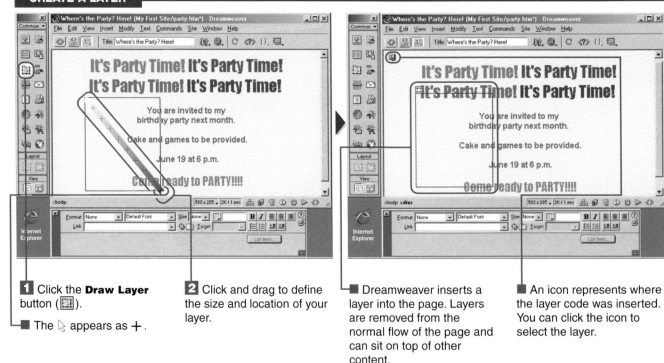

1 Click the **Draw Layer** button (☐).

■ The ⬚ appears as +.

2 Click and drag to define the size and location of your layer.

■ Dreamweaver inserts a layer into the page. Layers are removed from the normal flow of the page and can sit on top of other content.

■ An icon represents where the layer code was inserted. You can click the icon to select the layer.

How do I place one layer inside another?

Open the Preferences dialog box (click **Edit** and then **Preferences**). Click the **Layers** category and make sure the **Nesting** check box is checked. Close the window and click the **Insert Layer** button on the Objects panel. Click and drag inside an existing layer to nest a new layer inside it. When a layer is nested inside another, the layer's icon appears inside the enclosing layer.

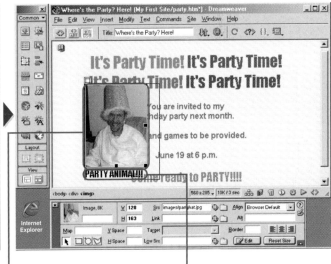

ADD CONTENT TO A LAYER

1 Click inside the layer.

2 Click a button in the Objects panel to insert an object.

3 Fill out any necessary dialog boxes to define and insert the object.

■ In this example, an image object appears inside the layer.

■ To add text, you can click inside the layer and type. You can also style the text in a layer.

RESIZE AND REPOSITION LAYERS

Every layer has specific position and dimension settings that define its place on the page. You can adjust the position and dimensions of a layer to make it fit attractively with the rest of the content on your page.

RESIZE AND REPOSITION LAYERS

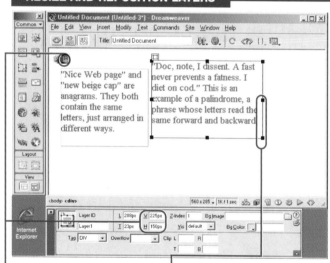

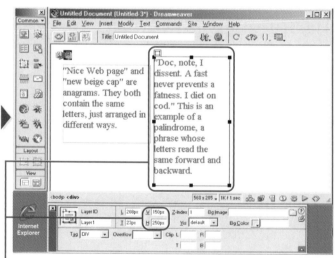

RESIZE A LAYER

1 Click the **Layer** button ([⬚]) to select the layer.

2 Type the new width of the layer in the W field and the new height of the layer in the H field.

■ Label the values **px** for pixels, **in** for inches, or **cm** for centimeters.

■ You can also click and drag on the layer's border handles to change its dimensions.

■ Dreamweaver applies the new dimensions to the layer.

How do I change a layer's visibility?

Select a layer, and then adjust the Vis (Visibility) menu in the Property inspector. The menu lets you make a layer visible or invisible, or have it inherit its characteristic from its parent (the enclosing layer).

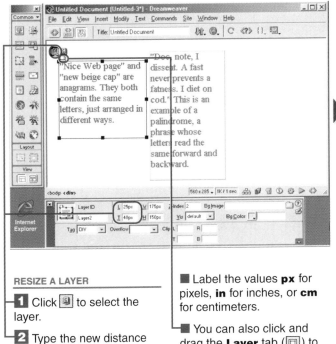

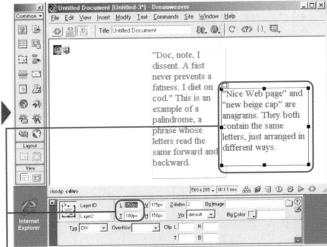

RESIZE A LAYER

1 Click 📖 to select the layer.

2 Type the new distance from the left side of the window in the L field and the new distance from the top of the window in the T field.

■ Label the values **px** for pixels, **in** for inches, or **cm** for centimeters.

■ You can also click and drag the **Layer** tab (📖) to change a layer's position.

■ Dreamweaver applies the new positioning to the layer.

ADD A BACKGROUND COLOR TO A LAYER

You can set the
background color of a
layer to make the layer
stand out or blend in on
a page.

ADD A BACKGROUND COLOR TO A LAYER

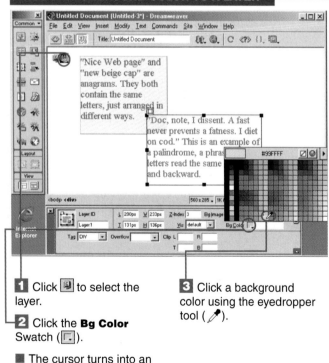

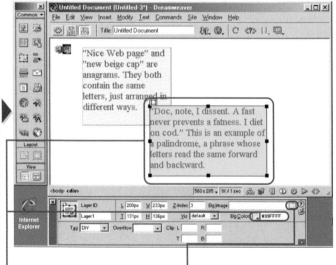

1 Click 🔲 to select the
layer.

2 Click the **Bg Color**
Swatch (🔲).

■ The cursor turns into an
eyedropper (✐).

3 Click a background
color using the eyedropper
tool (✐).

■ The layer background
changes to the new color.

■ In this example, the two
layers have different
background colors. The Web
page also has its own
background color.

■ Clicking **Bg Image** folder
(🔲) lets you select a
background image for the
layer.

234

CHANGE THE STACKING ORDER OF LAYERS

You can change the stacking order of layers on a page to change how they overlap one another. You can then hide parts of some layers under other layers.

Autumn Leaves,
Falling Leaves

Falling Leaves

CHANGE THE STACKING ORDER OF LAYERS

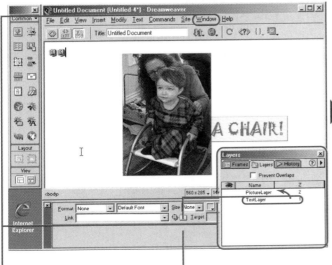

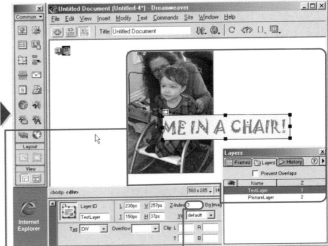

Note: The picture layer is over the text layer.

1 Click **Window** to open the drop-down menu.

2 Click **Layers**.

■ The layers in the page appear in the Layers panel.

3 Click and drag layer names to change the stacking order. Drag the name up to move a layer higher in the stack; drag down to send it down.

■ Dreamweaver changes the stacking order of the layers.

■ You can also select a layer in the Document window and change its Z-Index value in the Property inspector. Layers with greater Z-Index values are placed higher in a stack.

Ancient Treasur

CHAPTER 13

Implementing Behaviors

You can make your Web site more interactive by adding behaviors. This chapter shows you how to put these powerful features to use quickly.

You can add interactivity to your Web pages with behaviors. Behaviors let you create image rollovers, validate forms, check browser versions, and more.

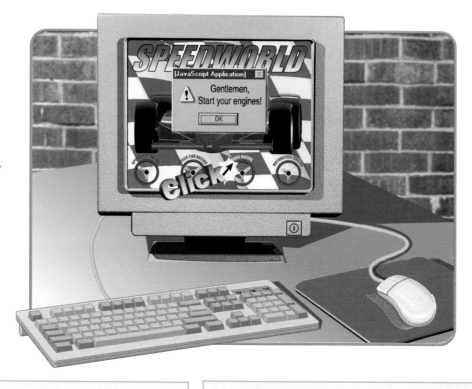

Behavior Basics

A *behavior* is a cause-and-effect feature that you set up in your Web page. You specify a user event, such as a mouse click, and the resulting action, such as a pop-up window appearing, that should take place when that event occurs.

JavaScript Effects

Dreamweaver builds behaviors with *JavaScript,* a popular programming language for adding dynamic features to Web sites. You apply behaviors to specific objects on your Web page using dialog boxes, then Dreamweaver writes the JavaScript code behind the scenes to create the behaviors.

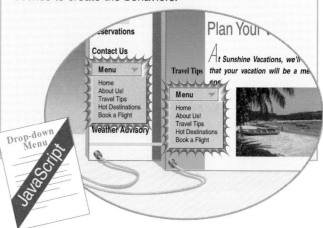

Behaviors and Browsers

Dreamweaver's standard behaviors all work in Version 4 or later of Microsoft Internet Explorer and Netscape Navigator. Some behaviors also work in earlier browsers.

Create Rollover Images

A *rollover* behavior replaces an image on your page with another in response to a cursor passing over it. Many Web designers apply the rollover behavior to navigation buttons on Web pages.

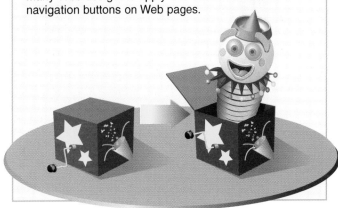

Validate Forms

You can keep users from entering erroneous information in Web-page forms by using a behavior to validate form fields. The behavior generates an alert if invalid data is submitted, and enables users to change their entries.

Check Browser Versions

Designing a page that works equally well in all browsers can be difficult, especially if you use advanced features such as style sheets and layers. You can use a behavior to check the brand of browser (Microsoft Internet Explorer or Netscape Navigator) as well as the version. The behavior can then forward a user to a page built specifically for that browser.

CREATE A ROLLOVER IMAGE

You can replace an image on your page with another in response to a cursor passing over it with a *rollover* behavior. Rollover effects are often applied to navigation buttons, where passing your cursor over the button causes it to light up or appear depressed, like a real button.

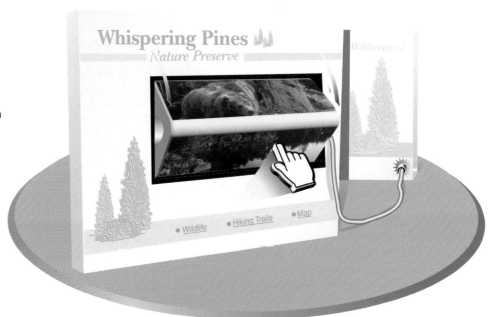

CREATE A ROLLOVER IMAGE

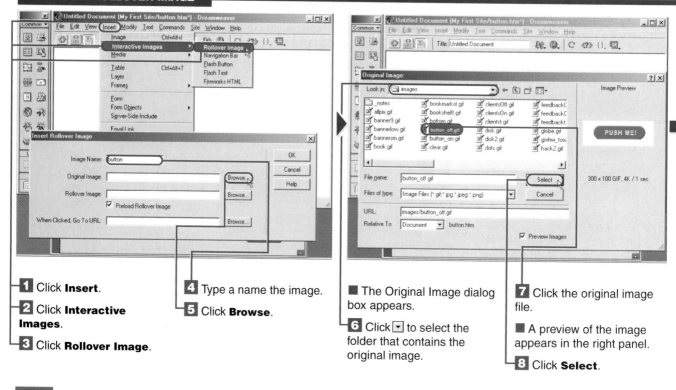

1 Click **Insert**.

2 Click **Interactive Images**.

3 Click **Rollover Image**.

4 Type a name the image.

5 Click **Browse**.

■ The Original Image dialog box appears.

6 Click ▼ to select the folder that contains the original image.

7 Click the original image file.

■ A preview of the image appears in the right panel.

8 Click **Select**.

How do I create interesting rollover buttons for my page navigation?

You can create interesting buttons to use for navigation in an image editor such as Macromedia Fireworks or Adobe Photoshop. Both programs include commands that let you easily create contoured or interestingly colored shapes (buttons) that you can then label with text. Some common ways to create the swapped version of a rollover button are to reverse its colors, add a border, or shift the art slightly so it looks like the graphic has been pressed down.

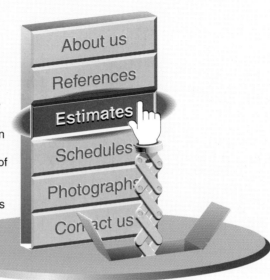

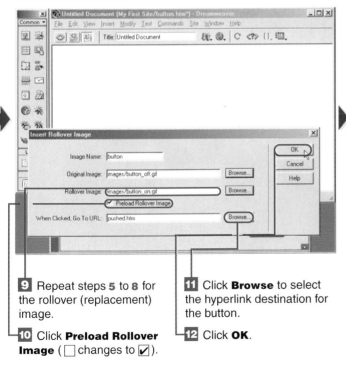

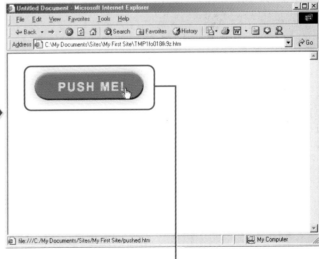

■9 Repeat steps **5** to **8** for the rollover (replacement) image.

■10 Click **Preload Rollover Image** (☐ changes to ☑).

■11 Click **Browse** to select the hyperlink destination for the button.

■12 Click **OK**.

■13 Preview the page in a Web browser.

Note: See page 60 for instructions on how to preview a Web page in your browser.

■ When you pass the cursor over the image, it is replaced with the rollover image.

CREATE A STATUS BAR MESSAGE

You can use a behavior to display a status bar message when a user rolls the cursor over a hyperlink. This message can describe where the hyperlink takes the user.

CREATE A STATUS BAR MESSAGE

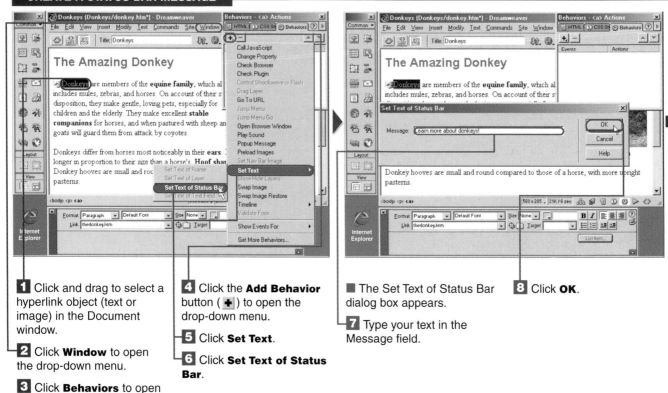

1 Click and drag to select a hyperlink object (text or image) in the Document window.

2 Click **Window** to open the drop-down menu.

3 Click **Behaviors** to open the Behavior panel.

4 Click the **Add Behavior** button ( ) to open the drop-down menu.

5 Click **Set Text**.

6 Click **Set Text of Status Bar**.

■ The Set Text of Status Bar dialog box appears.

7 Type your text in the Message field.

8 Click **OK**.

How do I cause the status bar message to disappear when I roll the cursor off my object?

You need to define a complementary `onMouseOut` action for your object. Repeat the steps below, but specify a blank message and use the `onMouseOut` event in the Behaviors panel. This causes the message to disappear when you roll the cursor off the object. (The `onMouseOut` action works in version 4.0 and later browsers.)

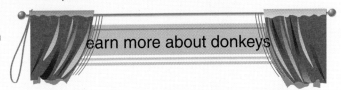

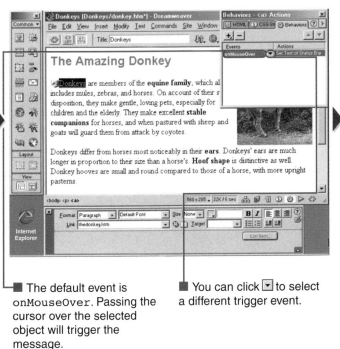

■ The default event is `onMouseOver`. Passing the cursor over the selected object will trigger the message.

■ You can click ▼ to select a different trigger event.

9 Preview the page in a Web browser.

Note: See page 60 for instructions on how to preview a Web page in your browser.

■ When you pass the cursor over the hyperlink, the message appears.

243

VALIDATE A FORM

You can double-check the information a user enters in a form to make sure it is valid. The validation process can include checking that postal codes have the correct number of characters and that e-mail addresses are in the correct format.

VALIDATE A FORM

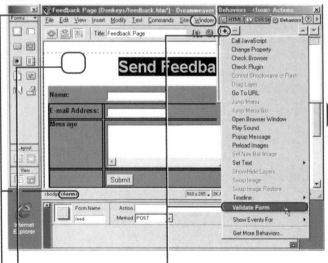

1 Click inside the red dashed box that defines the form.

2 Click `<form>` to select the form.

3 Click **Window** to open the drop-down menu.

4 Click **Behaviors** to open the Behavior panel.

5 Click the **Add Behavior** button ( ) in the Behavior panel to open the drop-down menu.

6 Click **Validate Form** to open the dialog box.

■ All the field names of the form appear in a list.

7 Click a form field.

■ You can click **Required** to require a value in the selected form field (□ changes to ☑).

8 Specify the type of data to accept in the form field.

■ You can repeat steps **7** and **8** for other fields.

9 Click **OK**.

244

What browser events can trigger validation?

If you need to validate a single field in a form, you can use the `onBlur` event to trigger validation. `OnBlur` causes validation to occur when the user clicks away from the field. If you need to validate multiple fields, you can use `onSubmit` for the trigger. `OnSubmit` causes validation to occur after the user clicks the **Submit** button.

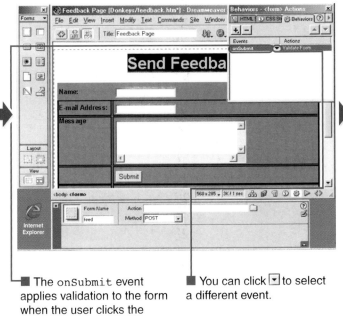

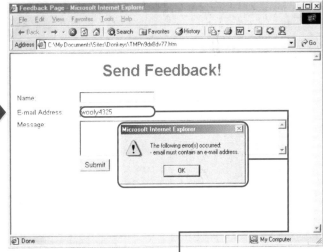

■ The `onSubmit` event applies validation to the form when the user clicks the submit button.

■ You can click ⏷ to select a different event.

10 Preview the Web page in a browser.

Note: See page 60 for instructions on how to preview a Web page in your browser.

■ If you submit the form with invalid content, the browser generates a pop-up alert.

OPEN A CUSTOMIZED BROWSER WINDOW

You can use a behavior to open linked information in a new, customized browser window. This enables you to keep the page that contains the link open on the user's computer.

This behavior is similar to the feature described on page 120.

OPEN A CUSTOMIZED BROWSER WINDOW

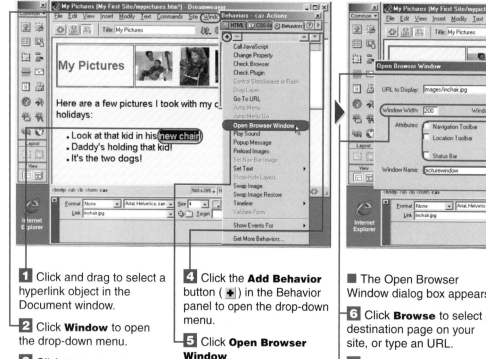

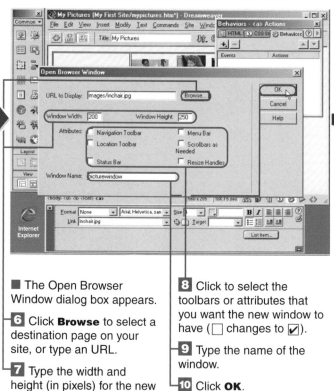

1 Click and drag to select a hyperlink object in the Document window.

2 Click **Window** to open the drop-down menu.

3 Click **Behaviors** to open the Behavior panel.

4 Click the **Add Behavior** button (+) in the Behavior panel to open the drop-down menu.

5 Click **Open Browser Window**.

■ The Open Browser Window dialog box appears.

6 Click **Browse** to select a destination page on your site, or type an URL.

7 Type the width and height (in pixels) for the new window.

8 Click to select the toolbars or attributes that you want the new window to have (□ changes to ✔).

9 Type the name of the window.

10 Click **OK**.

**Why would I want to keep toolbars from
appearing in a new browser window?**

Hiding toolbars lets you keep the
new browser window
compact and maximizes
the window space
available for content.
Before
hiding
the
toolbars for a new
window, you should
consider whether users
might need the features that
are on them (such as the Back and
Forward buttons).

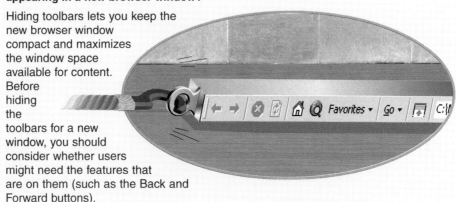

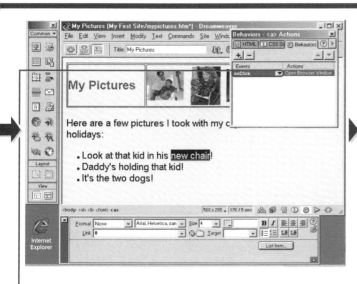

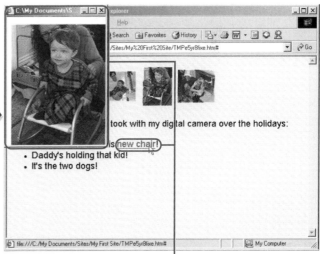

■ Make sure onClick is
the trigger event. You may
have to click ▼, **Show
Events For**, and then **4.0
and Later Browsers** to
make it available.

11 Type a pound sign (#) in
the Link field to prevent
pages opening in the old
window.

12 Preview the Web page in
a browser.

*Note: See page 60 for instructions
on how to preview a Web page in
your browser.*

■ When you click the
hyperlink, the new browser
window appears.

You can use a behavior to check the brand and version of a user's browser, and then forward the user to a page built specifically for that browser. This capability lets you present advanced features only to the users that can experience them.

CHECK A USER'S BROWSER

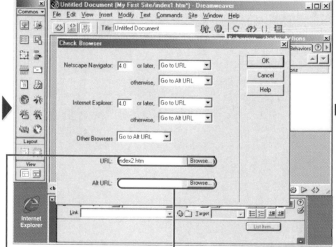

1 Click inside the Document window.

2 Click **<body>** in the tag selector.

■ Selecting the page body causes the behavior to execute when the page loads.

3 Click **Window** to open the drop-down menu.

4 Click **Behaviors** to open the Behavior panel.

5 Click the **Add Behavior** button (**+**) in the Behavior panel to open the drop-down menu.

6 Click **Check Browser**.

■ The Check Browser dialog box appears.

7 Click **Browse** to select a destination page on your site, or type an external URL.

■ If you want to send some users to a second page, click **Browse** to select the page, or type an external URL.

What features might I want to hide from users with older browsers?

Layers (covered on pages 230 to 236) can only be viewed in Version 4 or later browsers. Some JavaScript and style-sheet features also do not work in older browsers.

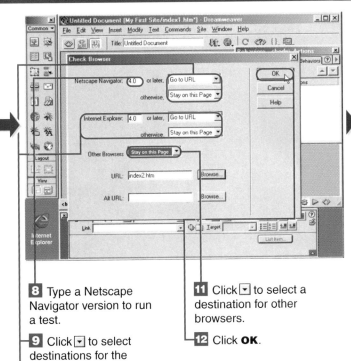

8 Type a Netscape Navigator version to run a test.

9 Click ⯆ to select destinations for the Navigator test.

10 Repeat steps **8** and **9** for Microsoft Internet Explorer.

11 Click ⯆ to select a destination for other browsers.

12 Click **OK**.

13 Preview the page in a Web browser.

Note: See page 60 for instructions on how to preview a Web page in your browser.

■ In this example, the Web page opens in Microsoft IE5. The browser is forwarded to a custom page.

CHAPTER 14

Implementing Timelines

Timelines enable you to animate your page by changing the position and other characteristics of elements over time. This chapter shows you how to create timeline animations.

You can add animation to your Web page by using timelines.

Animating Your Pages

Timelines enable you to manipulate the position, visibility, and other attributes of a Web page's layers over time. Because timelines rely on layers, timeline animation only works in Version 4.0 or later browsers. For an introduction to layers, see page 230.

Timelines Combine HTML and JavaScript

Timeline animations are created with JavaScript, which is able to change the HTML and style-sheet properties of a page over time. This combining of JavaScript, style sheets, and HTML is also known as *Dynamic HTML*. You define the characteristics of a timeline using the Timelines inspector; Dreamweaver then writes the JavaScript code behind the scenes to create the animation.

The Timelines inspector lets you create and edit animations on your page. You can click Window and then Timelines to open the inspector.

REWIND BUTTON

Moves the playback head to the first frame.

BACK BUTTON

Moves the playback head back one frame.

AUTOPLAY

Causes the animation to repeat indefinitely after it begins when checked.

CURRENT FRAME

Shows the current position of the playback head.

LOOP

Causes the animation to repeat indefinitely after it begins when checked.

PLAY BUTTON

Moves the playback head forward one frame, or plays the entire animation if you click and hold it.

KEYFRAMES

Contains details about a specific point of an object in an animated layer.

PLAYBACK RATE

Defines how many frames of the animation play each second.

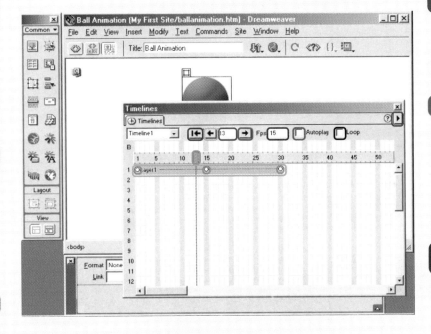

PLAYBACK HEAD

Defines which frame is currently playing in the Document window.

ANIMATION ROW

Defines the frames of an animation for a layer on your page.

TIMELINES MENU

Gives you access to timeline commands.

CREATE A STRAIGHT-LINE ANIMATION

You can create a timeline animation that moves a layer in a straight line on your page. A straight-line animation can enliven a page that otherwise consists of static text and images.

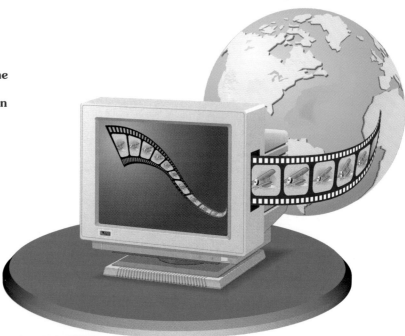

CREATE A STRAIGHT-LINE ANIMATION

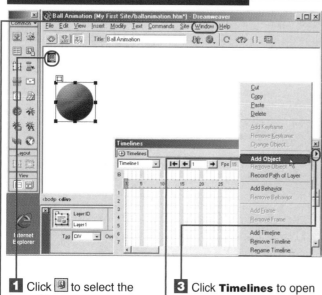

1 Click 🗗 to select the layer that you want to animate.

Note: See page 230 for instructions on how to add a layer to your page.

2 Click **Window** to open the drop-down menu.

3 Click **Timelines** to open the Timelines panel.

4 Click ▶ to open the Timelines menu.

5 Click **Add Object**.

■ If an alert box with layer attribute information appears, click **OK**.

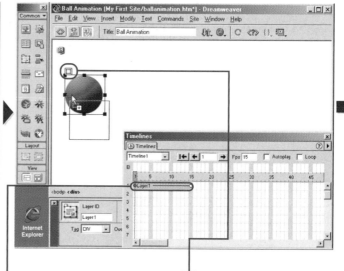

■ An animation bar appears on your timeline.

6 Click the keyframe at the beginning of the animation bar.

7 Click and drag the layer to its initial position.

254

**Can I create several straight-line
animations on a single Web page?**

Yes. Put each piece of
content that you want to
animate in its own layer, then
define an animation bar in the
Timelines inspector for each layer.
(To add each additional animation
bar to the Timelines inspector,
click a layer and use the
Add Object command in
the Timelines menu.)

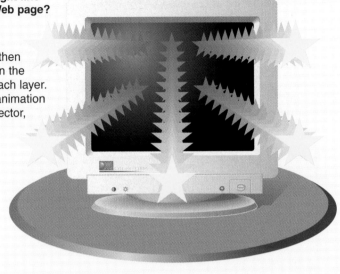

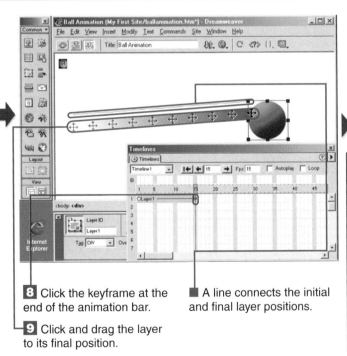

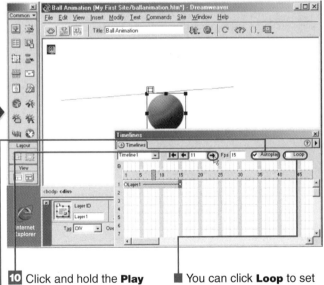

8 Click the keyframe at the
end of the animation bar.

9 Click and drag the layer
to its final position.

■ A line connects the initial
and final layer positions.

10 Click and hold the **Play**
button ➡.

■ The animation plays.

■ You can click **Autoplay**
to set the animation to play
automatically when the page
opens in a browser (☐
changes to ✔).

■ You can click **Loop** to set
the animation to play
indefinitely (☐ changes
to ✔).

■ To remove an animation,
click the animation bar and
then click **Delete** from the
Timelines panel menu.

CREATE AN ANIMATION BY DRAGGING A PATH

You can save time by recording a path instead of describing animation with many keyframes. To create animations that loop or curve, you can drag a layer along the intended path and have Dreamweaver record the path as you go. Recording a path can save you time because it lets you avoid having to describe the path with keyframes.

CREATE AN ANIMATION BY DRAGGING A PATH

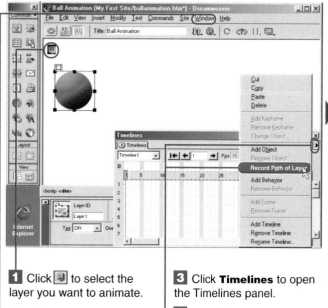

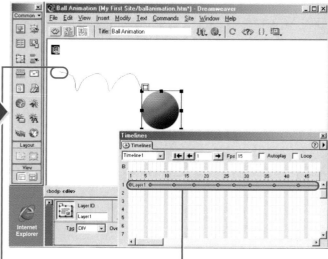

1 Click 🖳 to select the layer you want to animate.

Note: See page 230 for instructions on how to add a layer to your page.

2 Click **Window** to open the drop-down menu.

3 Click **Timelines** to open the Timelines panel.

4 Click ▶ to open the Timelines menu.

5 Click **Record Path of Layer**.

6 Click and drag the layer along the intended animation path.

Note: If after dragging, an alert box with layer attribute information appears, click OK.

■ Dreamweaver creates an animation bar describing the recorded path.

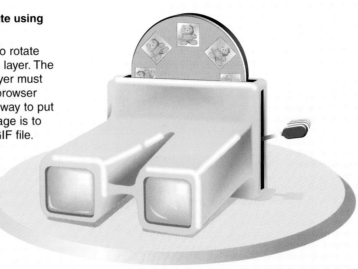

Can I cause a layer to rotate using timelines?

You cannot use timelines to rotate the content that is inside a layer. The animated content in the layer must stay perpendicular to the browser window as it moves. (One way to put rotating content on your page is to create it as an animated GIF file. You can create animated GIFs in Macromedia Fireworks.)

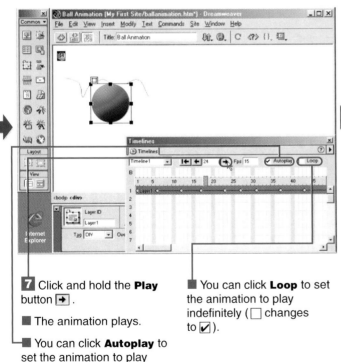

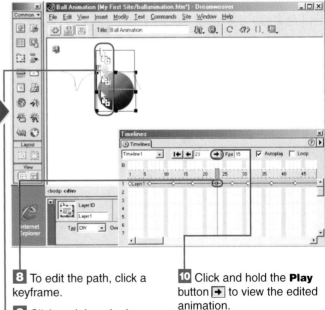

7 Click and hold the **Play** button ➡.

■ The animation plays.

■ You can click **Autoplay** to set the animation to play automatically when the page opens in a browser (☐ changes to ☑).

■ You can click **Loop** to set the animation to play indefinitely (☐ changes to ☑).

8 To edit the path, click a keyframe.

9 Click and drag the layer to a new position for that keyframe.

10 Click and hold the **Play** button ➡ to view the edited animation.

■ To remove an animation, click the animation bar and then click **Delete** from the Timelines panel menu.

CREATE A FLASHING ANIMATION

To draw attention to part of a page, you can make content inside a layer blink by changing the visibility of the layer in a timeline.

CREATE A FLASHING ANIMATION

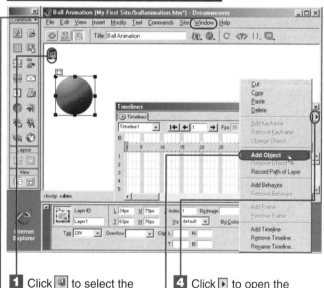

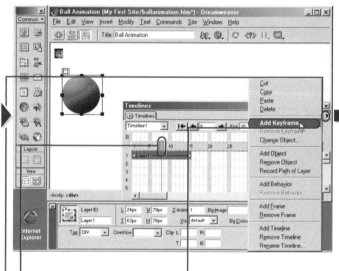

1 Click 🔲 to select the layer that you want to animate.

2 Click **Window** to open the drop-down menu.

3 Click **Timelines** to open the Timelines panel.

4 Click ▶ to open the Timelines menu.

5 Click **Add Object**.

■ If an alert box with layer attribute information appears, click **OK**.

6 Click and drag the playback head to the middle of the animation bar.

7 Click ▶ to open the Timelines menu.

8 Click **Add Keyframe**.

258

How do I shuffle positions of overlapping layers in a timeline?

Change the Z-indexes of the layers at a keyframe in the timeline. Layers are stacked according to what their Z-indexes are relative to other layers (the greater the Z-index, the lower the position in the stack). You can specify a layer's Z-index in the Property inspector.

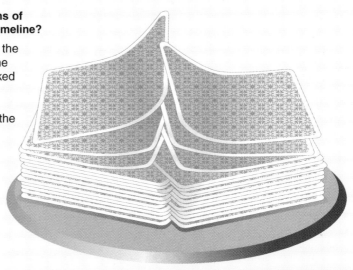

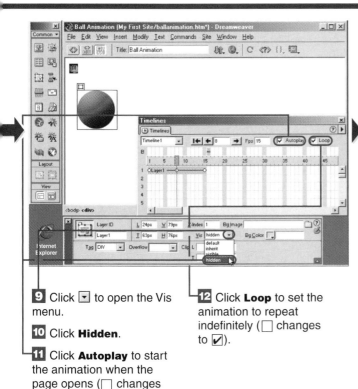

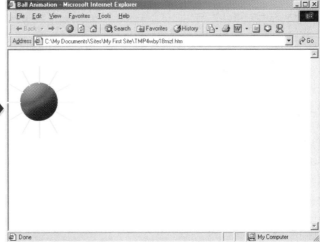

9 Click ▼ to open the Vis menu.

10 Click **Hidden**.

11 Click **Autoplay** to start the animation when the page opens (☐ changes to ☑).

12 Click **Loop** to set the animation to repeat indefinitely (☐ changes to ☑).

13 Preview the Web page in a browser.

Note: See page 60 for instructions on how to preview a Web page in your browser.

■ The object flashes on and off indefinitely.

CHANGE ANIMATION SPEED

You can speed up or slow down a timeline animation by changing its frame rate or by adjusting the number of frames that make up the animation.

CHANGE ANIMATION SPEED

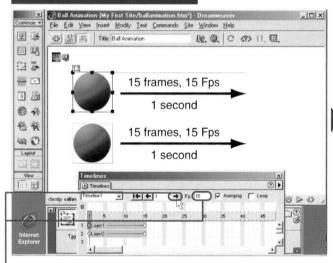

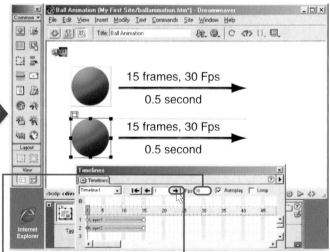

CHANGE THE FRAME RATE

1 Click and hold the **Play** button ➡ to preview the timeline animations on a page.

2 Type a new fps (frames-per-second) value for the animations (example: **30 frames-per-second**).

■ A higher value increases the animation speed, and a lower value decreases the animation speed.

■ The change in the fps rate affects all the animations in the timeline equally.

3 To preview the modified animations, click and hold the **Play** button ➡.

260

How high should I set my frame rate for animations?

Your average browser will not be able to display animations at rates faster than 15 frames per second. You will most likely want to use this rate as your ceiling. If you are running many animations on a page, and want to make sure all users will be able to play them smoothly, you may want to decrease the frame rate to less than 15 fps.

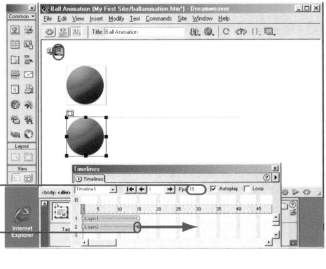

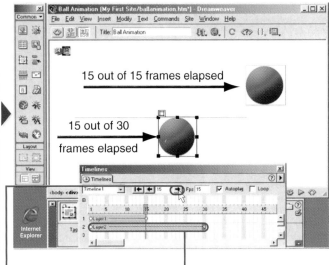

CHANGE THE NUMBER OF FRAMES

1 Click 🔳 to select an animated layer.

2 Click and drag the final keyframe of the selected layer.

■ Drag the keyframe left to decrease the number of frames, or drag it right to increase the number of frames.

3 To preview the modified animation, click and hold the **Play** button ➡ .

■ The layer that has more frames in its animation plays slower.

You can combine Dreamweaver behaviors and timelines so that clicking an image or hyperlink in your page plays an animation. This is an alternative to selecting Autoplay in the Timelines inspector, which causes an animation to automatically start when a page loads.

TRIGGER AN ANIMATION WITH A BEHAVIOR

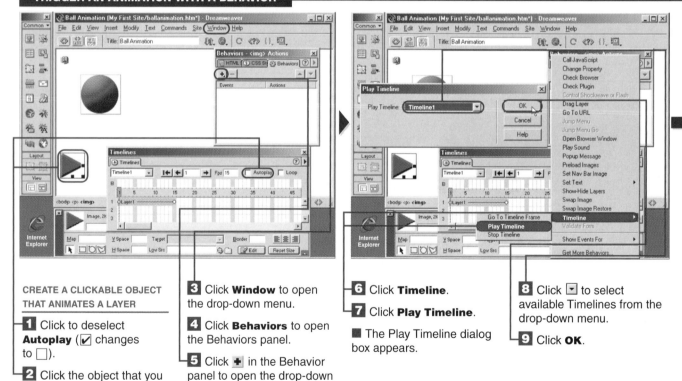

CREATE A CLICKABLE OBJECT THAT ANIMATES A LAYER

1 Click to deselect **Autoplay** (☑ changes to ☐).

2 Click the object that you want to trigger the animation.

3 Click **Window** to open the drop-down menu.

4 Click **Behaviors** to open the Behaviors panel.

5 Click ➕ in the Behavior panel to open the drop-down menu.

6 Click **Timeline**.

7 Click **Play Timeline**.

■ The Play Timeline dialog box appears.

8 Click ▾ to select available Timelines from the drop-down menu.

9 Click **OK**.

How do I create an animation that is stopped with a mouse click?

To create an animation that is stopped with a mouse click, follow steps **1** to **6** in this section, but click **Timeline** and then **Stop Timeline** in step **7**. Make sure the **Autoplay** box is checkzed in step **1**, so the animation runs when the browser opens the page.

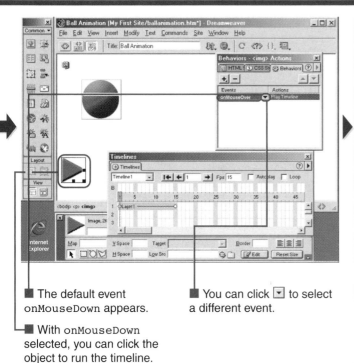

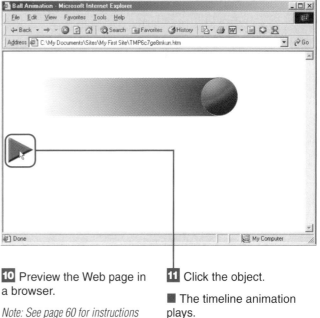

■ The default event onMouseDown appears.

■ With onMouseDown selected, you can click the object to run the timeline.

■ You can click ⬇ to select a different event.

10 Preview the Web page in a browser.

Note: See page 60 for instructions on how to preview a Web page in your browser.

11 Click the object.

■ The timeline animation plays.

CHAPTER 15

Publishing a Web Site

You can publish your completed Web pages on a server to allow the rest of the world to view them. This chapter shows you how to use the various publishing features of Dreamweaver.

PUBLISH YOUR WEB SITE

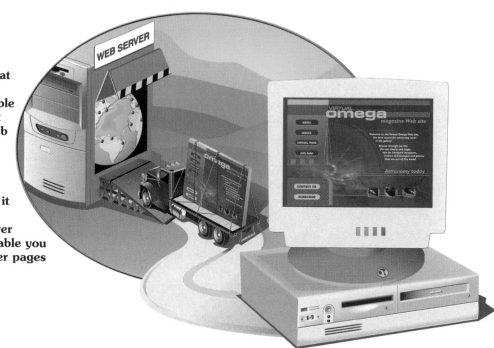

To make the pages that you have built in Dreamweaver accessible on the Web, you must transfer them to a Web server. A *Web server* is an Internet-connected computer running special software that enables it to serve files to Web browsers. Dreamweaver includes tools that enable you to connect and transfer pages to a Web server.

Steps for Publishing your Web site

Publishing your site content using Dreamweaver involves the following steps:

1 Specify where on your computer the site files are kept.

Note: This is done by defining a local site. See Chapter 4 for instructions.

2 Specify the Web server to which you want to publish your files.

Note: This is done by defining a remote site. See the section "Set Up a Remote Site" later in this chapter.

Note: Most people publish their Web pages on servers maintained by their Internet service provider (ISP) or by their company.

3 Connect to the Web server and transfer the files.

Note: The Site window gives you a user-friendly interface for organizing your files and transferring them to the remote site.

After uploading your site, you can update it by editing the copies of the site files on your computer (the local site) and then transferring those copies to the Web server (the remote site).

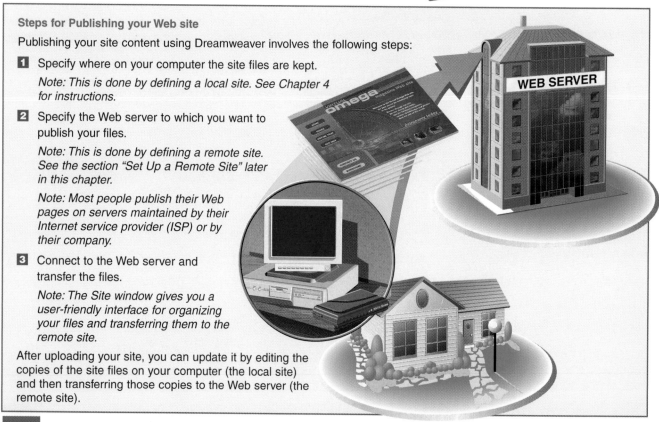

USING THE SITE WINDOW

The Site window lets you view the organization of all files in your site. You also upload local files to the remote site and download remote files to the local site in the Site window.

SITE WINDOWS VIEW

You can click 📋 and 🏠 to switch between viewing your site as lists of files or as a site map. See page 282.

SITE MENU

Lets you select from the different sites you have defined in Dreamweaver.

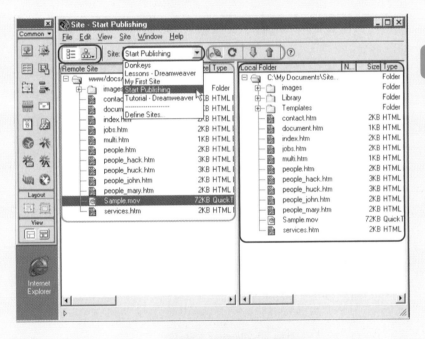

REMOTE SITE

The left pane displays the contents of your site as it exists on the remote Web server. To define a remote site, see page 270.

FILE TRANSFER

Buttons enable you to connect to your remote site, refresh the file lists, upload files to the remote server, and download files to the local site.

LOCAL SITE

The right pane displays the content of your site as it exists on your local computer. To define a local site, see page 30.

ORGANIZE FILES AND FOLDERS

You can use the Site window to organize the elements that make up your local and remote sites. The window lets you create and delete files and folders, as well as move files between folders.

Creating subfolders to organize files of a similar type can be useful if you have a large Web site.

ORGANIZE FILES AND FOLDERS

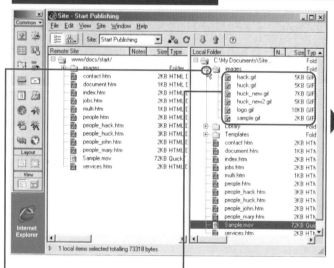

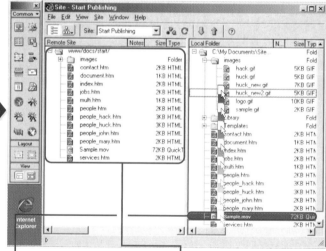

REARRANGE SITE FILES

1 Click **Window**.

2 Click **Site Files** to open the Site window.

3 Click ⊞ to view the files in a subfolder (⊞ changes to ⊟).

■ The folder contents display.

■ You can click ⊟ to close the subfolder.

4 Click and drag a file from the local site folder into a subfolder.

■ If a prompt appears asking if you want to update your links, click **Update**. This will keep your site links from breaking.

■ You can rearrange files the same way in the remote site pane. However, Dreamweaver cannot automatically update your links in pages on your remote site.

What happens to links when I move files?

When you move files into and out of folders, the hyperlinks and image referenced on those pages will most likely need updated (because document-relative references become invalid). Dreamweaver keeps track of any affected code when you rearrange files, and can update it for you when you move a file. This capability can save you time and help keep your site links from breaking.

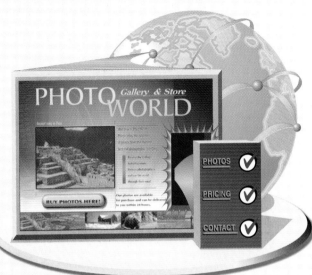

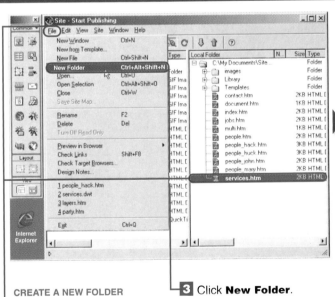

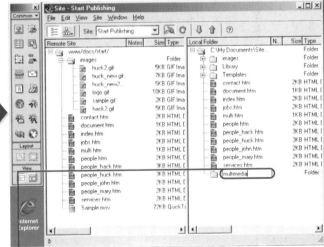

CREATE A NEW FOLDER

1 Click inside the local site pane.

2 Click **File**.

3 Click **New Folder**.

4 Name the new folder.

■ To create a new folder on the remote site, click inside the remote site and perform steps **2** to **4**.

The remote site is the place where the files of your site are made available to the rest of the world. You set up a remote site by specifying a directory on a Web server where your site will be hosted.

SET UP A REMOTE SITE

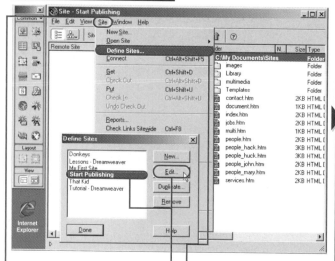

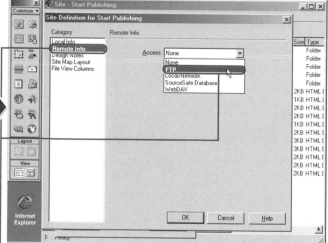

1 Set up a local site.

Note: See page 52 for instructions on setting up a local site.

2 Open the Site window.

Note: See page 267 for instructions.

3 Click **Site**.

4 Click **Define Sites**.

■ The Define Sites dialog box appears.

5 Click a site name from the list.

6 Click **Edit**.

■ The Site Definition dialog box appears.

7 Click **Remote Info**.

8 Click ⬛ to select an access method.

9 Click **FTP**.

■ If your Web server is mounted as a network drive (Windows) or as an AppleTalk or NFS server (Mac), or if you are running a Web server on your local machine, click **Local/Network**.

What happens if I change my Internet service provider (ISP) and need to move my site to a different server?

You will need to change your remote site settings to enable Dreamweaver to connect to the new ISP's server. Your local site settings can stay the same.

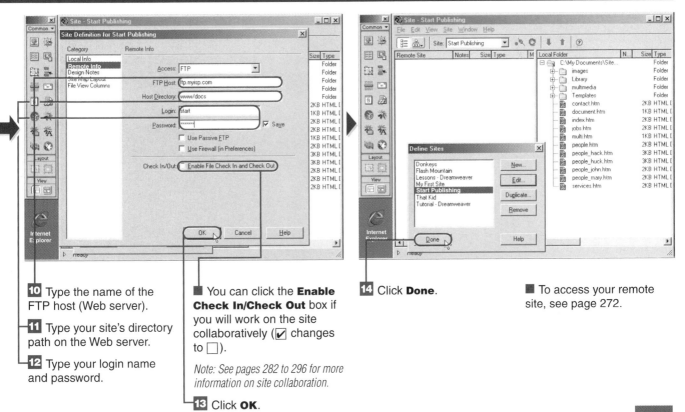

10 Type the name of the FTP host (Web server).

11 Type your site's directory path on the Web server.

12 Type your login name and password.

■ You can click the **Enable Check In/Check Out** box if you will work on the site collaboratively (☑ changes to ☐).

Note: See pages 282 to 296 for more information on site collaboration.

13 Click **OK**.

14 Click **Done**.

■ To access your remote site, see page 272.

CONNECT TO A REMOTE SITE

You can connect to the
Web server that hosts
your remote site and
transfer files between it
and Dreamweaver.
Dreamweaver connects
to the Web server by a
process known as *File
Transfer Protocol,*
or FTP.

CONNECT TO A REMOTE SITE

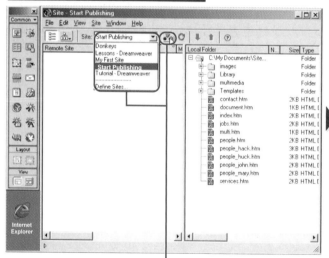

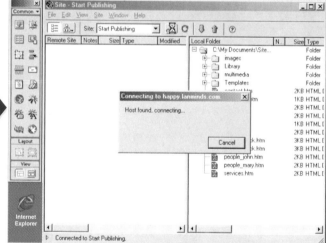

1 Set up a local site.

*Note: See page 52 for instructions
on setting up a local site.*

2 Set up a Remote Site.

Note: See page 270 for instructions.

3 Open the Site window.

*Note: See page 54 for instructions
on opening the Site window.*

4 Click ⏷ to select your
Web site.

5 Click the **Connect**
button (🖧).

■ Dreamweaver attempts to
connect to the remote site.

*Note: If it cannot connect to the site,
Dreamweaver displays an alert box.
If you have trouble connecting,
double-check the host information
you entered for the remote site.*

How do I keep Dreamweaver from prematurely disconnecting from the Web server?

You can click **Edit**, **Preferences**, and then **Site**. Then you can adjust the time that Dreamweaver lets pass between commands before it logs you off the server (the default is 30 minutes). Note that Web servers also have a similar setting on their end. So the server, not Dreamweaver, may sometimes log you off.

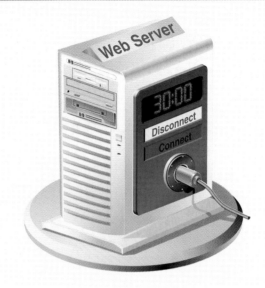

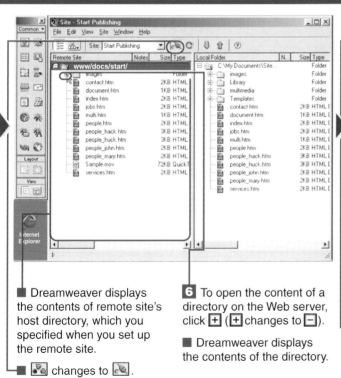

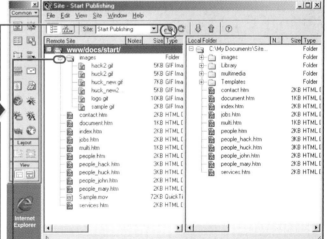

■ Dreamweaver displays the contents of remote site's host directory, which you specified when you set up the remote site.

■ 🖳 changes to 🖳.

6 To open the content of a directory on the Web server, click ⊞ (⊞ changes to ⊟).

■ Dreamweaver displays the contents of the directory.

■ You can click ⊟ to close a directory.

7 Click 🖳 to disconnect from the Web server.

■ Dreamweaver automatically disconnects from a Web server if you do not transfer any files for 30 minutes. You can change the disconnect period in Preferences.

Note: See page 30 for more information on Preferences.

273

UPLOAD FILES

You can upload site files from Dreamweaver to your remote site to make the files available to others on the Web.

UPLOAD FILES

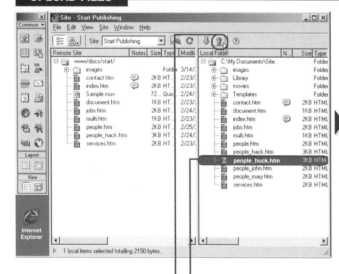

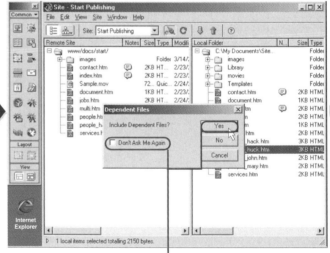

1 Connect to the Web server by using the Site window.

Note: See page 272 for instructions.

2 Click the file you want to upload.

3 Click the **Put** button (⬆).

■ An alert box appears asking if you want to include dependent files.

Note: Dependent files are images and other files associated with a particular Web page.

■ If you are uploading a frameset, dependent files include the files for each frame in the frameset.

4 Click **Yes**.

■ You can click here to avoid the alert box in the future (☐ changes to ☑).

**How do I stop a file
transfer in progress?**

You can click the **Stop
Sign** button, which
appears at the bottom of
the Document window
while a transfer is in
progress. You can also
press `Esc` (`⌘` +).

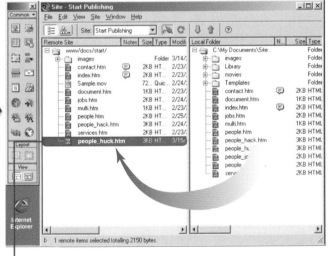

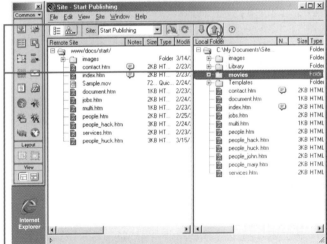

■ The files transfers from
your computer to the Web
server.

UPLOAD A FOLDER

1 Click a folder in the right
pane.

2 Click ⬆.

■ Dreamweaver transfers
the folder and its contents
from your computer to the
Web server.

DOWNLOAD FILES

You can download files from your remote site to Dreamweaver if you need to retrieve copies of your pages from the Web server.

DOWNLOAD FILES

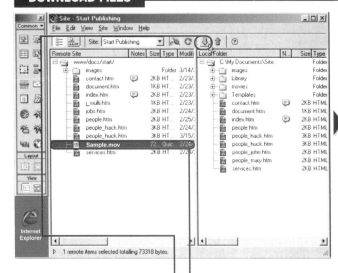

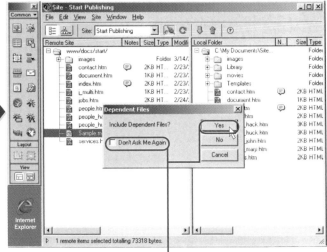

1 Connect to the Web server by using the Site window.

Note: See page 272 for instructions.

2 Click the file you want to download.

3 Click the **Get** button (⬇).

■ An alert box appears asking if you want to include dependent files.

Note: Dependent files are images and other files that are associated with a particular Web page.

■ If you are downloading a frameset, dependent files include the files for each frame in the frameset.

4 Click **Yes**.

■ You can click here to avoid the alert box in the future (☐ changes to ☑).

Where does Dreamweaver log errors that occur during transfer?

Dreamweaver logs all transfer activity (including errors) in a file-transfer log. You can view it by clicking **Window** (Windows) or **Site** (Mac), and then **Site FTP log.**

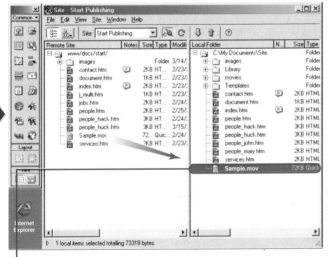

■ The file transfers from the Web server to your computer.

DOWNLOAD MULTIPLE FILES

1 Press and hold **Ctrl** (**Shift**) and then click to select the files you want to download.

2 Click ⬇.

■ The files transfer from your the Web server to your computer.

SYNCHRONIZE YOUR LOCAL AND REMOTE SITES

Dreamweaver can transfer files between your local and remote sites so that both sites have an identical set of the most recent files. This can be useful if other people are editing files on the remote site, and the files on your local site may not be the most recent.

SYNCHRONIZE YOUR LOCAL AND REMOTE SITES

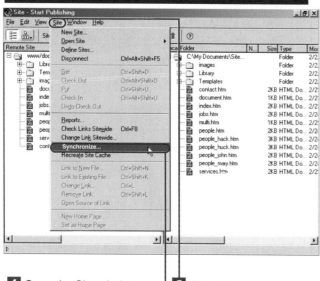

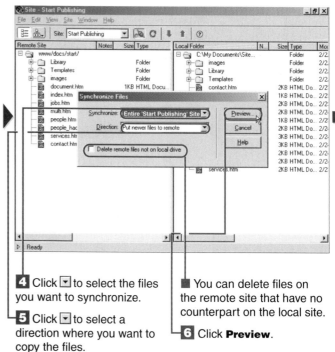

1 Open the Site window.

Note: See page 267 for instructions on opening the Site window.

2 Click **Site**.

3 Click **Synchronize**.

■ The Synchronize Files dialog box appears.

4 Click ▼ to select the files you want to synchronize.

5 Click ▼ to select a direction where you want to copy the files.

■ Transferring files in both uploading and downloading directions places the newest copies on both sites.

■ You can delete files on the remote site that have no counterpart on the local site.

6 Click **Preview**.

How can I see which files are newer on the local or remote site?

In the Site window, click **Edit** and then **Select Newer Local** or **Select Newer Remote**. Dreamweaver compares the modified dates of the two sets of files and highlights the newer ones. On a Macintosh, click **Site**, **Site Files**, and then **Select Newer Local** or **Select Newer Remote**.

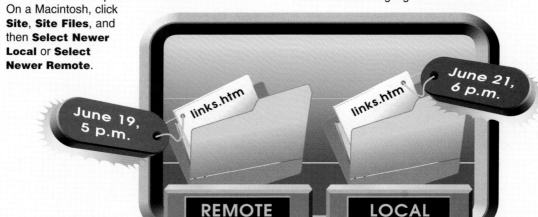

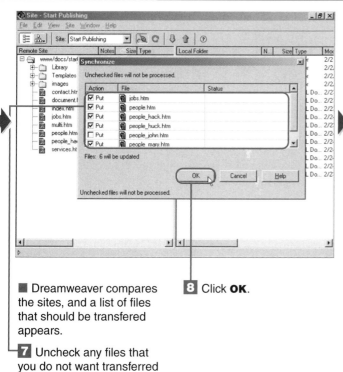

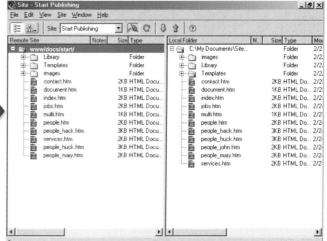

■ Dreamweaver compares the sites, and a list of files that should be transfered appears.

7 Uncheck any files that you do not want transferred (☐ changes to ☑).

8 Click **OK**.

■ The files are transferred and the Synchronize dialog box is updated.

9 Click **Close**.

■ The local and remote sites are now synchronized.

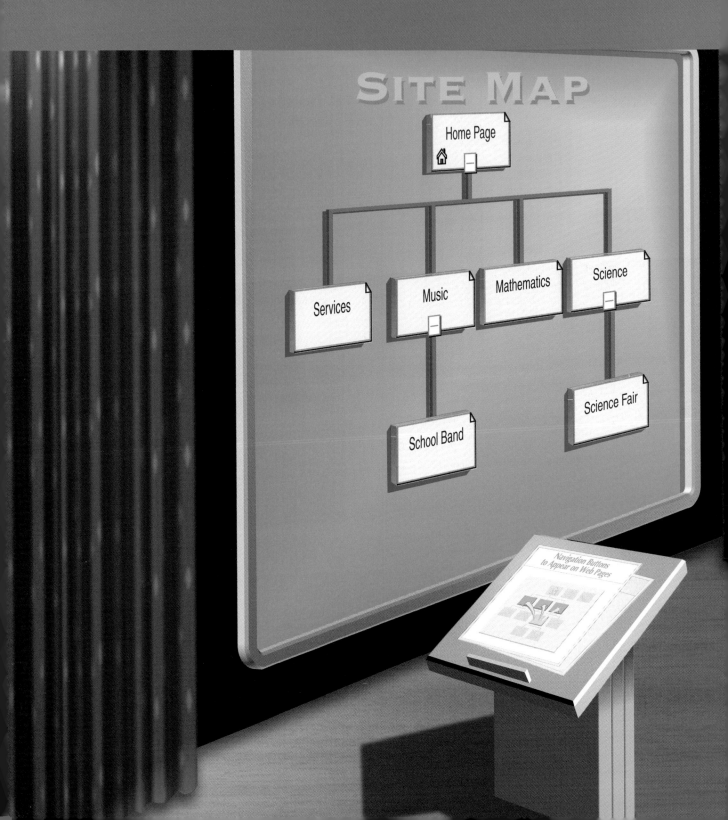

CHAPTER 16

Site Maintenance

Keeping the links of a site working and its content fresh can be as much work as creating the site. This chapter shows you how Dreamweaver can make site maintenance less of a chore.

USING THE SITE MAP

The Site Map view enables you to see your site in flowchart form with lines (which represent links) connecting your pages. This view highlights pages that have broken internal links, which can help you maintain your site.

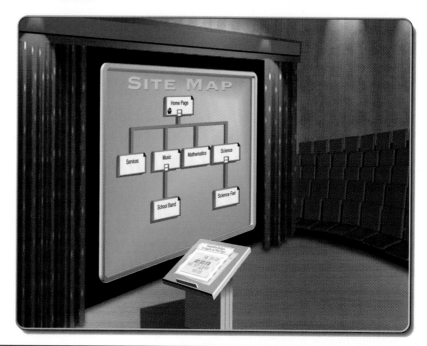

USING THE SITE MAP

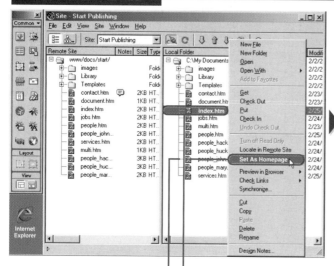

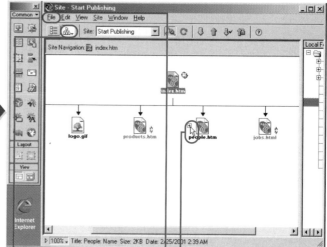

1 Open the Site window.

Note: See page 267 for instructions on opening the Site Window.

■ To create a site map in Dreamweaver, you must first define the home page of your site. It serves as the root file of your Site Map.

2 In the local site pane, right-click the file you want to use as your home page.

3 Click **Set As Home Page**.

4 Click the **Site Map** button (⬛).

■ A site map appears in the left pane. By default, the Site Map displays the site structure two levels deep beginning from the home page.

5 To view files below the second level, click ⊞.

■ To save the Site Map as a BMP image, click **File** and then **Save Site Map**.

How do I fix a broken link in the Site Map?

A broken chain icon in the Site Map means the link to a page is broken. You can fix a broken link by right-clicking the destination page and clicking **Change Link.** Links can break because a destination page is renamed or deleted.

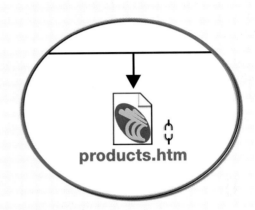

products.htm

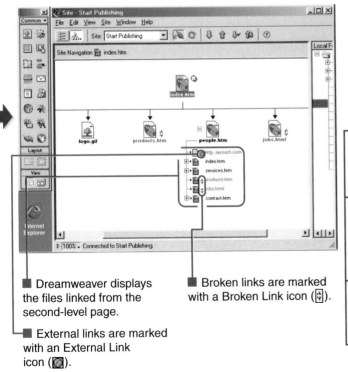

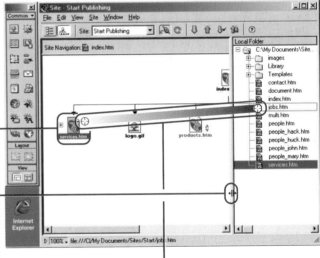

■ Dreamweaver displays the files linked from the second-level page.

■ External links are marked with an External Link icon (⬛).

■ Broken links are marked with a Broken Link icon (⬛).

6 Click and drag the Site window border to display both the Site Map and the local site.

7 Click a file in the Site.

8 Click and drag ⊕ to the file of your choice in the local site.

■ A new link is added to the top of the page selected in the Site Map.

■ You can double-click the page to open it.

MANAGE SITE ASSETS

You can view and
manage important
elements that appear in
the pages of your site
with the Assets panel.

MANAGE SITE ASSETS

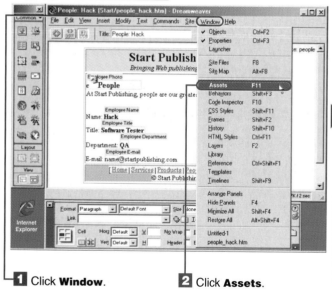

1 Click **Window**.

2 Click **Assets**.

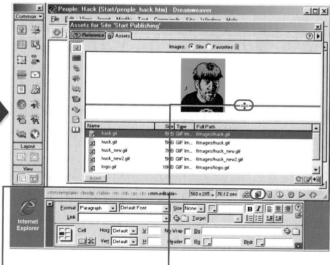

■ You can also click the
Assets icon (⬚) to open
the Assets panel.

■ The Assets panel
appears, displaying objects
from the selected category.

3 Click and drag the border
between the top and bottom
panes.

284

How are assets organized?

Items in the Assets panel are organized into the
following categories (top to bottom)

🖼	**Images**	GIF, JPG, and PNG images
🎨	**Color**	Text, background, link colors, and style-sheet colors
🔗	**URLs**	External Web addresses that are accessible from your site
🎬	**Flash Movies**	Flash-based multimedia
🎞	**Shockwave Movies**	Shockwave-based multimedia
📽	**Movies**	QuickTime and MPEG movies
📜	**Scripts**	External JavaScript or VBScript files
📋	**Templates**	Page layouts for your site
📚	**Library Items**	Reusable page elements

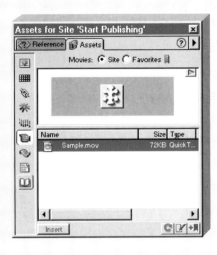

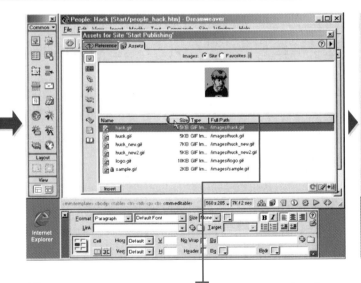

■ The panes assume the new dimensions.

4 Click a column heading.

■ The assets are sorted in ascending order. You can click the column again to sort in descending order.

■ To view other assets, click a different category button.

ADD CONTENT BY USING THE ASSET PANEL

You can add frequently used content to your site directly from the Assets panel. This technique can be more efficient than using a menu command or the Objects panel.

ADD CONTENT BY USING THE ASSET PANEL

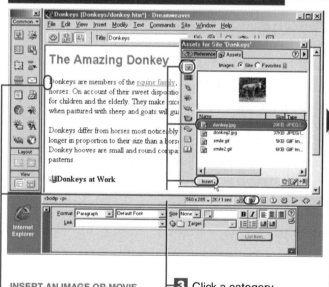

INSERT AN IMAGE OR MOVIE

1 Click inside the Document window where you want to insert the asset.

2 Click 📷 to open the Assets panel.

3 Click a category.

4 Click an asset.

5 Click **Insert**.

■ You can also drag and drop the asset from the panel to the Document window.

■ Dreamweaver inserts the asset into your Document window.

286

How do I copy assets from one site to another?

Click one or more items in the Assets panel, click **Copy to Site** in the Assets panel drop-down menu, and click the destination site. The assets appear in the Favorites list under the same category in the other site.

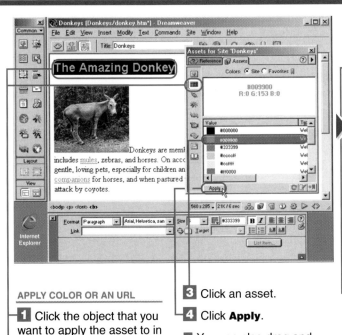

APPLY COLOR OR AN URL

1 Click the object that you want to apply the asset to in the Document window.

2 Click a category.

3 Click an asset.

4 Click **Apply**.

■ You can also drag and drop the asset from the panel onto the selected object in the Document window.

■ Dreamweaver applies the asset in the Document window.

SPECIFY FAVORITE ASSETS

To make your assets lists more manageable, you can organize items that you use often into a Favorites list inside each asset category.

SPECIFY FAVORITE ASSETS

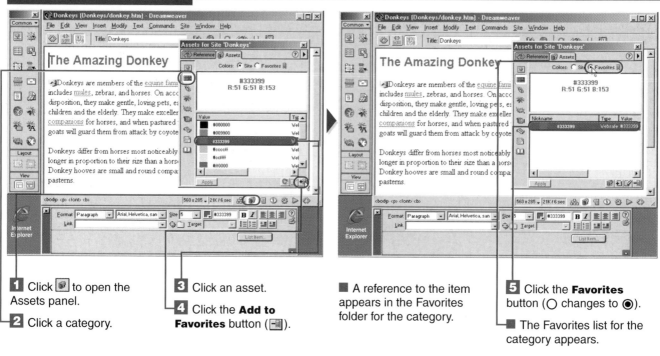

1 Click 🖼 to open the Assets panel.

2 Click a category.

3 Click an asset.

4 Click the **Add to Favorites** button (🖿).

■ A reference to the item appears in the Favorites folder for the category.

5 Click the **Favorites** button (○ changes to ◉).

■ The Favorites list for the category appears.

How do I remove an item from the Assets panel entirely?

You need to delete the item from your local site folder. You can right-click (option +click) the item in Site window (see page 267) and click **Delete** from the menu that appears. When you return to the Assets panel and click the **Refresh** button (⟳), the asset is gone.

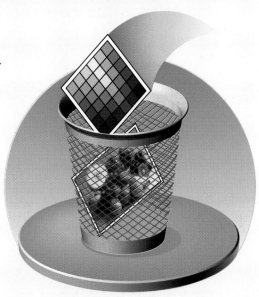

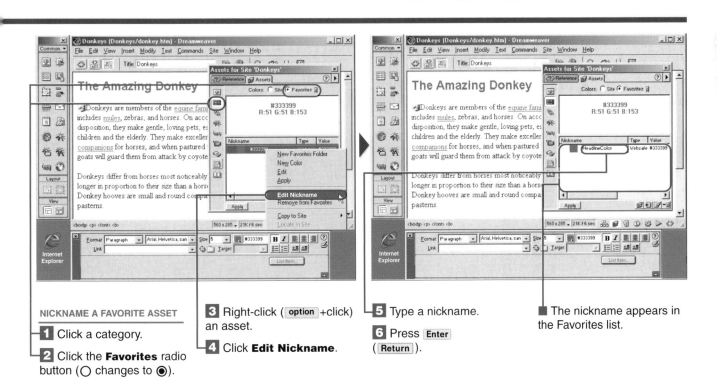

NICKNAME A FAVORITE ASSET

1 Click a category.

2 Click the **Favorites** radio button (○ changes to ●).

3 Right-click (option +click) an asset.

4 Click **Edit Nickname**.

5 Type a nickname.

6 Press Enter (Return).

■ The nickname appears in the Favorites list.

CHECK A PAGE IN OR OUT

Dreamweaver provides a Check In/Check Out system that enables several people to work collaboratively on the files of a Web site. When this system is on, others cannot work on site files that are checked out by you.

When the Check In/Check Out system is off, several people can check out the same file at once.

CHECK A PAGE IN OR OUT

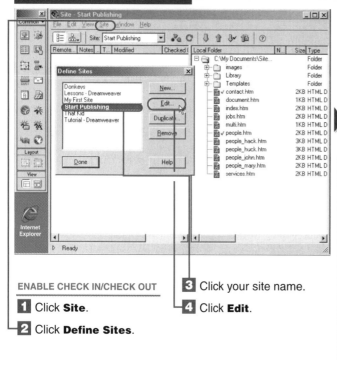

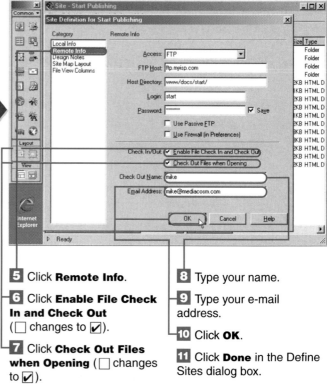

ENABLE CHECK IN/CHECK OUT

1 Click **Site**.

2 Click **Define Sites**.

3 Click your site name.

4 Click **Edit**.

5 Click **Remote Info**.

6 Click **Enable File Check In and Check Out** (☐ changes to ☑).

7 Click **Check Out Files when Opening** (☐ changes to ☑).

8 Type your name.

9 Type your e-mail address.

10 Click **OK**.

11 Click **Done** in the Define Sites dialog box.

How is a file marked as checked out?

When you check out a file, Dreamweaver creates a temporary LCK file that is stored in the remote site folder while the page is checked out. The file contains information about who has checked the file out. Dreamweaver does not display the LCK files in the Site window, but you can see them if you access your remote site with an FTP program.

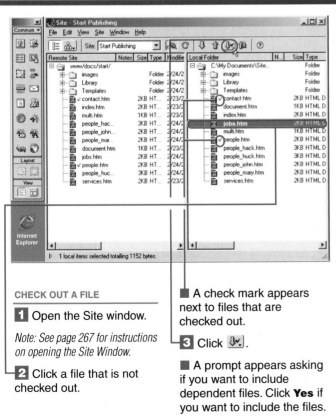

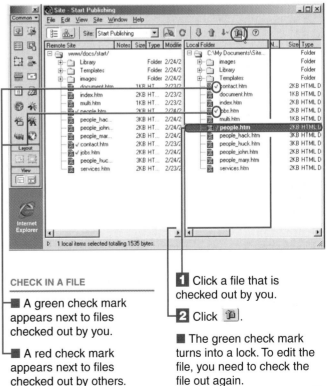

CHECK OUT A FILE

■1 Open the Site window.

Note: See page 267 for instructions on opening the Site Window.

■2 Click a file that is not checked out.

■ A check mark appears next to files that are checked out.

■3 Click 🖱.

■ A prompt appears asking if you want to include dependent files. Click **Yes** if you want to include the files.

CHECK IN A FILE

■ A green check mark appears next to files checked out by you.

■ A red check mark appears next to files checked out by others.

■1 Click a file that is checked out by you.

■2 Click 🖱.

■ The green check mark turns into a lock. To edit the file, you need to check the file out again.

MAKE DESIGN NOTES

You can attach accessory information, such as editing history and an author name, to your Web pages with Design Notes. Such notes can be useful if you are working on a site collaboratively, because they let you add information about the development status of a file.

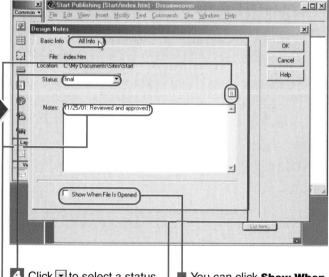

■ Design Notes are on by default when you create a site. You can turn them off in your site definition settings by clicking **Site** and then **Define Sites**.

1 Open the page where you want to attach Design Notes.

2 Click **File**.

3 Click **Design Notes**.

4 Click ▾ to select a status for the page.

5 Type any notes that are relevant to the page.

■ You can click 📅 to enter the current date in the Notes field.

■ You can click **Show When File Is Opened** to automatically show any Design Notes when a file is opened.

6 Click the **All Info** tab.

292

What are HTML comments?

Similar to Design Notes, HTML comments let you attach text information to your page that does not show up in the browser. HTML comments are bracketed by `<!--` and `-->` characters and are stored in a page's HTML. Design Notes offer more security than HTML comments because they are stored separately from the HTML file. Design Notes are stored in a `_notes` folder inside the local site folder.

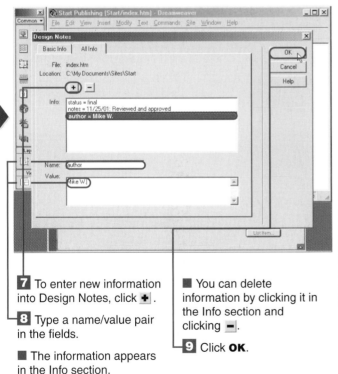

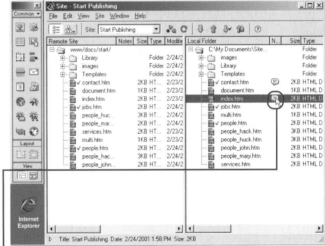

7 To enter new information into Design Notes, click ➕.

8 Type a name/value pair in the fields.

■ The information appears in the Info section.

■ You can delete information by clicking it in the Info section and clicking ➖.

9 Click **OK**.

VIEW DESIGN NOTES

1 From the Site window, double-click 💬 next to a file.

■ The Design Notes for that file open.

■ You can view the notes of a page by clicking **File** and then **Design Notes** when the page is open in the Document window.

RUN A SITE REPORT

A site report pinpoints any redundant HTML and missing descriptive information in your pages. It is a good idea to run a site report before you upload your site to a Web server.

RUN A SITE REPORT

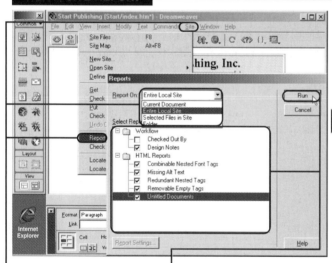

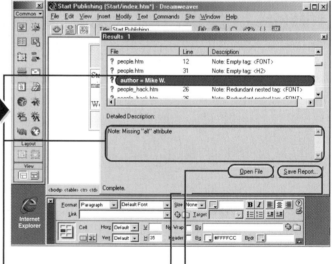

1 Click **Site**.

2 Click **Reports**.

3 Click the files where you want a report.

■ You can run a report on several files by `Ctrl` +clicking (`Shift` +clicking) the files in the Site window before opening the Reports dialog box.

4 Click the topics for which you want a report.

5 Click **Run**.

■ Dreamweaver creates a report.

6 Click an entry in the report list.

■ Details appear for the entry.

7 Click **Open File** to open the file for an entry.

8 Click **Save Report** to save the report as an XML file.

CHANGE A LINK SITEWIDE

You can search for and
replace all the hyperlinks
on your site that point to
a specific address. This
is helpful when a page is
renamed or deleted and
hyperlinks to it need
updating.

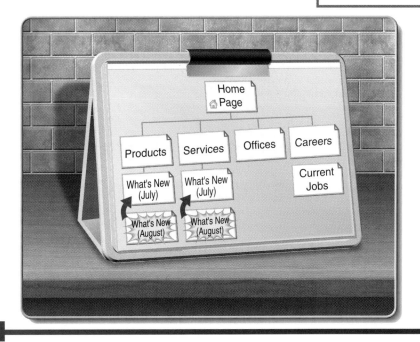

CHANGE A LINK SITEWIDE

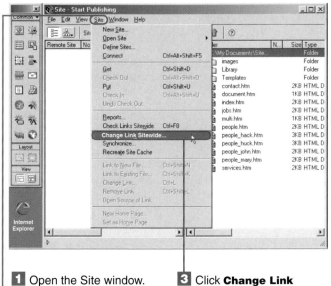

1 Open the Site window.

Note: See page 267 for instructions on opening the Site Window.

2 Click **Site**.

3 Click **Change Link Sitewide**.

4 Type the old hyperlink address you want to change or click 🖿 to select the file.

5 Type the new hyperlink address or click 🖿 to select the file.

■ The hyperlinks must start with a /, be an e-mail link, or be a full URL.

6 Click **OK**.

■ Dreamweaver finds and replaces the hyperlinks. A dialog box asks you to confirm the changes.

295

FIND AND REPLACE TEXT

The Find and Replace feature is a powerful tool for making changes to text elements that repeat across many pages. You can find and replace text on your Web page, text in your source code, or specific HTML tags in your pages.

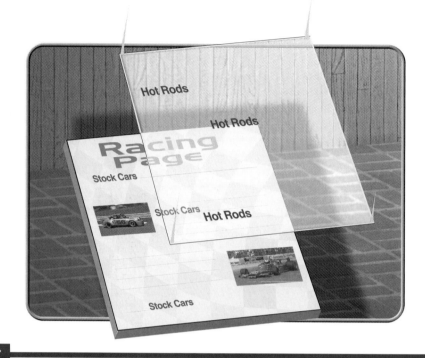

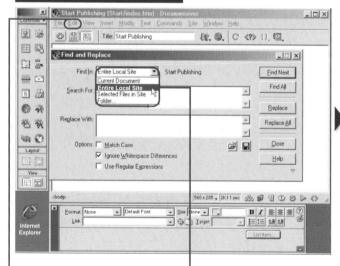

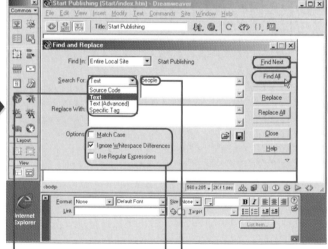

1 Click **Edit**.

2 Click **Find and Replace** to open the Find and Replace dialog box.

3 Click ▾ to select the files you want to search.

■ To search Selected Files in a site, `Ctrl` +click (`Shift` +click) the files in the Site window before performing step **2**.

4 Click ▾ to select the type of text for which you want to search.

■ For example, you can select **Text** (Advanced) to find text that is inside a specific tag.

5 Type a search query.

6 Click your search options (☐ changes to ☑).

7 Click **Find All**.

■ You can click **Find Next** to find instances of your query one at a time.

Why might I want to find and replace an HTML attribute?

You can replace attributes to achieve many things. You can change the alignment of the contents of a table (change `align="center"` to `align="right"` in `<td>` tags), change the color of specific text in your page (change `color="green"` to `color="red"` in `<font>` tags), or change the page background color across your site (change `bgcolor="black"` to `bgcolor="white"` in `<body>` tags).

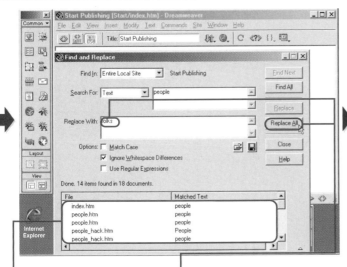

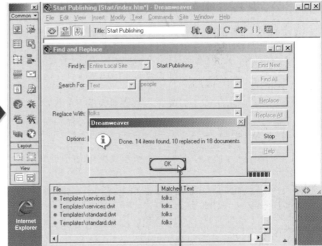

■ An alert box appears telling you if Dreamweaver found anything.

8 Click **OK** to close the alert box.

■ The results of your search appear.

9 Type your replacement text.

10 Click **Replace All**.

■ You can also click items in the found list and then click **Replace** to replace them individually.

■ An alert box may appear asking if you want to replace text in documents that are not open. Click **OK**.

11 Click **OK** to close the box.

INDEX

Symbols

(pound sign)
    in the Link field, 247
    preceding an anchor name, 115
    preceding hexadecimal codes for colors, 83
/ (forward slash) in HTML tags, 35
. (period), beginning class names, 228
<> (angle brackets) in HTML tags, 34–35

A

<a> tag, 41
Absolute font sizes, 80
absolute units, 225
access method for a remote site, 270
accessory windows, 14
Active Links, 123
Adobe Photoshop, 113, 241
Align drop-down menu, 91
alignment, 136, 137
alternate text, 103
animated GIF files, 257
animation, 252–263
Apply Template to Page command, 210
Assets panel, 196, 197, 284–285, 286–287, 289
Attach Style Sheet command, 229
attributes, 45, 49
audience for a Web site, 9
Autoplay check box, 253, 255, 257, 259
autostretch column, 149
Available Fonts list, 77

B

<b> (bold) tags, 35, 40
Back button in the Timelines inspector, 253
background, changing for a table, 132–133
Background button, 102
Background category, 227
background color, 102, 234
Background Image field, 101
background images, 100–101
Behavior panel, 242, 244
behaviors, 238, 239, 262–263
Bg Color button, 132, 133
Bg Color swatch, 234
Bg Image folder, 234

blank option in the Target menu, 120
blank pages, opening, 56
block-formatting tags, 39
<body> tags, 38
bold (<b>) tags, 35, 40
bold text, 78
Border Color button, 188
Border Width, 188
borders, 89, 129, 135

 (line break) tag, 39
broken links, 124, 283
browser windows, 95, 120, 246–247
browsers. *See* Web browsers
bulleted lists, 70–71

C

captions, adding to images, 131
Cascading Style Sheets (CSS). *See* style sheets
case sensitivity of HTML tags, 35
cells of tables. *See* table cells
center-aligned paragraphs, 65
centering images, 92–93
CGI script for a form, 152
Change Link command, 283
Change Link Sitewide command, 295
Character button, 74
check boxes, 160–161, 167
Check Browser dialog box, 248
Check In/Check Out system, 290–291
Check Links option, 124
Checked Value, 160, 161, 162, 163
Choose Local Folder dialog box, 52
classes. *See* style-sheet classes
Clean Up HTML command, 42
Clean Up HTML dialog box, 43
clip art. *See* images
code. *See* HTML code
Code and Design Views button, 36
Code Inspector, 36
Code Rewriting category in Preferences, 31
Code Rewriting option, 45
Code View button, 36, 64
color
    apply through the Assets panel, 287
    change hyperlinks, 122–123
    change text, 82–83
    change the background of a table, 132

INDEX

INDEX

INDEX

vertical space, adding above and below an image, 96
video clips, inserting, 104, 105
View Options menu, 21
Vis (Visibility) menu, 233, 259
Visited Links, 123

W

Web browser window, paragraph width in, 65
Web browsers, 5
    check the brand and version of, 239, 248–249
    display style definitions, 225
    make another available, 61
    preview Web pages in, 60–61
    standard behaviors and, 239
    style sheets and, 217
    view styles in, 223
Web editors, WYSIWYG compared to text-based, 21
Web pages, 4
    create, 35, 56, 210–211
    detach from templates, 211
    elements found on, 6–7
    move from one to another in a Web site, 108–109
    navigate to other, 168–169
    open, 54–55
    plan, 8

    position elements, 216
    preview, 60–61
    save, 58–59
    switch between open, 55
    total size of, 91
Web server, 5, 266, 273–277
Web sites, 5
    add hyperlinks to other, 110–111
    create framed, 174
    host, 9
    organize files in, 109
    plan, 8–9
    publish, 266
    update, 202–203, 212–213
    view in flowchart form, 282–283
windows, 14, 25
word processing documents, linking to, 116–117
World Wide Web (Web), 4
wrap attribute, defining for a multiline text field, 157
wrap text around images, 90–91
WYSIWYG, 21

Z

Z-Index values, 235, 259

Read Less, Learn More™

Visual

Simplified®

Simply the Easiest Way to Learn

For visual learners who are brand-new to a topic and want to be shown, not told, how to solve a problem in a friendly, approachable way.

All *Simplified®* books feature friendly Disk characters who demonstrate and explain the purpose of each task.

Title	ISBN	Price
America Online® Simplified®, 2nd Ed.	0-7645-3433-5	$27.99
Computers Simplified®, 5th Ed.	0-7645-3524-2	$27.99
Creating Web Pages with HTML Simplified®, 2nd Ed.	0-7645-6067-0	$27.99
Excel 97 Simplified®	0-7645-6022-0	$27.99
FrontPage® 2000 Simplified®	0-7645-3450-5	$27.99
Internet and World Wide Web Simplified®, 3rd Ed.	0-7645-3409-2	$27.99
Microsoft® Access 2000 Simplified®	0-7645-6058-1	$27.99
Microsoft® Excel 2000 Simplified®	0-7645-6053-0	$27.99
Microsoft® Office 2000 Simplified®	0-7645-6052-2	$29.99
Microsoft® Word 2000 Simplified®	0-7645-6054-9	$27.99
More Windows® 95 Simplified®	1-56884-689-4	$27.99
More Windows® 98 Simplified®	0-7645-6037-9	$27.99
Office 97 Simplified®	0-7645-6009-3	$29.99
PC Upgrade and Repair Simplified®, 2nd Ed.	0-7645-3560-9	$27.99
Windows® 95 Simplified®	1-56884-662-2	$27.99
Windows® 98 Simplified®	0-7645-6030-1	$27.99
Windows® 2000 Professional Simplified®	0-7645-3422-X	$27.99
Windows® Me Millennium Edition Simplified®	0-7645-3494-7	$27.99
Word 97 Simplified®	0-7645-6011-5	$27.99

Over 10 million *Visual* books in print!

with these full-color Visual™ guides

The Fast and Easy Way to Learn

 Discover how to use what you learn with "Teach Yourself" tips

Title	ISBN	Price
Teach Yourself Access 97 VISUALLY™	0-7645-6026-3	$29.99
Teach Yourself FrontPage® 2000 VISUALLY™	0-7645-3451-3	$29.99
Teach Yourself HTML VISUALLY™	0-7645-3423-8	$29.99
Teach Yourself the Internet and World Wide Web VISUALLY™, 2nd Ed.	0-7645-3410-6	$29.99
Teach Yourself Microsoft® Access 2000 VISUALLY™	0-7645-6059-X	$29.99
Teach Yourself Microsoft® Excel 97 VISUALLY™	0-7645-6063-8	$29.99
Teach Yourself Microsoft® Excel 2000 VISUALLY™	0-7645-6056-5	$29.99
Teach Yourself Microsoft® Office 2000 VISUALLY™	0-7645-6051-4	$29.99
Teach Yourself Microsoft® PowerPoint® 2000 VISUALLY™	0-7645-6060-3	$29.99
Teach Yourself More Windows® 98 VISUALLY™	0-7645-6044-1	$29.99
Teach Yourself Office 97 VISUALLY™	0-7645-6018-2	$29.99
Teach Yourself Red Hat® Linux® VISUALLY™	0-7645-3430-0	$29.99
Teach Yourself VISUALLY™ Computers, 3rd Ed.	0-7645-3525-0	$29.99
Teach Yourself VISUALLY™ Digital Photography	0-7645-3565-X	$29.99
Teach Yourself VISUALLY™ Dreamweaver® 3	0-7645-3470-X	$29.99
Teach Yourself VISUALLY™ Fireworks® 4	0-7645-3566-8	$29.99
Teach Yourself VISUALLY™ Flash™ 5	0-7645-3540-4	$29.99
Teach Yourself VISUALLY™ FrontPage® 2002	0-7645-3590-0	$29.99
Teach Yourself VISUALLY™ iMac™	0-7645-3453-X	$29.99
Teach Yourself VISUALLY™ Investing Online	0-7645-3459-9	$29.99
Teach Yourself VISUALLY™ Networking, 2nd Ed.	0-7645-3534-X	$29.99
Teach Yourself VISUALLY™ Photoshop® 6	0-7645-3513-7	$29.99
Teach Yourself VISUALLY™ Quicken® 2001	0-7645-3526-9	$29.99
Teach Yourself VISUALLY™ Windows® 2000 Server	0-7645-3428-9	$29.99
Teach Yourself VISUALLY™ Windows® Me Millennium Edition	0-7645-3495-5	$29.99
Teach Yourself Windows® 95 VISUALLY™	0-7645-6001-8	$29.99
Teach Yourself Windows® 98 VISUALLY™	0-7645-6025-5	$29.99
Teach Yourself Windows® 2000 Professional VISUALLY™	0-7645-6040-9	$29.99
Teach Yourself Windows NT® 4 VISUALLY™	0-7645-6061-1	$29.99
Teach Yourself Word 97 VISUALLY™	0-7645-6032-8	$29.99

ORDER FORM

TRADE & INDIVIDUAL ORDERS

Phone: (800) 762-2974
or (317) 572-3993
(8 a.m. – 6 p.m., CST, weekdays)
FAX: (800) 550-2747
or (317) 572-4002

EDUCATIONAL ORDERS & DISCOUNTS

Phone: (800) 434-2086
(8:30 a.m.–5:00 p.m., CST, weekdays)
FAX: (317) 572-4005

CORPORATE ORDERS FOR VISUAL™ SERIES

Phone: (800) 469-6616
(8 a.m.–5 p.m., EST, weekdays)
FAX: (905) 890-9434

Qty	ISBN	Title	Price	Total

Shipping & Handling Charges

	Description	First book	Each add'l. book	Total
Domestic	Normal	$4.50	$1.50	$
	Two Day Air	$8.50	$2.50	$
	Overnight	$18.00	$3.00	$
International	Surface	$8.00	$8.00	$
	Airmail	$16.00	$16.00	$
	DHL Air	$17.00	$17.00	$

Subtotal _____

CA residents add
applicable sales tax _____

IN, MA and MD
residents add
5% sales tax _____

IL residents add
6.25% sales tax _____

RI residents add
7% sales tax _____

TX residents add
8.25% sales tax _____

Shipping _____

Total _____

Ship to:

Name_____

Address_____

Company_____

City/State/Zip_____

Daytime Phone_____

Payment: ☐ Check to Hungry Minds (US Funds Only)
☐ Visa ☐ Mastercard ☐ American Express

Card # _____ Exp. _____ Signature_____